THE
SPIRIT
OF THE
DOG

An *illustrated* history

THE SPIRIT OF THE DOG

An *illustrated* history

Tamsin Pickeral
Photography by Astrid Harrisson

Foreword by Victoria Stilwell

BARRON'S

A Quintessence Book

First edition for North America and the Phillipines published in
2012 by Barron's Educational Series, Inc.

All inquiries should be addressed to:
Barron's Educational Series, Inc.
250 Wireless Boulevard
Hauppauge, NY 11788
www.barronseduc.com

ISBN: 978-0-7641-6549-8
Library of Congress Control No.: 2012939507

This book was designed and produced by
Quintessence Editions Ltd
230 City Road, London, EC1V 2TT

Project Editor	Elspeth Beidas
Editors	Heather Hayes, Rebecca Gee
Designer	Dean Martin
Additional Design	Alison Hau
Production Manager	Anna Pauletti
Editorial Director	Jane Laing
Publisher	Mark Fletcher

Colour reproduction by KHL Chromagraphics, Singapore
Printed in China by 1010 Printing International Ltd.

9 8 7 6 5 4 3 2 1

CONTENTS

FOREWORD *By Victoria Stilwell*

As someone who has dedicated my life to making the world a better place for people and their dogs, I am constantly amazed at the seemingly unending ability of this species to surprise, challenge, delight and enrich our lives. My primary role as a dog trainer and behavior expert is to help owners build healthier bonds with their dogs by gaining a better understanding the canine experience.

Over thousands of years, there have been many species that have succeeded in achieving varying degrees of domestication and/or ability to thrive in an increasingly mankind-driven world, but in my opinion today's dog stands alone in its ability to adapt, develop, maintain, and enjoy complex and co-dependent relationships with their human counterparts.

How is it that the modern dog became so successful in our strange, domesticated world? What specific characteristics did their wolf ancestors need to embrace and foster during the long journey through the gradual domestication process? How did one species evolve into such a stunningly diverse group of animals in terms of size, shape, and demeanor? What is so unique about dogs that allows them to share many of our emotional, physiological, and behavioral tendencies?

Modern behavioral science is at long last beginning to answer some of these questions, but in order to truly understand our canine companions, we must also look back at their development as a species and appreciate the sometimes overlooked power inherent in the relationship our two species have forged with one another.

This book is an astoundingly beautiful and informative testament to where our dogs have come from. Not only has Tamsin succeeded in beautifully and clearly laying out for us how individual groups and breeds of dogs came to be, she has also woven the fascinating personal history of our relationship with each breed into the journey. By exploring the roles played by various types of dogs in our long and sometimes tortured history, *The Spirit of the Dog* does not stop at providing valuable breed history and information, but also helps us understand how and why some of best-loved companions look, act, and feel the way that they do today.

Astrid's stunning photography is the ultimate complement to Tamsin's narrative. I've worked with many photographic artists who specialize in the canine form, but the artwork in this book is some of the most exquisite I have ever seen.

Given the monumental task of cataloging the history of dog breeds, their place in our lives, and why they are so important to us today, Tamsin and Astrid have truly created a masterpiece which also celebrates the individuality and unique bond shared between man and dog. Whether one is a "dog person" or not, the impact that these amazing animals have had on our wildly disparate cultures through the centuries is undeniable, so it is thus not simply an academic exercise in physiological history to read this book, it is also a window into an ongoing discussion regarding why dogs are what they are and how we can most effectively, humanely, and respectfully live up to the responsibility we inherited when their domestication process first began. It is a discussion which, when coupled with such mastery of language and art, one does not tire or outgrow.

As a dog lover, trainer, and owner, I can only hope that you enjoy reading and absorbing this book as much as I do.

Victoria Stilwell

Celebrity Dog Trainer, Author, and TV Personality.

INTRODUCTION

More than any other creature, dogs have infiltrated the very fabric of our lives; they are our most trusted and loyal friends, quick to forgive, eager to please, and always a listening ear. They do not judge us, they entertain us, and they provide comfort. Their companionship and sensitivity, intelligence, apparent empathy with human emotions, and even humor have contributed toward a unique canine/human bond, one that is precious and often underestimated. There is in the spirit of the dog something with which people can identify, a type of kinship that evokes our long, combined history—one in which the dog padded alongside our ancestors, fought in their wars, found their food, protected their homes and livestock, and kept them warm at night. Dogs have rescued people and enriched lives, their unwavering loyalty has been a constant in an uncertain world, and no one need be excluded. There is truly a dog for all, such is their diversity, from the very large to the tiny, the sweet to the macho, the energetic to the downright lazy, and in almost every assortment of color, coat, frame, voice, and character.

These eminently versatile animals are utilized in myriad ways, perhaps more so than any other domestic animal. They figure in ancient superstitions and mythology, where they were aligned with gods and goddesses and were greatly revered. They have taken explorers to the North and South Poles, and have been invaluable to cultures living within the Arctic Circle. Superlative dogs have long been traded as diplomatic gifts among nations, they trek through mountains to find missing persons, detect bombs and illegal substances, and protect when required. Fortunes have been won and lost on dogs at the racetrack, and dreams made and shattered in the show ring. Service dogs provide essential aid for the deaf, blind, and physically challenged, while others have rid ships, homes, and factories of vermin. They have tended to livestock, looked after children, and been the subject of paintings and stories for many hundreds of years, more recently featuring in television programs, cartoons, and Hollywood movies. So far reaching is the appeal of dogs that their image has been used to sell everything from paint to tobacco and music to washing detergent. There are few areas in life in which the dog has not been of some influence, so readily have they journeyed with us with their camaraderie and joie de vivre. Notwithstanding that, dogs also have been and continue to be a vital source of food in some cultures.

Clear archeological evidence suggests that this long relationship originated at least 14,000 years ago. Primary sources of information are burial sites, many of which feature domestic dogs interred with human remains; one example is the Bonn Oberkassel grave in Germany, c. 14,000 B.P. (Before Present). That dogs were buried with people underlines the nature and strength of our special relationship with them, but within some complex spiritual systems dogs were also assigned the role of protective entity and guide to the spirit world. Dog graves have been discovered in every major landmass with the exception of Antarctica, and dogs have been linked to virtually every major cultural group throughout their history.

Archeological evidence has provided pointers to the history of the dog that are visually quantifiable, but the history has been and continues to be further unraveled (and complicated) by the scientific study of genetics. The results conflict, and the issue of the domestic dog's origins remains highly debated. What is uncontested is that the domestic dog evolved from the gray wolf, though exactly when this occurred, the length of time it took, and the geographic location are argued. Doglike fossils have been found in Europe and Eurasia, with the oldest, in the Goyet Cave, Belgium, dating to c. 31,700 B.P.; these have been described as more pre-historic dog than wolf and could represent an evolutionary stage between the two.

Currently the most quoted date of domestication is given as around 14,000–15,000 B.P.. There are three main areas cited as the birthplace of the domestic dog, all supported scientifically, but none absolutely conclusively. The first is the Middle East, confirmed by the wealth of archeological finds in this region; second is Europe or Southwest Asia; and third is the southern part of East Asia, south of the Yangtze River. The date of domestication, based on the study of mitochondrial DNA in dogs worldwide, has been put forward by Savolainen et al, 2002, Pang et al, 2009, and Ding, Savolainen et al, 2011.

What drove this momentous evolutionary event can only be guessed at. Perhaps young gray wolves, attracted to the hearths and discarded food of early humans, found life within the human circle to be more beneficial than that outside it; possibly wolf cubs were captured and raised in the domestic environment. Over time there occurred changes to the animals' jawbones and teeth, a reduction in their overall body size, and modification of their behavior. Yet it has not been proved conclusively whether domestication occurred once in one location, or several times in different locations.

A study undertaken in 2004 (Parker et al), suggests that the oldest dog types are divided into four groups: Asian Spitz-type breeds (Shar Pei, Shiba Inu, Akita, and Chow Chow); the primitive African Basenji; Arctic Spitz-type breeds (Alaskan Malamute and Siberian Husky); and the sight hound-types (Afghan and Saluki). How the progression from gray wolf to different types of dogs occurred is unclear, but it is suggested that as human cultures progressed, dogs developed to fulfill roles required of them, particularly within agriculture and farming. Artistic, literary, and archeological evidence from the ancient cultures of the Middle East and Europe from around 6,000 B.P. indicates different types, most obviously sight hounds, mastiffs, small dogs, and various types of hounds for hunting. As early cultures migrated from Central and East Asia they took their dogs with them, and these evolved in response to their new environments as well as their new functions. Southern East Asia or Central Asia may be cited as the "birthplace" of the domestic dog, but the Middle East and Europe became the "stage" where many of the early types developed their specific characteristics.

Of the proliferation of dog breeds today, the majority have only been established within the last few hundred years. Prior to this, dogs exhibited clear types (which are referred to as "breeds" in this book) and were bred specifically to be the best at their given job, but pedigrees and records were not kept, or have not survived. Breeds as they are recognized today are associated with a range of specialized kennel clubs; breed standards have been drawn up, and breed clubs formed to protect and promote these through competitive endeavors such as dog shows and field trials. The dog breeds are categorized into various groups within the different kennel clubs—such as the international Fédération Cynologique Internationale (FCI), American Kennel Club (AKC), and British Kennel Club (KC). The groups are largely based on the breed's use; examples are "Herding" in the AKC (which includes the livestock breeds), "Gun Dog" in the KC, and "Sight Hounds" in the FCI, although each of the kennel clubs categorizes the breeds slightly differently. The chapters in this book represent a personal selection of breeds and do not necessarily correlate to any kennel club categorization.

Each breed in this book is listed as either modern or historic. Modern breeds are those that have developed within the last few hundred years, while all others are considered historic (clearly, some of these are far older than others). Some breeds, such as the Cavalier King Charles Spaniel, have historic roots but have been recognized only recently. Further, each breed is also described as "rare," "moderate," or "common." This is an approximation of breed numbers internationally and is meant as a guide only—particular breeds are populous in some countries, and in others they are virtually unknown.

Much of the early history of the dog and particular dog breeds relies on unsubstantiated legends, while scientific theories are proved, disproved, and proved again. We do know that the dog was the first animal to be domesticated, or perhaps it simply chose us. Certainly, dogs aligned themselves with us, and us with them, and we have lived together for the most part in symbiosis. And the spirit of the dog, that intangible quality that touches the human soul, is unquantifiable and humbling in its integrity. Few, if any, animals are so consistently loyal, forgiving, and loving, or protect and comfort us when we need them. Dogs, as companions to kings and paupers and all in between, are indeed our best friend. But make no mistake: we may consider ourselves the superior race, but the dogs have the last laugh, claiming the warmest, most comfortable spot in the house, dragging us for walks in the pouring rain, and training us to throw a ball, again and again and again . . .

CHAPTER 1
ELEGANCE AND SPEED

Sight hounds are in effect the Thoroughbred of the dog world. They are built for speed and athleticism and are the fastest breed of dog. They are also one of the oldest types of dog. Their collective history is extraordinary and it is marked by its close association with monarchs and rulers. Sight hounds are undoubtedly the dogs of the nobility, and their elegant form has appeared more frequently in the arts than that of any other canine type.

As their name implies, sight hounds hunt by sight. They are universally prone to great speed and stamina, and have a distinctive athletic frame. They also have dolichocephalic skulls, which means that the length of their head is proportionally longer than the width. This characteristic, which is also seen in wolves and wild dogs, allows them a wide field of vision and differs from most other domestic dogs, which have predominantly been bred to have shorter and wider heads. The sight hound is best equipped to hunt on open terrain, where it can see its quarry, and is most often long in the leg, which gives it a greater length of stride and a capacity for the fast coverage of ground. Sight hounds are known for being independent, intelligent dogs, characteristics that are demonstrated by their problem-solving skills and their ability to hunt largely without human direction. Once a sight hound is after its quarry, it is essentially on its own and must track, capture, and hold, kill, or retrieve it until the hunter catches up. Unfortunately the dogs' innate intelligence can work against them in terms of the human/dog relationship, because intelligence does not necessarily translate into obedience: you threw the stick, you go and get it.

Most often sight hounds are noted for their extremely affectionate nature towards their owner, but they can be aloof with strangers. The polarity of their behavior—able to hunt and kill a coyote, jackal, or wolf and yet be quiet and devoted—is extreme, and it is partly this nature that has led to these dogs occupying an unusual place in the domestic environment. Since records began, they have lived alongside their owners and been treated as a domestic pet on the one hand and as a valued hunting companion on the other. This is at odds with many other working and hunting dog types that have been kept in kennels and maintained purely for their working function, an arrangement that is still seen today with some gundogs, guard dogs, working scent hounds, and livestock guardians.

The precise origins of the specific sight hound type remain unknown, with the exception of the Whippet, which was developed in nineteenth-century England. Sight hounds are most commonly thought to have developed in Mesopotamia, part of the Fertile Crescent and an area corresponding to modern-day Iraq, northeastern Syria, southeastern Turkey, and southwestern Iran or Eastern Europe. Although recent studies suggest that the domestic dog originated around 15,000 years ago in southern East Asia, it is believed that sight hounds developed their type in the aforementioned Middle Eastern area. Ceramic fragments discovered at the prehistoric site of Susa, east of the Tigris river in Iran, depict dogs with clear sight hound characteristics, popularly thought to be Salukis, and date to around 4000 B.C.E. Primitive rock paintings uncovered at Jebel Ouesslat, Tunisia, dating to between 7000 and 5000 B.C.E., portray sight hounds of Sloughi-like appearance. Images of sight hounds started to appear more frequently during the times of the ancient cultures of Egypt and then Greece and Rome, and the great tombs of ancient Egypt have revealed mummified sight hounds as well as painted and sculpted likenesses.

Sight hounds have appeared consistently throughout history alongside well-known, powerful individuals and were given as significant diplomatic and political gifts until the early twentieth century. Alexander the Great (356–323 B.C.E.) liked to hunt with sight hounds because they could keep up with his horse, and he imported a number of them from the Segusian tribe who lived southwest of the Rhine in Gaul. In the eleventh century, the English king, Canute, is popularly said to have banned commoners from owning Greyhounds because they were impinging on royal hunting, although no written records survive to substantiate this claim. Centuries later, in 1619, the American Virginia Assembly banned the sale of Greyhounds to Native Americans, again to protect their hunting "rights." However, sight hounds were imported in large numbers to North America, and hunting using the dogs became popular entertainment, but also a valuable method of vermin control. General George Custer (1839–76) was an ardent dog enthusiast and took his Greyhounds and Deerhounds with him on military campaigns. His favorite Deerhound, Tuck, died alongside the general at the ill-fated Battle of Little Big Horn in 1876.

Sight hounds were also popular in the European courts, especially those of France, Spain, and Italy. King Louis XI of France (1423–83) lavished attention on his Greyhounds: he commissioned a scarlet velvet collar adorned with twenty pearls for one, and provided another with its own bed and night clothes. Such was the bond between the aristocracy and their Greyhounds that when Robert the Bruce's wife, Elizabeth, was imprisoned in 1306 by Edward I (1239–1307), she insisted on being incarcerated with " . . . three Greyhounds and a sober and wise servant to make her bed." Queen Victoria (1819–1901) and Prince Albert were enthusiastic dog owners, too, and had a variety of breeds, including Greyhounds and Borzoi, the latter of which were gifted by Tsar Alexander II and Tsar Alexander III. The queen's devotion to certain breeds instigated a fashion for them among the general populace.

The original use of the sight hound as a hunting dog has become obsolete in many countries, and they are now used in the sports of racing and lure coursing. In lure coursing, the dogs chase a mechanical lure across a set pattern of twists and turns (and sometimes obstacles) that is intended to simulate live prey. The criteria for judging vary in different countries, but can include points for speed, agility, endurance, intelligence, and enthusiasm. Although the role of sight hounds has changed over the millennia, their basic nature has remained constant. These dogs can switch from being a powerful, super-athlete to being a happy, domestic companion with great ease.

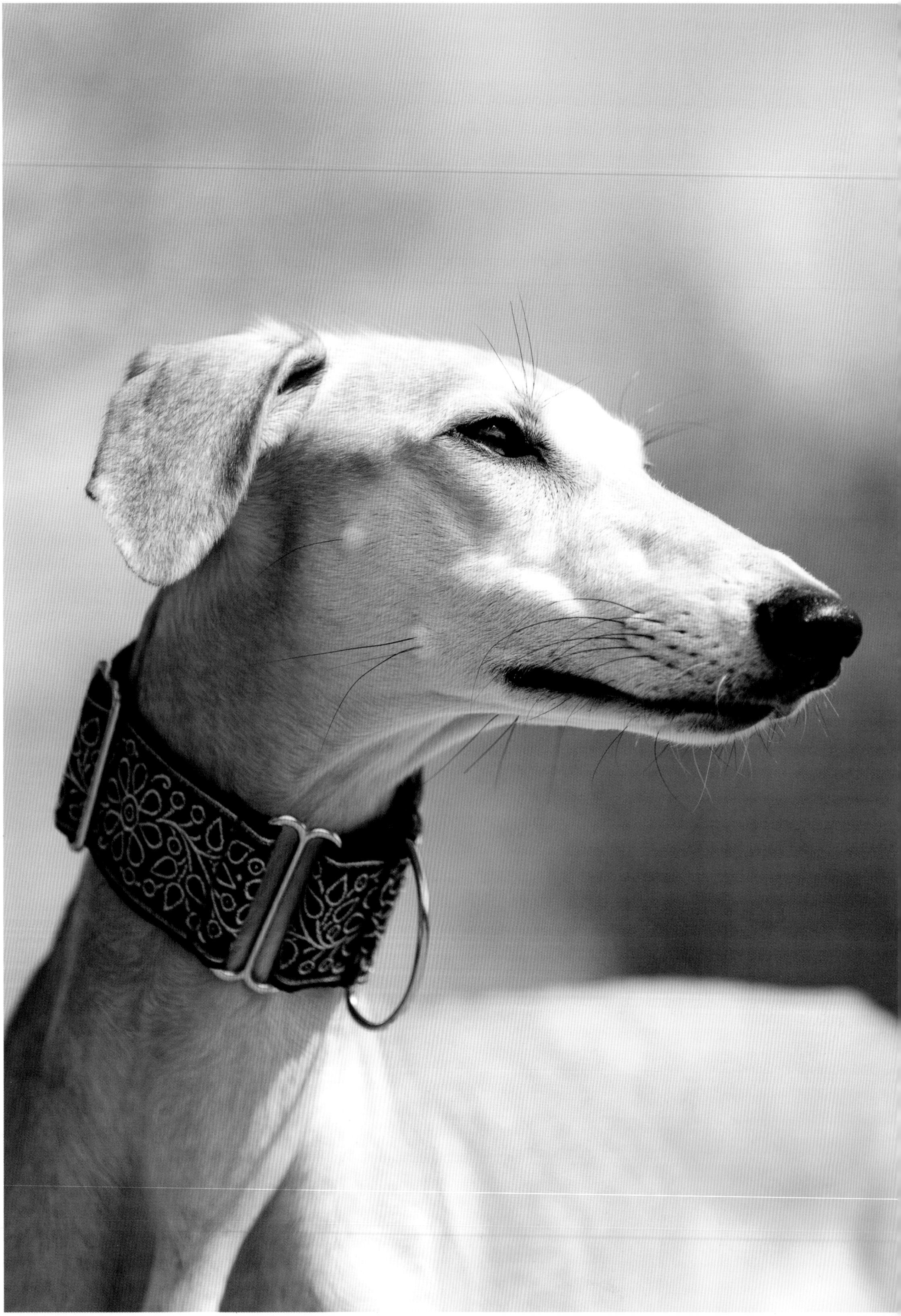

SALUKI

ANCIENT – MIDDLE EAST – RARE

SIZE

Males 23–28 in./females proportionately smaller

APPEARANCE

Graceful, athletic, intelligent. Long, narrow head; black or liver nose; oval "far seeing" eyes. Long ears with long silky hair; long, muscular neck; sloping shoulders; deep, narrow chest; broad back; muscles arched over loins; wide hip bones; low-set, long curved tail with feathering on underside

COLOR

Black and tan, white, cream, golden, fawn, red, grizzled, tricolor, any of these colors and white. Two types of coat: feathered with smooth, short fur with longer hair on ears, tail, and feet; smooth coated with smooth and short fur

APTITUDE

Originally for coursing gazelles, hares, and fox; lure coursing; racing; companion; showing

THE SALUKI IS REPUTED to take its name from either the ancient Arab city of Saluk or the Syrian town of Seleukia. It is one of the first dog breeds to have developed and is most associated early in its history with ancient Mesopotamia, which roughly corresponds to modern-day Iraq, northeastern Syria, southeast Turkey, and southwest Iran. This area is rich in ancient excavated sites that have revealed evidence of domestic dogs with Saluki-like characteristics. These include artifacts from the Sumerian Empire and the region of Sumer settled between 4500 and 4000 B.C.E., and particularly from the prehistoric site of Susa in Iran, where many ceramic fragments have been found that attest to the presence of the Saluki.

From early times, the Saluki was known as the "royal dog of Egypt," and mummified remains of Saluki appearance have been discovered in ancient Egyptian tombs alongside their owners. However, the Saluki truly owes its heritage to the nomadic tribes that roamed across the huge interior of the Middle East. These were predominantly the Bedouin Arabs to whom the Saluki was known as El hor, "the noble one" and as a "gift from Allah." The Bedouins concentrated on producing an animal of supreme beauty and unmatched speed and endurance.

Salukis were kept and used for hunting gazelle, hares, rabbits, fox, and other small prey to provide a valuable food source. The dogs were worked in packs and hunted in conjunction with a hawk. The hawk would be released to find the prey and would indicate its whereabouts by hovering in the air. The Saluki would then be unleashed to tear after the prey, followed by the hunter on horseback. Islamic customs dictate that the hunter must kill the prey in a certain way, so the dogs were trained to capture and hold, but not to kill the quarry. Salukis had to develop enormous stamina and strength for the pursuit, which was over soft, sandy terrain, or very harsh, rocky land. Despite the fragile and elegant appearance of the Saluki, it is an extremely strong dog with great endurance.

The Saluki developed slightly differently within the various Bedouin tribes and regions of its Middle Eastern home and today exhibits a fair range of body types in terms of frame weight and height. It is also seen in two clear types of coat: smooth and feathered.

The nomadic nature of the Bedouins encouraged the spread of the Saluki throughout the Middle East and the breed became widely dispersed. It is thought to have arrived in China by the time of the Tang Dynasty (618–907 C.E.), and an early pictorial reference appeared in a painted mural in the tomb of Prince Zhanghua (died 684 C.E.) near XiAn. A likeness appears in a number of Chinese artworks, seen most beautifully in *Two Saluki Hounds* (1427) by Emperor Hsuan-tsung (reigned 1426–35).

The first Saluki to land on American soil was imported by Colonel Horace Fisher from Thebes in 1861, but the breed did not take off until the 1920s. The American Kennel Club recognized the breed in 1927, and in the same year the Saluki Club of America was established. Salukis became steadily more fashionable through the 1930s, helped by the establishment of the important Diamond Hill Kennels in Rhode Island. Owned by Mr. Aldrich, these kennels went on to produce many Saluki champions. Today the Saluki is deeply cherished by all who know it and has a core of enthusiastic breeders and admirers, although it remains in relatively low numbers.

SLOUGHI

ANCIENT – MIDDLE EAST/NORTH AFRICA – RARE

SIZE
Males 26–29 in./females 24–27 in.

APPEARANCE
Classy, athletic, dignified. Fairly long head and muzzle, black nose and lips. Large, dark, intelligent eyes, triangular ears, folded down, carried close to head. Long, strong, arched neck; narrow chest; long, strong, flat back, muscular hindquarters; long, hare feet; tail in line with croup, carried no higher than top of back

COLOR
Any shade of light sand to mahogany red fawn, with or without black mask and brindling. Excessive white unacceptable. Smooth, short, fine coat

APTITUDE
Hunting gazelles, hares, fox, jackals, wild boar, any small game in native land, lure coursing, racing, showing, companion

THE SLOUGHI, ALSO KNOWN AS THE Bedouin Greyhound or Arabian Greyhound, is a North African desert dog, most closely associated with the nomadic Bedouins of Algeria, Tunisia, Libya, and Morocco, although its ancestors probably hailed from the Middle East. The Sloughi is an ancient breed about whose origins very little is known or documented. This includes its antiquity, which is projected to between 7000 and 5000 B.C.E., based on primitive rock paintings found at Jebel Ouesslat, Tunisia, that depict sight hounds of Sloughi-like appearance. Most commonly, the Sloughi has been confused with the Saluki, a Middle Eastern sight hound, but recent mitochondrial DNA testing has definitively shown that these two dogs are different breeds. Nevertheless, they do have physical similarities, and both breeds have developed along parallel lines, nurtured within ancient nomadic cultures.

The Sloughi is not considered a "normal" or "dirty" dog by the Arab Bedouins, whose Muslim beliefs find dogs unclean. Instead the Sloughi is revered and treated by the Bedouins in much the same way as the Saluki. Both breeds were considered a gift from Allah and "clean," unlike other dogs referred to as *kelb*; they were in fact perceived as totally different from all other types of dog. The Bedouins kept their Sloughi in their tents with them and exercised strict breeding policies, which allowed only purebred Sloughis to breed in order to keep their heritage true. The

earliest written account of these dogs came from General Daumas (1803–71), a French general and writer who was posted to Algeria in 1835. He wrote a number of books about the local cultures, including a lengthy description of the Sloughi. According to Daumas, the dogs were so revered that the family would give them their own blankets in order to keep warm. They were also decorated with exotic jewels and collars and fed only the best meats; the puppies, if necessary, were breast fed. They were treated as family members and grieved for accordingly on their death. Daumas spoke of their legs being branded, their ears cropped, and their bodies decorated with henna paints.

Ear cropping protected the Sloughis during the ferocious jackal and wild boar hunts in which the breed excelled. Long, flapping ears gave the jackals something to rip and tear, whereas closely cropped ears were harder to grasp. Some communities, particularly in Tunisia, still practice ear cropping, because they believe that it helps a dog's hearing and protects it against fly bites. Decorating the dogs with henna paint and branding them is also still practiced and is deeply rooted in tradition. In Morocco, the henna is believed to be good for the dogs' bones, while in Tunisia dipping their feet in henna is thought to ward off the "evil eye." The inside of the front legs is sometimes branded with horizontal lines because this practice is thought to improve the strength of the legs, and branding and tattooing are part of Bedouin tradition in some areas.

The Sloughis that were taken to France during the period of French control of Algeria from 1830 to 1962 are thought to be the earliest to have left their homeland. The Dutch artist August Johannes Legras (1864–1915) is known to have traveled in Algeria and Tunisia in the late 1800s, and returned to the Netherlands with several Sloughis. It was in both France and the Netherlands that the dogs were most fashionable at this time. The first official breed standard was published in France in 1925 by the French Sight Hound Association, and the Sloughi was

considered to be a French breed until Algeria gained independence in 1962. Morocco is now the country that represents the breed within the Fédération Cynologique Internationale, the international dog breed organization.

The fate of the Sloughi in its homeland during French occupation was rather catastrophic. During this period, hunting with sight hounds was prohibited and the dogs could be shot on sight, which led to a huge decline in breed numbers; this coincided with periods of political unrest that greatly affected the wealthy native breeding kennels. Since the mid-twentieth century, however, there have been renewed efforts to preserve this ancient breed.

The history of the Sloughi in the United Kingdom and the United States is a short one, and breed numbers in both these countries remain very low, although the breed is supported by a body of dedicated and knowledgeable individuals. The first Sloughi, a dog called Tagiurie el Sian, arrived in the United States in 1973, and in 1979 another two were imported from Germany and four from France. Key figures in the breed's early American history were Jacques and Ermine Moreau-Sipiere, French breeders of Sloughis who had established their kennels in France in 1976. They moved to the United States in 1979, and in 1981 the first litter of American-born Sloughis arrived at their Moreau-Sipiere International Sloughi Kennels in California. The Moreau-Sipieres went on to establish the American Sloughi Association in 1989, which was recognized in 2010 as the National Parent Club of the breed by the American Kennel Club. The Sloughi Fanciers of America Association was formed in 1988 and it is now the National Parent Club of the Large Gazehound Racing Association. Another key figure on the American Sloughi circuit is Dr. Dominique de Caprona, who has written extensively about the breed. He established the prestigious Shi'Rayan Kennels, and the first litter of Shi'Rayan puppies was born in 1993.

Traditionally the Sloughi was always bred and raised in close proximity to its family and, accordingly, acted as a guard dog to the family home. These characteristics perpetuate with this ancient breed, and the dogs behave in an aloof manner toward strangers, but are very affectionate and loyal to those they know. Consequently, the Sloughi is not a dog that does well if it is left on its own for extended periods of time.

ELEGANCE AND SPEED

BORZOI

ANCIENT – RUSSIA – MODERATE/RARE

SIZE
Males minimum 28 in./females minimum 26 in.

APPEARANCE
Elegant, regal, very well balanced through their frame. Long, narrow, slightly domed head, often with a "Roman" nose. Small ears, lying flat; dark, almond-shaped eyes. Deep but narrow through chest; back slightly curved; broad, very powerful loins. Long tail, set low, gracefully curved

COLOR
All acceptable. Coat silky, flat or wavy, or rather curly, short on head and ears, longer on body

APTITUDE
Originally coursing wolves, lure coursing, racing, companion, showing

THERE ARE FEW BREEDS OF DOG that are brave, strong, or fast enough to capture a wolf, but the Russian Borzoi is one, and this ability is all the more remarkable given its elegance and beauty. Its tall, slender frame; long, silken coat; and regal nature disguise a steely character and supreme athletic nature. It is a sensitive dog that is affectionate toward its owner, and although it has a long association with royalty and the sport of coursing, the modern Borzoi is primarily kept as a pet. However, it is still used for lure coursing and racing, and, in some areas of the United States, for hunting coyotes, too.

In Russia the word *borzoi* is a generic term that is applied to any "fast" sight hound type of dog, of which historically there was a large number. The ancestors of these agile Russian hounds were ancient types of sight hound, such as the Saluki, that developed across the Middle East and Central Asia. These crossbred with native Russian working dogs to produce athletic and agile dogs that are able to withstand the Russian climate. Early references were made to "hare coursing dogs" in 1260 at the court of the Grand Duke of Novgorod, and in 1613 the Imperial Tzar's kennels were built at Gatchina and used for breeding sight hounds.

The breed was associated with the ruling classes and was used for the sport of coursing; chasing small game such as hare, rabbit, or fox, and large game, such as wolf; and hunting. The dogs were widely known as Russian Wolf Hounds, and were only called Borzoi from 1936. Hunting wolves was seen as a particularly heroic endeavor, given the aggression and violence of the prey, and the dog's bravery and skills were reflected on to the owner. Typically, once a wolf was spotted a pair or "brace" of Borzoi was let loose to pursue it, one on either side, and bring it down by attacking either side of its neck. The dogs would then hold the wolf until the hunter arrived to either release it or dispatch it with a knife.

In 1861 serfdom in Russia was abolished, the kennels were closed, wolf hunting went out of fashion, and the hounds' numbers began to fall. In 1873, with the hounds seriously threatened, the Imperial Association for the Propagation of Hounds was formed to protect them, and in the following year the first dog show was held in Russia. It was from this period onward that the "modern" Borzoi began to take shape, with more unilateral breeding for specific type and rigorously documented pedigrees.

The first Borzoi to be imported to the United States was a pair bought by Paul Hacke in 1888 from an exhibition in Paris. Hacke imported several dogs from the Imperial Kennels at Gatchina and was also the first American to visit Russia to source Borzoi. He was followed by Charles Stedman Hanks, who traveled to St. Petersburg to purchase Borzoi and established a breeding kennel at his estate in Massachusetts. Joseph Thomas was the most influential figure in the early American history of the Borzoi: he established the O'Valley Farm Kennels in Connecticut. The American Kennel Club first registered Borzoi in 1892, and in the same year the first Borzoi Club was founded in the United Kingdom.

Despite its success across the United States, the United Kingdom, and much of Europe, the breed suffered catastrophically during the Russian Revolution (1917–18). At the same time, as a result of World War I, breeding programs in the United Kingdom were reduced dramatically. Interest in the Borzoi has since been rekindled, and the breed is supported in the United States, Australia, and Europe, and particularly in Germany and Canada.

AFGHAN HOUND
ANCIENT – AFGHANISTAN – MODERATE

SIZE
Males 27 in./females 24–26 in.

APPEARANCE
Elegant and powerful. Head is long, carried high, and has distinctive topknot of hair. Eyes triangular in shape, dark color preferred for their "eastern" expression. Ears low on head with long, silky hair. Medium-length back; muscular front end; deep chest; long legs; powerful, angulated hindquarters; and low-set tail ending in a "ring." Slender-framed dog with prominent hip bones

COLOR
All acceptable. Coat is short along top of back and long and silky over rest of body

APTITUDE
Hunting hares and gazelles in native land, lure coursing, showing, companion

THERE IS LITTLE DISPUTE regarding the antiquity of this breed, often described as the "king of dogs," but its precise origins are the subject of debate. Several legends feature the Afghan Hound, including the story that the Afghan accompanied Noah on his ark, and the tale that the elegant hounds aided Isis, the Egyptian goddess of motherhood and fertility, as she searched for her husband, Osiris. The Afghan Hound belongs to the sight hound group of dogs, which is one of the oldest, and genetic testing has shown that it has little divergence from wolves on some markers. The breed's ancestors developed in the Middle East thousands of years ago and over time moved east through Persia (Iran) and into Afghanistan, which is recognized today as the Afghan Hound's country of origin.

There were many different types of sight hound that lived across the vast interiors of the Middle East. These native hounds, including the Tazi and Taighan—ancestors of the modern Afghan Hound—were an essential component of life, and have historic associations with both upper and lower castes. For poor farming communities in the rugged geographical and climatic extremes between mountains and hot desert, Afghan Hounds were fundamental to daily life. They were, and often still are, used for guarding sheep, goats, and the homestead, and particularly for hunting. The Afghan Hound that lived in these rural communities was not the groomed and silky dog of Western countries, but a rugged, working dog; its slender frame belied its tremendous power, stamina, speed, and agility. Consequently, it was also valued by the wealthy ruling shahs, who used the dogs for hunting as sport.

In the late 1800s army officers returning to Britain from India, Pakistan, Afghanistan, and Persia brought various types of sight hound with them, and they were often referred to as Persian Greyhounds or Barukzy Hounds, before the name "Afghan Hound" was adopted. Public interest in these exotic dogs was considerable, and increased further when they were exhibited at dog shows in the early 1900s in classes for "Foreign Dogs." The most significant dog in the history of the "modern" Afghan was Zardin (c. 1902–c. 1914), who was imported to England from India in 1907 by Captain John Barff. In the same year, Zardin won the Foreign Dogs class at the Kennel Club Show at Crystal Palace and caused such a sensation that Queen Alexandra requested his presence at Buckingham Palace. After the initial enthusiasm, however, interest diminished, and during World War I the exotic hound dogs all but disappeared in the Western world. Their fortunes were revived in the postwar years, and in 1925 the first UK Afghan Hound breed standard was published, based on a description of Zardin made in 1906 by the *Indian Kennel Gazette*. In 1907 the Afghan Hound was officially recognized as a breed in the United Kingdom.

In the 1920s two types of Afghan Hound were brought to the United Kingdom, and these have given rise to the "modern" Afghan. Firstly, in 1921, Major Bell Murray imported a significant group of Afghan Hounds and established a kennel in Scotland. These dogs, referred to as Bell-Murrays, came from Baluchistan—a large desert region of southern and southwestern Afghanistan—and they were distinctive in appearance because they were taller and longer in frame than previous types and had a sparser coat variety. The second group was imported in 1925 by Major and Mary Amps. Their dogs, referred to as Ghaznis, came from the mountainous areas of Kabul and had thicker coats and stockier frames. Within two decades, the two types had been blended together in the United Kingdom and had given rise to the type seen today. Two exceptions were the Dutch Van De Orangje Manege Kennel that bred only Ghazni-type hounds (originally sourced from the United Kingdom) and the Katwiga Afghan Hound Kennel in Germany, which continued the Ghazni breeding.

From the 1920s onward Afghan Hounds were exported from the United Kingdom to North America, Canada, Australia, Asia, and Europe. The first Afghans arrived in the United States in 1922, and several kennels were established, including the Dunwalk Kennels on the East Coast. The breed was accepted by the American Kennel Club (AKC) in 1926, at which point the stud book was opened. Despite these early imports, the real foundation of the Afghan Hound in the United States can be traced to 1931, when Zeppo Marx—the youngest of the Marx brothers—imported two Afghans, Westmill Omar and Asra of Ghazni. Unable to care for the dogs while filming, Zeppo passed them on to Mr. McKean (a breeder of Wire Fox Terriers), who owned Prides Hill Kennel in

Connecticut. In 1934 McKean imported Badshah of Ainsdart, and together these three Afghan Hounds formed the nucleus of the breed in the United States. Badshah's brother, Tufan, was also brought to the United States, and two more dogs, Saki of Paghman and Tazi of Beg Tute, were exported in the 1930s, direct from Afghanistan.

The Afghan Hound Club of America was formed in 1940, and in 1948 an American breed standard was written and accepted by the AKC. In 1950 an Afghan Hound, Turkuman Missims Laurel, won the Hound Group class at the Westminster Kennel Club Dog Show, and in 1957 the Afghan Shirkhan of Grandeur became the first hound breed to win the Best in Show at Westminster. While the Afghan has increased in popularity in the West, in its homeland it seems to have all but disappeared because of war, a lack of record keeping, and nonselective breeding.

Part of the great attraction of Afghan Hounds is their regal beauty and elegance, which disguises their tremendous strength and stamina. Universally, they are extremely loyal and affectionate dogs and make excellent pets, although they do require a very high level of care and maintenance because of their long, silky coat.

GREYHOUND

ANCIENT – BRITAIN – COMMON

SIZE

Males 28–30 in./females 27–28 in.

APPEARANCE

Powerful, elegant, regal. Long, narrow head, fairly wide between ears; good length of muzzle; powerful, chiseled jaw. Oval eyes, dark with intelligent expression. Small, fine-textured ears, folded back but semi pricked when alert. Long, elegant, arched neck; long, muscular, broad back; powerful, slightly arched loins. Deep chest,

fairly well-sprung ribs, well tucked up at flanks. Straight front legs with plenty of bone, very muscular hindquarters with hocks well let down. Long tail, rather low set, gently curved

COLOR

Black, white, red, blue, fawn, fallow, brindle, or any of these colors broken with white

APTITUDE

Coursing, lure coursing, racing, showing, companion

THE HISTORY OF THE GREYHOUND is long and lively; these dogs have changed little in appearance over several thousand years and they are one of the most distinctive of dog breeds. Throughout its history the Greyhound has been associated with royalty, nobility, heads of state, and leading political figures. The dogs have been extensively traded throughout the world, used as significant diplomatic gifts particularly during the Renaissance in Europe, and historically have appeared more frequently in works of fine art than any other breed. They are also the fastest breed of dog in the world.

The exact origins of the Greyhound are undocumented. Traditionally, theories center on either the Middle East or the ancient cultures of eastern Europe. The breed is commonly linked to images of Greyhound-like dogs found in the Middle East, and particularly Egypt, that date to around 2900 to 2751 B.C.E. Other Greyhound-like dogs can be seen on artifacts recovered from the tomb of Tutankhamun. Tomb imagery often featured such dogs, which suggests that the animals were highly regarded as eternal companions, a tradition that was reawakened centuries later in medieval Europe when stone effigies of Greyhound-like dogs were placed at the end of tombs.

In 2004 Dr. Heidi Parker, Dr. Elaine Ostrander, and colleagues produced a scientific study into the genetic structure of the purebred dog. The results were extensive,

and revealed that the Afghan and Saluki are the oldest of the sight hound breeds. More extensive study was undertaken to research the division between breeds, and the surprising results of this put the Greyhound, along with the Borzoi and Irish Wolfhound, into the same genetic cluster as several of the European herding breeds, such as the Belgian Tervuren, Collies, and Shelties. The scientists concluded that the Greyhound and Borzoi addition to this cluster indicated they were either progenitors to or descendants of the herding group. This is still somewhat contested; however, these results, combined with historical evidence, have led some experts to conclude that the Greyhound originated in southeastern England around 2,000 to 2,500 years ago.

Moreover, it is Britain with which the Greyhound in its present form is most closely associated. Greyhound types may have been brought to Britain during the late Neolithic period or early Bronze Age by the Beaker people. The Beaker (or Bell Beaker) culture was spread across western Europe, and the Beaker people were defined by their common use of a specific style of pottery. Then, in the fifth century B.C.E., the ancient Celts arrived in Britain from Europe and they are also credited with bringing sight hounds with them. For centuries prior to the Roman invasion of Britain in 43 C.E., there had been extensive trading between Britain and Europe. Accounts by the Greek historian, Strabo (c.63 B.C.E.–24 C.E.), indicate that dogs formed part of the trades during the first century B.C.E.

From the earliest times, the Greyhound has had a strong association with the ruling classes. Greyhound types appear in the Julius Work Calendar, an early Anglo-Saxon calendar made in Canterbury with illustrations depicting seasonal activities: the Greyhound types appear in a boar hunt depicting the month of September. The use of the Greyhound in the hunt was further cemented through the Forest Laws. First thought to have been formalized by William the Conqueror (c. 1028–87), these laws reserved large areas of the country for hunting by the aristocracy and prevented "commoners" from owning Greyhounds. The commoners, however, also valued these dogs for their ability to procure food through hunting, and many written accounts exist pertaining to those arrested for hunting with their Greyhounds in the forests.

Greyhounds were popular across Europe, particularly in Italy, Spain, and France, where they were kept and bred in large numbers by the aristocracy and were traded between families for large sums of money. Throughout the European courts, favorite Greyhounds lived in luxury: eating, dining, and sleeping with their esteemed owners.

During the sixteenth century, hare coursing with Greyhounds became extremely popular in the United Kingdom and mainland Europe. The first official coursing club was formed in 1776 in Swaffham, Norfolk, and in 1858 the National Coursing Club (NCC) was established to regulate the sport. Coursing reached the height of its popularity in the United Kingdom during the nineteenth century, by which time it had crossed the class divide and people from all stations in life—from farmers and tradesmen to gentry—participated. The NCC established the original Greyhound stud book in 1882 and has run it ever since to register all British Greyhounds.

During the nineteenth century, Greyhounds were still very much part of the royal household. Queen Victoria (1819–1901) and Prince Albert (1819–61) were particular Greyhound enthusiasts. Prince Albert's favorite dog, Eos, was brought from Germany and became his almost constant companion for ten and a half years. Queen Victoria wrote that Albert was beside himself with grief when Eos died.

The first Greyhounds to arrive in America were brought by the Spanish conquistadores during the sixteenth century, and sadly their role was grisly. Greyhounds, along with Mastiffs, were used extensively by the conquistadores for hunting Native Americans, and the Greyhounds were able to outrun any man and bring him down with its powerful jaws. Twenty dogs, including Greyhounds and Mastiffs, were taken on Christopher Columbus's second voyage in 1493 and classed as "weapons." In 1539 Hernando de Soto landed in Tampa Bay with nine ships, various supplies, horses, and numerous dogs, including his favorite Greyhound, Bruto. This dog earned dubious fame for his

aggression against the Native Americans, to such an extent that when he died his death was kept secret so his reputation could continue to terrify people.

In 1585 Sir Walter Raleigh shipped Greyhounds to Virginia to hunt deer and game, and from this time onward the breed was used more exclusively for this endeavor. As a sight hound, the Greyhound is unsurpassed and it is a brilliant, quick, and efficient killer of game. It was used widely by the colonists for hunting, primarily for entertainment and sport. In 1619 the Virginia Assembly forbade the sale of English dogs, specifically Greyhounds, to Native Americans, in order to protect their own hunting interests. By the mid-1800s Greyhounds were being shipped to the United States in large numbers from Ireland and England, mainly for vermin control in the Midwest. At the same time, Colonel George Armstrong Custer (1839–76) used two Greyhounds for tracking Native Americans on his first campaign. Custer was fond of Greyhounds and is said to have owned twenty-two of the dogs.

By the 1890s coursing had become popular in the United States, and a number of clubs had been established. There was also great public interest in the sport of dog showing, which began in the 1870s, and the Greyhound was among the most popular to be exhibited. The formation of the American Kennel Club (AKC) in 1884 increased interest in showing, and Greyhound owners then formed the Greyhound Club of America in 1907.

The development of Greyhound track racing from coursing began in the United Kingdom and Ireland in 1876, when the first enclosed coursing track was used. It was also in 1876 that the first track race featuring a mechanical lure was run in the United Kingdom. It was introduced by an American, Owen Patrick Smith. Smith invented the first oval Greyhound track with mechanical lure in 1907 and established tracks across the United States. A year earlier, the National Greyhound Association (NGA) was formed to register all racing Greyhounds; the AKC registers nonracing Greyhounds and will accept dogs also registered with the NGA; however, the NGA will not accept Greyhounds registered with the AKC. In 1947 the American Greyhound Track Operators Association was founded and became a national organization in 1960. Greyhound racing remains a popular sport in the United Kingdom, United States, Ireland, Europe, and Australia.

ELEGANCE AND SPEED

IBIZAN HOUND

ANCIENT – MIDDLE EAST/IBIZA – MODERATE

SIZE
Males 23½–27½ in./females 22½–26 in.

APPEARANCE
Slender, athletic, deerlike. Long, narrow head; flesh-colored nose; intelligent, amber eyes; very large, erect ears. Long, muscular neck, upright upper arm; long straight front legs. Level, strong back, sloping slightly from hip to tail; tail low set and long, may be carried high

COLOR
White or any shade of red in solid color or any combination of these. Smooth coated with short, hard hairs, or wire coated with short to medium-length wiry hair

APTITUDE
Rabbit hunting, lure coursing, racing, companion

THE IBIZAN HOUND takes its name from the Spanish Balearic island with which it is most associated, but it actually developed in the Middle East at some point in prehistory. Many images of animals with clear Ibizan Hound characteristics that date to at least 3,000 B.C.E. have been discovered. These visual representations appear most frequently on tombs, such as the tomb of Tutankhamun, and often depict the Egyptian god of the dead in the Ibizan Hound form.

It is to the Phoenicians, however, that the spread of the Ibizan Hound is most commonly attributed. The Phoenicians established an ancient maritime trading culture, and by the eighth century B.C.E. they had founded settlements on the island of Eivissa, modern-day Ibiza, and had taken their hunting hounds with them. When the Ibizan Hound became obsolete in the Middle East, it continued to flourish on the Spanish islands, and as such became known as the Ibizan.

The Ibizan Hound was kept specifically to hunt rabbits, at which it excelled, and for the provision of food rather than sport. The dog was not pampered or treated as a family member but was considered as working livestock. Native farmers kept and bred only the best dogs, breeding for speed, athleticism, and hunting abilities. The Ibizan Hound is unusual in its ability to work on sight, sound, and scent, and all three senses are highly developed in the breed. It is efficient at hunting rabbits and is trained to capture and retrieve, rather than to catch and kill. It should have a soft mouth and return to the hunter with the prey still alive. Traditionally, Spanish farmers kept one or two dogs for hunting; they were able to hunt alone or in a brace. Today, the dogs may hunt in a pack of fifteen, and will cooperate together well.

The Ibizan remains one of the most distinctive hound breeds thanks to its mobile, large, and upright ears. It is found primarily across Spain and also in France, Italy, Switzerland, the United Kingdom, and the United States, but exists in relatively low numbers. The first Ibizan Hounds in the United States arrived in 1956, imported by Colonel and Mrs. Seoane from Rhode Island, and Ibizans are used popularly for lure coursing and racing. The breed was recognized by the American Kennel Club in 1976, and the first Ibizan breed champion was Ch Sunking Eterna of Treybeau, owned by Dean Wright. There is also a variety of Ibizan Hound that has a wire-haired coat, although this type remains relatively low in number in the United States, and indeed worldwide. Currently the top, winning, wire-haired Ibizan Hound in US history is Ch Grypons Stellar Eminence, who was born in 2000. She has won five Best in Shows and the much-coveted Best of Breed at the Westminster Kennel Club Dog Show.

In the United Kingdom, well-known early Ibizan Hounds were Leo the Brave, imported by John West; Sol, bred by Mrs. Holt; and Ivicen Cleopatra, bred by Diana Berry. The first UK show champion was Ch Ivicen Julius, bred by Sue Jenkins. The Ibizan Hound is promoted and preserved in the United Kingdom by an active breed club that strives to maintain the breed's original and fundamental qualities. The Ibizan is an active and intelligent dog with a huge jumping ability that requires a well-fenced yard. It is also playful and, on the whole, excellent with children, enjoying taking part in games and even tree climbing. Equally, it has retained its excellent hunting skills and can be prone to "selective hearing" to the recall when off the lead.

IRISH WOLFHOUND
ANCIENT – IRELAND – MODERATE

SIZE

Males minimum 32 in./females minimum 30 in.

APPEARANCE

Of great size and commanding appearance, muscular, balanced, powerful, and athletic. A noble head carried high; long muzzle; powerful jaws; kind, oval-shaped eyes. Small, velvety ears. Long, muscular neck; broad, sloped shoulders; very deep chest. Long back, belly drawn up, very powerful hindquarters. Long, slightly curved tail carried low

COLOR

Brindle, gray, red, black, pure white, fawn, and wheaten. Rough, coarse coat, particularly wiry under jaw and over eyes

APTITUDE

Originally for wolf hunting, lure coursing, showing, companion

THE MAGNIFICENT IRISH WOLFHOUND is one of the great dogs of history. Its story stretches far back and is woven into the very fabric of Irish folklore and legend; these dogs epitomize valor and loyalty, and they have, over time, accompanied warrior, hunter, and royalty alike. They were among the most valued dogs in early history, serving as guardians, affectionate companions, and ferocious hunters as required. Today the Irish Wolfhound is no longer called on for hunting wolves, but is instead one of the most charming and delightful companion dogs—for those with a large enough house and yard.

The origins of the Irish Wolfhound are unclear, but it is likely the dogs were descended from, or were closely related to, the Greyhound, which in turn is believed to have developed in either the Middle East or Eastern Europe. There is no documentary evidence to reveal how or when these massive dogs arrived in Ireland, the country with which they are most closely associated. One of the earliest references to what was probably the Irish Wolfhound dates to around 279 B.C.E. and to descriptions of the sacking of Delphi in Greece by the ancient Celts, accompanied by massive, ferocious hounds. By this time, the dogs had developed their own characteristics, which separated them from the Greyhound, namely, their huge size and a heavier frame. They are the tallest and largest of all the hound breeds and have been bred specifically for size.

The Celts reputedly took large numbers of Wolfhounds to Scotland during invasions in the first century C.E. and more again in the fifth century. These dogs would have been an early influence in the development of the Scottish Deerhound. The first clear written reference to the Wolfhound, however, was made in 391 C.E. in correspondence between the Roman Consul, Quintus Aurelius Symmachus, and his brother, Flavinius, in which Flavinius thanked the consul for sending seven of the dogs to Rome to fight in the arena. Mention of the dogs occurs frequently in ancient Irish tales, and the coat of arms of the early Irish kings bore the harp, shamrock, and Wolfhound, with the motto "Gentle when stroked, fierce when provoked" underneath. The dogs were referred to by the Celtic word *Cu*, roughly meaning "Greyhound." Such was the Celts' regard for their dogs as symbols of bravery and power that the word *Cu* was often added to the names of ancient warriors and chieftains.

It is fitting that the Irish Wolfhound should be linked to Ireland's patron saint, St. Patrick (c. 387–c. 460). At the time Patrick was born, the dogs were in great demand by the Romans in Europe and were extremely valuable. Patrick, fleeing from slavery in Ireland, begged passage on a ship setting sail for Gaul. The ship was loaded with valuable Wolfhounds that were destined to be sold to the Romans, but the dogs were unmanageable and wild. Patrick was able to calm them, thus endearing himself to the ship's captain. Later, when the ship beached on the Gaul coastline, he prayed for a herd of wild pigs and directed the dogs to kill them, so providing much needed food for everyone. Many years later, he was again associated with the Wolfhound, this time on his return to Ireland to bring Christianity to the country. A local chieftain called Dichu journeyed to the boat to dispatch the stranger and his religion, and took his giant, ferocious Irish Wolfhound, Luath, with him. When Dichu saw Patrick, he ordered his dog to attack, but Patrick knelt and prayed, and Luath stopped his charge and crept forward to nuzzle his hand. This is cited as the saint's first miracle in Ireland and impressed Dichu so much that he gave Patrick a barn for his new church and embraced the new religion.

The contrast between the Irish Wolfhound's ability to be highly aggressive and utterly passive is enormous and was a characteristic used to great advantage historically. It resulted in the breed being kept within the family home as a companion, while also being used for hunting and guarding. A well-known early Irish Wolfhound was the dog Gelert, who was given by King John (1166–1216) to the Welsh Prince Llywelyn the Great in around 1210. Gelert was fiercely protective of Llywelyn, his wife Joan, and their young son Dafydd. During a military expedition, Llywelyn left Dafydd under the guardianship of Gelert, which he had done many times before. When he returned, he saw that the tent had been ripped and there were bloodstains on the ground. Gelert was covered in blood and crouched by the remains of the tent. Normally the dog would have bounded toward his master, but he did not move and Llywelyn, still riled from the day's skirmishes, thought the dog had killed his son. He felled Gelert with his sword and rushed to the tent, only to find his son safe and sound, and the body of a mangled wolf lying nearby. Llywelyn realized that Gelert had killed the wolf to protect Dafydd. The Welshman was beside himself with grief, and Gelert was buried in a favorite spot by their home.

In the fifteenth century, each county in Ireland was required by law to keep at least twenty-four Irish Wolfhounds to control the wild wolf population. From the Middle Ages to the seventeenth century, the dogs were sought after across Europe and were frequently given as politically motivated gifts between the various royal houses of the continent, including England, France, Spain, Sweden, Denmark, and Poland. They were also sent to Persia and India. The dogs were traded abroad so extensively that they became scarce in their own country, in turn leading to a resurgence of the wolf population. In an effort to counteract the imbalance, Oliver Cromwell (1599–1658) issued a prohibition on the export of the dogs from Ireland, which helped to preserve their numbers for a short time. However, by the early years of the eighteenth century the wolf had been hunted to extinction and the Wolfhound had become redundant. The dogs began to fall from fashion, and their numbers dwindled to almost nothing. It was not until the nineteenth century, when there was a renewed interest in Irish nationalism and its important Celtic past (in which the Wolfhound had been so important), that there was a revival of the breed.

The modern Irish Wolfhound owes its existence to the efforts of several enthusiasts led by Major H. D. Richardson, a Scot living in Dublin who wrote a number of articles about the breed in 1841. He located several Wolfhounds in Ireland and established a breeding program, using some outcrosses to other similar breeds. His breeding program was taken up by Sir John Power of Kilfane, Mr. Baker of Ballytobin, and Mr. Mahoney of Dromore, who bred the dogs between 1842 and 1873. Another key figure was Captain George Graham, a Scot living in England and an authority on the Scottish Deerhound. He began breeding Irish Wolfhounds (in England) and was determined that the old breed should be saved. He had to introduce some Scottish Deerhound blood and other breeds such as the Borzoi, Great Dane, and a "Great Dog of Tibet." There was much controversy over the revival of the breed, and some people claimed that the original breed had disappeared and that the regenerated breed was not true to origin. Clearly, the enthusiasts, such as Graham, felt differently. Graham bred Wolfhounds for twenty years in order to try and reestablish the breed, and a breed standard was eventually produced under his supervision in 1886. He was also instrumental in establishing the Irish Wolfhound Club in 1885. The breed suffered again during both world wars, and by the end of 1945 it is estimated that nearly all Irish Wolfhounds in the United Kingdom were closely related to one dog, Clonboy of Ouborough. In order to counteract excessive inbreeding, the American Irish Wolfhound Club sent over the dog Rory of Kihone, and his breeding activities greatly helped. A further US dog, Barney O'Shea of Riverlawn, was also used in the United Kingdom, although less extensively.

Today the Irish Wolfhound is bred in its homeland and across the globe from Europe to Russia, the United States, and Australia. These dogs are extremely popular among enthusiasts, although they are still fairly moderate in number. They make excellent family pets, but are very large dogs and require substantial room inside and outside to be comfortable, and as such are not suited to city life.

SCOTTISH DEERHOUND
ANCIENT – SCOTLAND – RARE

SIZE
Males 30–32 in./females minimum 28 in.

APPEARANCE
Powerful, athletic, dignified. A large, rough-coated Greyhound-like dog. Long, narrow head; long, tapering muzzle. Strong jaws covered with long, wiry hair. Dark eyes, soft ears set high and folded back. Strong, long neck; long back; deep chest; broad, powerful hips and hindquarters. Long tail can be straight or slightly curved when still, curved when moving but carried low

COLOR
Any shade of gray, though dark gray preferred; gray brindle; yellow; red; fawn; minimal white on chest, toes, and tip of tail allowed; white on head or collar not acceptable. Coat is wiry on body, neck, and hindquarters and softer on head and belly

APTITUDE
Deer hunting, lure coursing, showing, companion

THE SCOTTISH NOVELIST Sir Walter Scott (1771–1832) described his adored Scottish Deerhound, Maida, as "the most perfect creature of heaven." She was painted by Sir Edwin Landseer (1802–73) and appears alongside Scott in a statue by John Steell that forms part of the Scott memorial in Edinburgh. Maida was not in fact a purebred Deerhound—her father was of Pyrenean blood—but had come from the kennels of Deerhound breeder Alasdair MacDonell of Glengarry (1773–1828). Nonetheless, Scott cherished her as his Deerhound, and it is this level of affection that is typical of Deerhound owners. These majestic dogs are rare now, but the breed is supported by dedicated enthusiasts who concur that once a Deerhound has entered a family, the family can never be without one.

The Deerhound's origins are contested, and no documentation survives surrounding its earliest development, although it is closely related to the Greyhound and even more so to the Irish Wolfhound. Swift running hounds that probably originated in either the Middle East or Eastern Europe are known to have been in Scotland since very early times, and records indicate that Irish Wolfhounds were taken there in the first century C.E., and would have crossed with native dogs. Remnants of Roman pottery dating from this time found in Argyll reveal a deer hunt using a number of very large rough-coated dogs, undoubtedly the Deerhound's ancestor. Although Scotland was subjected to numerous invasions, the country still presents relative geographic isolation, which allowed its Deerhounds to develop specific characteristics based on environment and use. Much like its relatives, the Greyhound and Wolfhound, the Deerhound has changed very little physically over the centuries. The dogs became perfectly adapted to hunting stag and deer over the rough highlands and lowlands of Scotland and are the most efficient of any breed with this quarry. Their frame is heavier than that of the Greyhound and their coat is wiry and long, thus offering better protection against the harsh environment. Although the Greyhound is the fastest dog in the world on the flat, the Deerhound will outrun it over rocky, hilly terrain.

By the sixteenth century, the Deerhound was firmly established as the preserve of nobility among whom deer coursing was popular. The dogs were typically worked singly or in pairs to bring down the quarry and either kill it or restrain it until the hunter arrived. Despite being a sight hound, the Deerhound also has a good sense of smell, making it even more valuable as a hunting animal. Much like its relative, the Irish Wolfhound, the Deerhound was (and still is) treated as part of the family and is at its best when kept indoors and in human companionship rather than being kenneled. It is noted for its extremely affable and affectionate temperament, and it is this quality, together with its skill at deer coursing, that resulted in the breed being jealously guarded by the Scottish chieftains and noble families. This degree of exclusivity meant that few Deerhounds of quality were found outside their native territory, and the breed declined. When the Scottish clan system collapsed in 1746 after the Battle of Culloden, the breed was virtually wiped out. The large estates were broken up and sold in smaller plots, and the place of the Deerhound was threatened.

By the 1830s there were only two main breeding lines of Deerhound—the Applecross in western Scotland and the Lochaber in the middle—and breeders turned to outside crosses, such as Borzoi, to sustain the breed. The demise was cemented further by the development of breech-loading rifles in the 1800s, which changed the nature of hunting. Coursing dogs became unfashionable, replaced by the more efficient and deadly firearm. Two brothers helped to turn around the fortunes of the Deerhound, Duncan McNeill (later Lord Colonsay) and Archibald, who established a breeding program to regenerate the breed. The Colonsay Deerhounds quickly became highly regarded and were noted for being yellow or fawn.

In the United States the Deerhound slowly gained credence for hunting coyotes, wolves, and rabbits. General George Armstrong Custer (1839–76) was a particular enthusiast of the breed and owned at least three, including his favorite, Tuck. Before the disastrous Battle of Little Big Horn in 1876, Custer sent away all his dogs, except Tuck who was by Custer's side as he fought. Custer and his entire company of men died in battle, as did Tuck.

The American Kennel Club registered the first Deerhound in 1886, the same year that the Deerhound Club was established in the United Kingdom. In 2011 the Deerhound Foxcliffe Hickory Wind won Best in Show at the Westminster Kennel Club Show, New York.

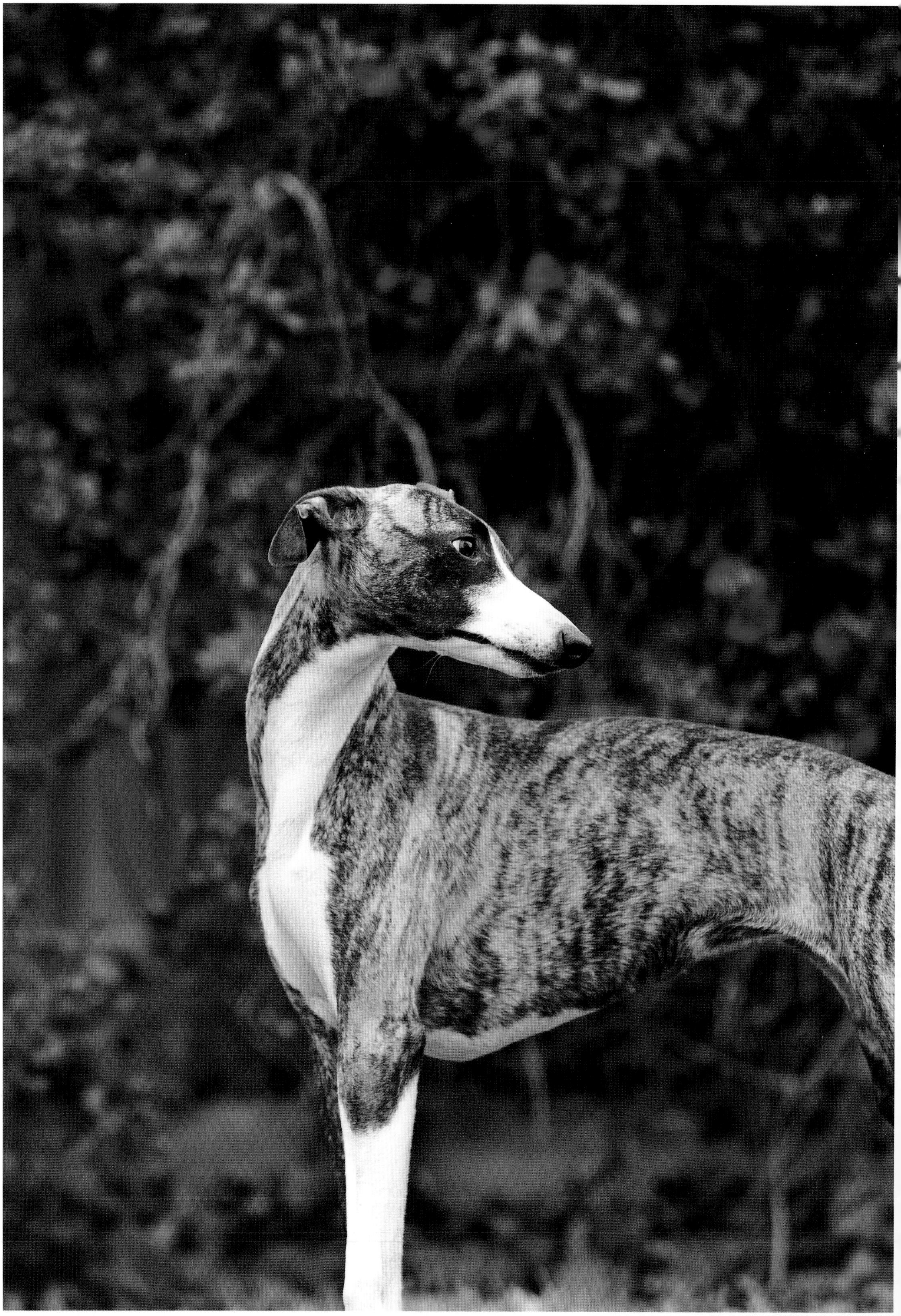

WHIPPET
MODERN — ENGLAND — COMMON

SIZE
Males 19–22 in./females 18–21 in.

APPEARANCE
Moderate-boned, graceful, athletic. Elegant head, long in profile; round to oval-shaped eyes; powerful jawline. Small, rose-shaped ears. Long, arched neck; long, muscular back; chest very deep; well-sprung ribs, definite tuck up.

Strong hindquarters, well-developed muscles. Long, tapering tail, carried in slight curve when moving

COLOR
Any color. Coat single layered, short, smooth

APTITUDE
Hunting small game, coursing, racing, showing, companion

THE ORIGINS OF THE WHIPPET are simply not known. It is widely held that these beautiful, elegant, small sight hounds have been in existence for many hundreds of years, and artistic representations showing similar hounds date back to prehistory. Whether these depict small Greyhounds or Whippets is not known. Similar type small sight hounds appear frequently in the art of the Renaissance: two particularly striking examples are Albrecht Durer's *The Vision of St. Eustachius* (c. 1500) and an illustration titled "The Month of January" attributed to Gerard Horenbout (c. 1510–20). Small sight hounds of Whippet type were popular across Continental Europe, where they were typically described as "levriers," a term applied to a variety of sight hound types. The confusion over terminology can be seen in an exquisite painting of Louis XV's two dogs, Misse and Turlu, by the French court artist, Jean-Baptiste Oudry (1686–1755). The dogs are described as "Greyhounds" but are quite clearly Whippets, given their size relative to the foliage.

The modern Whippet is closely associated with the northern reaches of nineteenth-century England, where it became extremely popular with miners and factory workers around Manchester, Liverpool, and the colliers of Lancashire, Yorkshire, Durham, and Northumberland. The game little dog, with its terrific turn of speed and wonderful temperament, was sometimes referred to as the "poor man's Greyhound," because it was cheaper and easier

to keep than its larger relative. It was also crossbred with various terriers, including the Bedlington Terrier, to produce small, athletic dogs for nonpedigree racing. The Whippet, too, was the poacher's friend, because it had the speed of a Greyhound, the attributes of a sight hound, and great tenacity. Despite its delicate appearance, the Whippet is a tough and enduring hunter. It will chase any quarry that it sees moving and, with its terrific speed, will invariably capture it.

The Whippet is the fastest dog of its size and can reach a staggering 35 miles per hour (56 kph) over a short distance. The early Whippets were often called "snap dogs," for the speed and power with which they make their first bite in an attack, either on prey or if they are threatened themselves by another aggressor. A popular early sport among the rural working classes involved seeing how many rabbits a Whippet could "snap" up in an enclosure. An offshoot from this was rabbit coursing, in which the Whippets were sometimes run after rabbits more than twenty times in one day. Whippets are still used for hunting rabbits in countries where this is legal. It was, however, for racing that the Whippet was most popular, and early Whippet races were held on alleyways between workers' houses in industrial towns. As popularity for the sport grew, tracks were developed, and races were held over a distance of 200 yards (183 m). A system of handicapping was introduced, based on the dogs' weight and previous winning form. The dogs' owners would stand behind the finish line and wave a piece of rag to encourage the dogs to run toward them. This practice lent the Whippet the nickname "rag dog." Whippet racing is far from obsolete and remains largely based in northern England and Scotland, but also takes place in North America, Canada, and parts of Europe.

Although this charming dog developed in England, it was first recognized as a distinct breed in the United States. The earliest Whippets to arrive in the United States were brought by British mill operators who settled in Massachusetts, and this area became a center for Whippet breeding and racing. As the sport and breed gained in popularity, it spread south to Maryland and in particular to Baltimore, where the most prestigious track was at Green Spring Valley. Races held here were described as "conducted by gentlemen for gentlemen," in reference to an abstinence of wagering on the track, when betting was largely outlawed during Prohibition (1920s–1930s) and for many years afterward. Despite this, rural Whippet racing of an "underground" nature was rife with gambling and heartily supported. It was also in Maryland, at Riviera Beach, that the first electric and circular track was built for Whippets. It was modeled on greyhound tracks with electric hares and was a departure for Whippets, who had until then raced primarily in straight lines. Circular or oval track racing became very popular in the United States because it afforded better viewing for spectators and did not need human runners to encourage the dogs.

It is thought that the great US showman P. T. Barnum introduced the circular Whippet track to England when he opened his traveling circus show at London's Olympia arena in 1889. In 1924 Edward, Prince of Wales paid a visit to Boston, Massachusetts, and stayed with his friend, leading Whippet enthusiast Bayard Tuckerman Jr. During the royal visit, Tuckerman organized impromptu Whippet racing in the grounds of his estate, and the prince was so taken by the dogs that he commissioned a Boston jeweler to make a number of 18-carat gold ladies' bracelets and men's tie pins featuring Whippets. In 1928 Whippet racing found its way to Bermuda, where electric starting boxes were used, and US dogs were imported for racing. By this time, Whippet racing had spread across the eastern and southern states and into western regions, as well as up into Canada, South Africa, and across much of Europe.

The first Whippet to be registered by the American Kennel Club was born in 1885 in Philadelphia. He was registered in 1888, but the breed was not recognized by the British Kennel Club until 1891. In 1899 the first breed club in the world for the Whippet, the Whippet Club, was opened in England. Since that time, these elegant and intelligent dogs have understandably grown in popularity and, with their loving nature, are highly valued today as pets and working dogs.

CHAPTER 2
BEAUTY AND ENDURANCE

The distinctive beauty of the spitz-type dog has perhaps overshadowed its incredible versatility and strength. The dogs have been used as companions, but also for hunting, guarding, herding, and pulling sleds, as well as for search and rescue. Moreover, some cultures have relied on the large working type of spitz dog, particularly in the wilderness of the Arctic. Locked in relative geographic isolation and within the icy, snow-bound reaches of an inhospitable landmass, the dogs were called upon for a wide range of roles. Significantly, only the strongest and hardiest survived, and the physical demands made on them almost certainly resulted in a natural selection of the fittest. The ancient working spitz types of this region developed into phenomenally strong dogs. They were impervious to extreme weather—their double coats are largely waterproof—and they were also noted for their affectionate nature that had been honed though millennia of coexisting with humankind.

It is not known when these Arctic dogs were first harnessed, but the realization that they could be utilized for transport and hauling had a profound effect on the largely nomadic cultures of the far north. The use of dogs for transportation vastly increased the distances traveled, which in turn greatly improved the opportunities for hunting, and once game was killed, it could be brought home with ease. The dogs themselves were also used for hunting, for protecting the home, and for babysitting infants. As hunter/gatherer cultures became herding cultures, the dogs were employed to move livestock (reindeer) and guard them. Dog pelts were made into highly insulated clothing, and the Samoyedes in particular gathered the wool from their dogs to spin into yarn; on occasion the dogs were also eaten. Centuries later these same Arctic spitz types were adopted by Westerners and used to explore both the North and South Poles. During these expeditions many of the dogs suffered greatly and died, as did many early explorers. Accounts indicate that dead dogs were fed to those that were still alive, and dog meat was used to sustain people when necessary.

The Arctic spitz-type dog was widely used during the Klondike Gold Rush (1897–99) and the Nome Gold Rush (1899–1909) to transport people and equipment as they searched for their fortunes. Around the same time, the sport of mushing (dog sledding) became popular. Teams of dogs were pitted against each other in the All Alaska Sweepstakes from the early 1900s to 1917, and the sport took off in North America, Canada, and later Northern Europe. Today the Iditerod Race is held annually from Anchorage to Nome and covers a distance of 1,150 miles (1,850 km). It is a grueling trial and testament to the courageous, tenacious spirit of the dogs that take part, although they inherently love to run and pull.

The general nomenclature "spitz" describes a type rather than a breed of dog, and today covers a great many different breeds. All of these share similar physical characteristics, which can include a tail that curls over the back; small, triangular, erect ears; pointed muzzles; and thick coats. Although there is a core group of truly ancient primitive spitz-type breeds that were typically working dogs, there is also a great number of far more recent breeds that exhibit spitz-like characteristics. These are primarily the smaller, nonworking spitz-type breeds, many of which were developed in Europe within the last few centuries and are related to the more ancient spitz type. The ancient spitz type is largely considered to be the oldest and most primitive of dog types, and differs the least from its wolf ancestors. Recent DNA testing has shown that a number of spitz-type breeds, including the Alaskan Malamute, Siberian Husky, Samoyed, Japanese Akita-Inu, Chow Chow, and Basenji rank among the oldest in the world. Several of these breeds developed over millennia in almost total geographic isolation and with virtually no influence from other dog types. This means that until the nineteenth century, when they came into Western focus, they remained very pure to their original evolutionary lines.

The spitz type is largely considered to have evolved in Central or Southeastern Asia in the first instance. As primitive cultures migrated, they took their dogs with them, and the dogs then developed unique characteristics within their geographic location. The extraordinary Basenji—native to Central Africa—evolved with a much finer coat than Arctic spitz types, but exhibits clear spitz-like, primitive characteristics. In Africa they lived on the fringes of primitive cultures and are most associated with the Pygmy cultures of Central Africa. They were used chiefly for hunting, at which they excel.

It was as a hunter that the Asiatic spitz type, characterized by the Chinese Chow Chow and the Japanese Akita-Inu, was so prized. Both these breeds, which are of ancient, primitive origin, were noted for their courage and tenacity when hunting or guarding, and sadly, in the case of the Japanese spitz types, when pitted against one another in dog fights. The modern Chow Chow is a rather different figure from its ancestors, which were noted for their athleticism and speed. Like their Arctic relatives, these dogs were historically used for hauling loads. Chow Chows became fashionable in the late nineteenth and early twentieth centuries among the rich and famous, particularly the "Hollywood set."

Northern Europe is also closely associated with spitz types, and the far northern countries of Finland, Sweden, and Norway are home to a number of breeds, such as the Norwegian Elkhound, that have much in common with their Arctic relatives: they have double coats and are widely used for hunting big game. A number of much smaller spitz-type breeds have developed in Europe (primarily), including the vivacious Finnish Spitz and Norwegian Lundehund, which have been used historically for hunting birds, and the Dutch Keeshond (also called the Wolfspitz). Germany is home to a number of spitz types, collectively referred to as German spitz, and these include the tiny, nonworking, and very popular Pomeranian. German spitz dogs gave rise to the American Eskimo Dog when they were imported to the United States from the seventeenth century onward.

ALASKAN MALAMUTE
ANCIENT – ALASKA – COMMON

SIZE	bushy tail, quite high, carried over
Males 25 in./females 23 in.	back when working
APPEARANCE	**COLOR**
Large, powerful, big boned.	Any shade of gray from light to
Attractive, broad head; large	black with white shading, white
muzzle; black or brown nose.	mask, any shade of sable or red with
Dark, almond-shaped eyes,	white shading, or all white. Double
small, triangular, thick ears,	coated. Top layer coarse, thick,
normally pricked; strong neck;	under layer soft, dense, woolly
muscular front end; heavy leg	**APTITUDE**
bones; deep chest; very powerful	Originally heavy sled pulling,
hindquarters; large feet;	showing, companion

THE MAGNIFICENT ALASKAN MALAMUTE is a powerful, intelligent, and dignified dog that has been used in diverse ways to benefit humans. It has sustained Eskimo life, been at the forefront of polar expeditions, served in the Klondike Gold Rush, facilitated the US Postal Service in remote Arctic regions, and been called upon by the military in both world wars. The Alaskan Malamute is a no-nonsense working breed with superlative stamina and endurance as well as the ability to withstand extremely frigid weather; in more recent years it has also adapted to being a companion animal, based on its lovely, affectionate nature.

Recent DNA testing has revealed that this spitz-type dog is among the earliest of dog types. It is believed to have developed in Central Asia, establishing its characteristics in the vast interior of Siberia, before being taken at some point in prehistory by nomadic tribes from Central Asia to Siberia and eventually to North America. Anthropological evidence suggests the presence of Eskimo culture at Cape Krusentern in northwest Alaska by around 1850 B.C.E. Geographically isolated and within an unrelenting ice-bound landscape, the early Eskimo's life depended on being able to travel to find food. It is not documented at which point Alaskan Malamutes were first used for transport and hauling, but the realization that these phenomenally strong dogs could be harnessed and attached to sleds made a profound difference to these isolated communities.

The Alaskan Malamute dogs were very valuable to the Eskimos and were treated humanely and fed well. They were also selectively bred, with only the strongest, most reliable dogs being used, and as such their numbers remained relatively low. They were closely guarded by the Eskimo and not readily passed out of their ethnic culture, which resulted in the fairly small foundation stock from which the modern Alaskan Malamute has descended.

In 1896 rich gold deposits were discovered in the Klondike river in the remote Yukon region of northwest Canada, sparking the Klondike Gold Rush. Alaskan Malamutes were recognized as the most efficient type for hauling huge loads, and the price of the Alaskan Malamute soared to around $500 a dog. Unsurprisingly, cross-breeding occurred as prospectors bred Malamutes with smaller, faster breeds and the larger St. Bernard to try to "improve" on nature.

Alaskan Malamutes also proved indispensable to Arctic and Antarctic expeditions and provided transport and hauled supply sleds for Roald Amundsen (1872–1928) in his exploration of the South Pole from 1910 to 1912, for example. Admiral Richard Byrd (1888–1957) also used Malamutes during expeditions to Antarctica from the 1930s to 1950s, and they continue to be used in this capacity today. The main source of his Malamutes was the Chinook Kennels in New Hampshire. The Seeleys, who established the kennels, founded a breeding program to most closely reproduce the original Alaskan Malamute from the Kotzebue Sound area, and they were instrumental in influencing the American Kennel Club (AKC) to recognize the breed. The Alaskan Malamute Club of America was formed in 1935, and in the same year the breed was recognized by the AKC, although they initially allowed only a short period of registration. Many dogs were lost during World War II, and the surviving registered bloodline base became very small. Today all registered Alaskan Malamutes trace back to original dogs from Alaska.

SIBERIAN HUSKY
ANCIENT — SIBERIA — COMMON

SIZE
*Males 21–23½ in./females
19–21 in.*

APPEARANCE
*Powerful, athletic, lively. Skull
slightly rounded on top;
medium-length muzzle; black,
liver, or flesh-colored nose.
Almond-shaped eyes, any shade of
blue, brown, one of each, or
parti-colored; triangular-shaped,
erect ears, high on head; proud,*
*arched neck; well-sloped
shoulders; straight front legs; oval
feet. Deep chest; strong, straight
back; powerful hindquarters;
well-defined hock joint. Tail of
fox-brush shape, carried curved
over back or trailing*

COLOR
*All colors. Coat thick and double
coated*

APTITUDE
Sled pulling, showing, companion

THE SIBERIAN HUSKY is the fastest of the purebred Arctic sled-pulling breeds and has consequently been one of the favorite breeds for use in competitive dog sledding. Matching its speed with a rugged constitution and great determination, the Siberian Husky is an extremely affectionate dog by nature, and will likely greet an intruder with as much enthusiasm as it greets its owner. A Siberian Husky makes an excellent pet for the informed dog owner but requires a high level of competence, understanding, patience, and exercise. It is an intelligent, independent dog and is also pack oriented, doing best in company, whether canine or human.

Siberian Huskies are spitz-type dogs of ancient origin, directly descended from Chukchi dogs. The Chukchi originated in Central Asia before migrating northeast, and taking their dogs with them. They settled on the remote Chukchi peninsula, the most northeastern extremity of Asia. The Reindeer Chukchi kept herds of reindeer, and their dogs were used as hunters and pack animals. The Maritime Chukchi lived in permanent settlements along the coast. Research suggests that they were the first to depend on their dogs for survival. Over centuries of relative isolation, the Chukchi dog evolved to suit perfectly its climate, terrain, and purpose, being able to withstand extreme weather on scarce food and pull relatively light loads very quickly over long distances.

It is unclear when the Chukchi dog was "discovered" outside its territory, but it was probably by the Russians who began their exploration, conquest, and colonization of Siberia in the sixteenth century. As a result of the Russian occupation, Siberian tribes no longer lived in isolation, and trade between the indigenous Siberian tribes, Alaskan fur traders, and whalers became common. The first documented importation of Siberian dogs to Nome, Alaska, occurred in 1908, and they were called simply "Siberian dogs." The addition of "Husky" to the name does not appear in print until 1929, just before the breed was recognized by the American Kennel Club.

Although sled races had existed previously, the first organized race did not take place until the early twentieth century. Albert Fink was instrumental in formalizing the dog-sledding competitions in Nome, and in 1908 formed the Nome Kennel Club and served as its first president. In 1909 the first Siberian Husky team took part in the All Alaska Sweepstakes race—408 miles (656 km) in total— which started in Nome. The team was owned by a Russian fur trader called William Goosak, but his driver was inexperienced and they finished in third place. However, a young Scotsman who had participated in the race realized that the dogs had great abilities and procured sixty Siberian Huskies from Siberia. He entered the dogs in three teams in the All Alaska Sweepstakes in 1910 and placed first, second, and fourth. Suddenly the racing abilities of the Siberian Husky were appreciated.

A number of Siberian Huskies were sourced for the Norwegian explorer Roald Amundsen (1872–1928) in preparation for his expedition to the North Pole in 1914. The dogs were given to Leonhard Seppala, a resident of Nome, to train for the expedition, but as World War I broke out, Amundsen canceled his plans. Seppala went on to race the dogs with great success, and won the Sweepstakes race in 1915, 1916, and 1917. The Siberian Husky's greatest achievement came during the "Serum

Run." In 1925 Nome had succumbed to a rapidly spreading diphtheria epidemic, and the collection of a life-saving serum would involve a 600-mile (965 km) round trip. Seppala left Nome with a team of twenty Siberian Huskies to collect serum that was being delivered to Nulato, some 300 miles (483 km) away. Meanwhile, Territory officials added dog teams all along the trail. Seppala met the serum at Shaktoolik and headed back toward Nome through one of the worst storms in memory. Seppala turned the serum over to Charles Olson at Golovin, who gave it to Gunnar Kaasen at Bluff. Kaasen, with his lead dog Balto, completed the final leg to Nome. There is a statue of Balto in Central Park, New York, honoring all twenty sled dog teams that participated. The grueling Iditarod Trail Sled Dog Race, held annually since 1973 between Anchorage and Nome, includes as checkpoints many of the roadhouses used during the Serum Run and honors the heroism of the Serum Run drivers and dogs.

After the Serum Run, Seppala and his dogs traveled widely through the United States and won many sledding competitions. He went into partnership with Elizabeth Ricker, a Siberian Husky enthusiast, and together they established a kennel at Poland Spring, Maine. This kennel supplied many racing dogs throughout North America before it closed in 1931. Seppala passed his Siberian Huskies to Harry Wheeler of Quebec, who established his well-known kennel with the "of Seppala" prefix. All registered dogs today can trace their ancestry back to the dogs from either the Seppala/Ricker kennel or Harry Wheeler's kennel. Other important early kennels in the United States were Eva Seeley's Chinook Kennel and Lorna Demidoff's Monadnock Kennel, both in New England.

The breed was officially recognized by the American Kennel Club in 1930, and the first breed standard was drawn up in 1932. During World War II, the dogs were used extensively by the military as search and rescue dogs. In the same period, the first Siberian Huskies are thought to have arrived in Britain, although the first documented ones were in 1968 and belonged to Mr. and Mrs. Profitt. The first to be registered belonged to a US lieutenant commander, and these two produced the first registered litter in Britain in 1971. The Siberian Husky has become increasingly popular on both sides of the Atlantic since the 1970s, as has the sport of dog sledding.

SAMOYED
ANCIENT – SIBERIA/RUSSIA – COMMON

SIZE
Males 21–23½ in./females 19–21 in.

APPEARANCE
Distinguished, good tempered, balanced. Wedge-shaped head, medium-length muzzle, black (preferred) nose and lips. Dark, almond-shaped eyes; triangular, erect ears, set well apart. Strong, arched neck; sloped shoulder; straight front legs; large, flattish feet; hair growth between toes. Medium-length, broad, powerful back; deep chest; very muscular hindquarters. Long tail, profusely covered in hair, carried over back to side, may be down when resting

COLOR
White, cream, or biscuit, white and biscuit. Double-coated, thick coat. Outer layer harsh, water repellant; undercoat soft, woolly

APTITUDE
Herding reindeer, pulling sleds, guardian, agility, showing, companion

THE DISTINCTIVE AND NOBLE SAMOYED, originally called a Bjelkier, is often referred to as "the smiling dog," and with good reason. This dog has one of the sunniest dispositions of any dog breed, with an inherent amiability that is rarely lacking and that has been a consistent feature of the breed. Multitalented and beautiful in appearance, this versatile dog traces its lineage to prehistory; it is closely aligned to its wolf heritage, and because of the isolated nature of its home, the breed remained largely undiluted by other dog types for much of its history.

The breed is named after the Samoyedes, ancient nomadic people of Asiatic origin who formed part of the earliest tribes of Central Asia and migrated northwest into the Arctic, taking their dogs with them. Sandra Olsen, head of anthropology at the Carnegie Museum of Natural History in Pittsburgh, Pennsylvania, has written about archeological evidence recovered from the Copper Age site at Botai in northern Kazakhstan, which includes dog skulls and skeletons similar to the modern Samoyed; this indicates the presence of this dog type farther south. However, it was in the frigid northern reaches of the Arctic that the dog developed its distinguishing characteristics.

The Samoyede people inhabited lands that were uninhabitable to most, choosing the vast, open, snowy tundra that stretched from the White Sea on the northwest coast of Russia to the Yenisei river. Within this area they chiefly inhabited the Taimyr peninsula of northwest Siberia. Their lives were inextricably bound to those of the reindeer, which they tracked and hunted, following their migratory routes as the animals searched for food. Their dogs were indispensable and an integral part of daily life. When the people were hunting, the dogs were left to guard the home, sometimes even the children, or they would accompany the hunter, aiding in the hunt, pulling the sled, and carrying home the game. Over time, the Samoyedes were able to change from being hunters to herders, and they established herds of reindeer that they managed. When this occurred, their dogs were used for watching the livestock and for herding purposes. They were all-around versatile dogs that were particularly useful for their hauling powers. The Samoyedes treated their dogs as family members and with great affection; they were allowed in their tents (*choom*), fed well, and cared for. This constant close companionship from so early in its history, and for so long, contributed largely toward the Samoyed's unfailingly kind and loyal disposition.

The dogs and the Samoyedes lived an isolated existence for hundreds of years, during which time the breed's characteristics were fixed. Although the Samoyede population is now greatly reduced, there are still some Samoyedes who continue their seminomadic existence. Little was known about the Samoyedes' dogs until the early seventeenth century, when the Russians began to explore and colonize vast areas of Siberia. The quality and beauty of the dogs were quickly recognized, and they were drafted into use pulling sleds for both the explorers and the Russian tax collectors. In the nineteenth century the dogs began to acquire international appeal, primarily because of European explorers. One of the first explorers to rely on the Samoyed was the Norwegian Fridtjof Nansen (1861–1930), who procured the services of Alexander Trontheim, a Russian employed by the Russian government to source dogs. Nansen had thoroughly researched the Samoyed and deemed it the best of the Arctic dogs for his needs. He attempted to reach the North Pole in 1895 using his dog team, but was unsuccessful. He did, however, travel farther north than anyone else at that time, although none of the dogs survived. Grisly details of the expedition reveal that as food sources ran out and the dogs weakened, Nansen killed the poorest to feed to the strongest. His explorations influenced many who came after him, including the Duke of Abruzzi, brother to the King of Italy, who consulted Nansen and sourced 120 Samoyeds through Trontheim. Roald Amundsen (1872–1928) also used Samoyeds as the leaders in his sled team during his expedition to the South Pole between 1910 and 1912.

The earliest Samoyed dogs to arrive in England were diplomatic gifts from Russia. The dogs had come into the Russian royalty's favor because of their exotic looks and friendly nature, and they were treated, along with a number of other breeds, as important gifts. Ties between the Russian and British royal families at that time were complicated but strong. In 1894, Queen Victoria's (1819–1901) granddaughter, Alexandra (Alix), married Nicolas II of Russia (1868–1918), the last emperor of the country. Alix and Nicolas frequently sent gifts of dogs, including Samoyeds, to her uncle, the Prince of Wales, later King Edward VII (1841–1910) and his wife, Alexandra. One of their Samoyeds was immortalized by Carl Fabergé, who created a miniature chalcedony dog with rose diamonds. The dog had been given to Queen Alexandra in 1899 by Major F. G. Jackson, leader of the Jackson-Harmsworth Expedition to Franz Josef Land (1895–98).

The breed was established in the United Kingdom by Ernest Kilburn-Scott and his wife, Clara. Ernest worked for the Royal Zoological Society and traveled extensively. He was very taken with the Samoyed and purchased dogs from explorers, as well as directly from Siberia. In the 1880s he brought a puppy back to the United Kingdom, and it instantly caused a stir. Although the Samoyed was not exclusively white in its homeland, white quickly became the preferred color in England. Scott acquired more pure white dogs from abroad and began to breed them in earnest. The Kennel Club allowed the breed to be shown in the Foreign Dog class, and in 1909 Kilburn-Scott founded the Samoyede Club, at which point "Samoyede" became the dog's official name, instead of "Bjelkier." The Kennel

Club recognized the dog as a distinct breed in 1912, and in 1923 the "e" was dropped from the name. Kilburn-Scott and Major F. G. Jackson became influential breeders of the Samoyed and sold a number of their dogs to explorers for expeditions. In 1920 the Samoyed Club was amalgamated with the Ladies' Samoyed Association to form the Samoyed Association, which still preserves the interests of the breed.

The Russian Revolution (1917–18) and the years after World War I had a devastating effect on the Samoyed in Russia. The export of the dogs was largely halted, and many of the dogs that had been kept by the royal family were slaughtered. As such, most of the breeding stock was located in England, Europe, and the United States. A number of the Kilburn-Scott dogs were sold to the United States between 1892 and 1912, and twelve of these are now regarded as the foundation dogs of the breed in America. In 1920 Kilburn-Scott moved to the United States, but Clara and the dogs remained in the United Kingdom, and she devoted much time and energy to popularizing the breed. One of the great early sires was the British champion dog Kara Sea, who has figured prominently in the pedigrees of Samoyeds on both sides of the Atlantic.

An early Samoyed in the United States was the Russian champion Moustan of Argenau, who arrived in 1904, and he was the first Samoyed to be registered with the American Kennel Club. By 1920 around forty Samoyeds had been registered; in 1923 the Samoyed Club of America was formed and drew up the breed standard. In the 1930s the Snowland Kennels, Pennsylvania, owned by Helen Harris, was influential in the breed's establishment across the country, and her dogs contributed to the opening of a number of other kennels, including the White Way Kennel, California, owned by Agnes Mason. Mason's dogs were used for sledding, and a number of them were trained to parachute from small aircraft to help in rescue operations. One of her dogs, Soldier Frosty of Rimini, was so exemplary during active service in World War II that he received a Good Conduct Medal and a Victory Medal.

The Samoyed has more than proved its versatility and adaptability throughout the years and overwhelmingly to the benefit of humankind. It makes a wonderful, intelligent, and affectionate pet and is most happy when given a job to do. No matter what it suffers, the Samoyed remains unfailingly cheerful.

AKITA

ANCIENT – JAPAN – COMMON

SIZE
Males 25–28 in./females 23–26 in.

APPEARANCE
Solid, powerful, intelligent. Large, broad head, forming a blunt triangle; small triangular-shaped eyes; small, strongly erect ears, wide at base, rounded at tip, carried slightly forward over eyes in line with back of neck. Comparatively short, muscular neck; strong shoulders; straight, heavy-boned front legs; wide, deep chest; back slightly longer than height of dog at withers; powerful hindquarters; moderate tuck up. Large, full tail, set high, carried curled over back

COLOR
Any including white, pinto, or brindle. Coarse, straight outercoat; soft, dense undercoat

APTITUDE
Originally hunting large game, dogfighting, now showing, companion

THE AKITA IS A MODERN DOG BREED that was not defined and categorized until the twentieth century. However, the origins of the Akita stretch far back in time, and its colorful history has been the subject of great debate. Within recent years the controversy has intensified as a result of the divergence of the breed into two types: the American Akita and the Japanese Akita-Inu. Kennel clubs across the world are divided on this issue: the American Kennel Club (AKC) considers both types to be variations of the same breed and registers the dogs simply as Akitas, whereas the UK Kennel Club, Fédération Cynologique Internationale, and Japanese Kennel Club regard the two types as different breeds.

The development of the modern Akita is most closely associated with Odate City (referred to as "Dog City" from the 1880s) and the surrounding countryside of the Akita Prefecture, in the northern end of Honshu Island. The area is rugged, isolated, and known for its harsh winters. Throughout the Akita province there were a number of regional dogs that shared similar characteristics, seen in the modern Akita, and were referred to as Matagi-Inu. These were native Japanese dogs of ancient spitz type with thick double-coated coats, strong frames, pricked ears, and curled tails. The Matagi-Inu were used primarily for hunting large game, such as bear, wild boar, and deer, and were trained to track, capture, and hold the prey until the hunter arrived. They were also valued as guard dogs, because they were loyal and affectionate to loved ones but also fiercely protective. These dogs were popular throughout the Akita Prefecture and were kept by nobles and farmers alike.

Historically, the Akita is associated with dogfighting, and many centuries ago wealthy families used to keep fighting dogs for competition. By 1870, dogs were being specifically bred for fighting in the area directly around Odate City, because dogfights were supposed to encourage the Samurai warrior's fighting spirit. This association has done much to tarnish the reputation of the Akita in contemporary Western circles, but the modern Akita is a lovely breed and greatly removed from its heritage.

By 1854, Japan's borders had opened to the West and a number of imported dog breeds, including Mastiffs, German Shepherds, and Great Danes, had arrived in Japan. Crossbreeding with native Japanese dogs gave rise to the Tosa Inu (Japanese Fighting Dog). As dogfighting became popular, particularly in Odate, Tosa Inu dogs were brought into the area because they tended to be bigger and more aggressive than the local Matagi-Inu dogs. Inevitably much crossbreeding occurred, fueled by the establishment of an organization in Odate in 1899 to oversee dogfighting, and the construction of a special arena. This led to a rapid decrease in distinct native types, and, in response, the Japanese government passed legislation in 1919 to start reconstructing a number of breeds, classing them as natural monuments. In 1927, Mr. Shigeie Izumi, the Odate town manager, established the Akita-Inu Preservation Society to promote uniformity in the dogs' characteristics. The name "Akita" was officially adopted in 1931, when it was recognized as a breed, and the first Japanese Akita breed standard was written in 1938.

The "new" Akita breed was given great publicity in 1932 in a newspaper article that documented the story of a very faithful Akita, Hachi-Ko. Hachi-Ko was born in 1923 in

Odate and owned by Eizaburo Ueno, a professor and lecturer at Tokyo University. Ueno took Hachi-Ko as a puppy to Tokyo, and each day the dog would walk with Ueno to the train station then sit and wait for him to return. One day in 1925 Ueno had a fatal stroke at work. Hachi-Ko continued to wait every day for his master to return, and even when he had been rehomed the dog would run away to wait at the station. Hachi-Ko kept up his vigil for ten years, mourning his dead master, and became a national hero. In 1934 a statue of Hachi-Ko was erected at the station, and the following year the dog died; the news of his death inspired people from all over the country to lay flowers at his statue.

American author and political activist Helen Keller (1880–1968), who was also deaf and blind, traveled to Japan in 1937 and heard the story of Hachi-Ko. When she arrived in Akita Prefecture she requested one of the dogs, and when she returned to the United States she was sent a puppy called Kamikaze-go. He quickly succumbed to distemper and died, but in 1939 she was sent his brother, Kenzan-go, to whom she became devoted.

The first half of the twentieth century was a difficult time for the Akita in Japan. During World War II, many dogs were confiscated because their fur was used to make military clothing; the police were permitted to capture and take all dogs, except German Shepherds, which were used by the military. Food was in scarce supply for humans, let alone dogs, and dogs were also consumed. Consequently, by 1945, very few Akitas had survived, and those that had exhibited three different types: the original Matagi-Inu hunting dog (Ichinoseki line), the crossbred fighting dog (Dewa line), and the Shepherd Akita, the result of crossing with German Shepherds.

After the war, there was a renewed effort to crystalize the characteristics of the Akita and to salvage the breed. This occurred using the two main lines: Ichinoseki and Dewa. As the Akita was being reestablished in Japan, it was also becoming popular in the United States, with dogs of mainly Dewa lines. A number of US officers returned home with Akitas, and breeding began in earnest with an emphasis on a heavier-boned type of Akita, of any color. The AKC recognized the Akita in the Miscellaneous class in 1955 but did not approve the Akita standard and moved it into the Working Group until 1972. Foundation stock from Japan was imported to the United States until 1974, when the AKC banned the registration of any Japanese stock because it did not recognize the Japanese Kennel Club. Recognition of the club was approved in 1992, but these intervening years are significant in the divergence in type between the US and Japanese dogs. Now, the US type is referred to as the Akita, and those of Japanese heritage as Japanese Akita-Inus. These two types are now viewed as totally separate breeds (in the United Kingdom, Japan, and other countries) and differ considerably in appearance. The US Akita is a larger, heavier dog than its Japanese relative and has been bred along the original fighting dog bloodlines. The Japanese Akita-Inu is much more Oriental in expression; this dog is largely derived from the bloodlines of the original hunting type of dog, the Matagi-Inu, and is finer, smaller, and more foxlike in appearance. There are strict color restrictions on the Japanese dog, which are not in place in the United States. The Japanese Akita-Inu has only four recognized colors and is very specific with regard to markings.

The Kennel Club in the United Kingdom did not split the breed into Akita (US type) and Japanese Akita-Inu until 2006. These dogs had first arrived in the United Kingdom in the early 1930s and one was exhibited at Crufts in 1936. From this time onward, dogs were imported from Japan and the United States, and the two types were interbred. In 2001 the Japanese Kennel Club prevented the sale or export of their Japanese Akita-Inus to any country that did not distinguish between the two types. In 2006 the Kennel Club (UK) announced that the breed would be split on genotype (not phenotype), which meant that only dogs that had three generations of Japanese pedigree could be registered as Japanese Akita-Inu. The Japanese Akita-Inu is still in its early days in the United Kingdom; the official club was given Kennel Club approval in 2007, and in the same year Crufts held the first show classes for the breed.

Both Akita and Japanese Akita-Inu make devoted and loyal, although often independent, pets. These dogs have a unique and rather aloof nature; they do not tolerate fools and are not an ideal pet for every family. However, for the responsible dog owner they are lovely, friendly, and characterful dogs and typically are good with children. Historically, the Akita was used as a "child minder" to watch over children and was said to bring the child luck.

CHOW CHOW

ANCIENT – CHINA – COMMON

SIZE
Males/females 17–20 in.

APPEARANCE
Lionlike, solid, powerful, dignified; a muscular dog with heavy bone and characteristic scowling but dignified expression. Dark brown, almond-shaped, deep-set eyes, placed well apart and obliquely. Small, moderately thick, triangular ears carried stiffly erect with slight forward tilt. Mouth and tongue ideally solid black. Strong, nicely arched neck, short, compact. Close-coupled body with deep, broad, and muscular chest. Hindlegs have little apparent angulation and appear almost straight when viewed from the side. Tail set high and carried close to back at all times

COLOR
Clear colored, solid, or solid with lighter shadings in the ruff, tail, and featherings. Can be red, black, blue, cinnamon or cream. Two types of coat: rough or smooth, both are double coated with a soft woolly undercoat

APTITUDE
Originally guarding, herding, hunting, pulling carts, food

AN ANCIENT CHINESE FAIRY TALE recounts that when the world was created and the stars were placed in the sky, a few pieces of sky fell to the earth and were licked up by a Chow Chow, forever staining the dog's tongue. The breed's dark bluish-black tongue is one of its highly distinctive characteristics, alongside its lion- or bearlike appearance. The Chow Chow is a quiet, dignified, and noble dog, noted for its independent nature and loyalty. Over the millennia of its long history, the Chow has proved to be versatile and, surprisingly given its sturdy frame, was once noted for its hunting abilities and speed.

Two popular theories surround the origins of this dog, whose antiquity has been proved recently through DNA testing that revealed that it is directly descended from the earliest dogs. The Chow is thought to have developed in the Arctic Circle and gradually moved south into Mongolia, Siberia, and China. One theory suggests that it was the result of a cross between the equally ancient Tibetan Mastiff and the Samoyed, although this seems unlikely because the Samoyed does not have the Chow's blue-black tongue. It is possible, in fact, that the Chow gave rise to the Samoyed and other similar breeds such as the Norwegian Elkhound, Keeshond, and Pomeranian. The Chow is widely believed to be one of the ancestors of the spitz-type breeds, and its antiquity is undisputed. An alternative theory claims that the Chow developed in China, the country with which the dog is most closely associated. A less popular (and unlikely) theory relates the Chow to the extinct prehistoric Hemicyon, which lived approximately 16 to 11 million years ago. The Hemicyon is described as a "dog bear," and its relative, the smaller Simicyon (extinct), is said to have given rise to the Chow, which does have a bearlike appearance.

Ancient artifacts dating to the Chinese Han Dynasty (206 B.C.E.–220 C.E.) reveal dogs of clearly Chow-like characteristics; one piece (c. 150 B.C.E.) depicts eight hunters with nets accompanied by eight Chow-like dogs setting off on a partridge or quail hunt. Small pottery statuettes of a similar date confirm that the dog's appearance has changed little since then. Although these artworks suggest a date of development, it is believed that the dogs were in existence as early as 3000 B.C.E. and were used by nomadic Mongolian tribes throughout Mongolia and China for their fierce guarding abilities and for hunting. Later, as Buddhism developed (sixth century B.C.E.), the dogs were adopted as guard dogs by Tibetan monasteries, and some rural monasteries still breed Chows today; interestingly, these dogs were typically of the blue coat variety. Their courage and highly developed sense of smell were recognized early in the breed's history, and they were used extensively for hunting wolves and other smaller game.

Dogs were a significant part of the royal Chinese household, and by 1000 B.C.E. records indicate that the palaces employed official "dog feeders." By the Tang Dynasty (618–907) Chows were an integral feature of the imperial household and one of the more favored breeds. The emperors owned them in vast numbers and used them for hunting. The Chow was also used in diverse ways by the general population. The dog's tremendous coat allowed it to withstand the Chinese winters easily and the Chow was widely employed in a working capacity. Apart from making an excellent guard dog and hunter, it was also used for herding livestock and pulling sleds. Unfortunately, the Chow was also a valuable food source and sought after for its pelt. Many small dog farms existed in northern China where the dogs were raised specifically as consumables and for their fur.

The origin of the breed's name is debatable. Chow, or Chou, is Chinese slang for edible, and the term "chow" is a colloquial Western term for food, too. It is also thought that the name "Chow Chow" derived from pidgin-English in the eighteenth century and was used by ships' captains to describe their various cargoes. Furthermore, it is possible that the name comes from an ancient word, *chao,* meaning "dog of great strength."

The earliest account of the Chow in the West was written in 1781 by Reverend Gilbert White (1720–93). His description was based on a pair of Chows that belonged to his neighbor, who had brought the dogs to the United Kingdom from India. The breed was slow to gain publicity in the United Kingdom, although it came to public attention in the early 1800s when several dogs were imported to London Zoo and exhibited as "Wild Dogs of China." In 1879 a black Chow named Chinese Puzzle was imported to the United Kingdom and exhibited at Crystal Palace Dog Show the following year, which sparked great interest in the exotic breed. The first Chow was entered in the Kennel Club Stud Book in 1894, and in 1895 the Chow Chow Club was established.

In 1890, the first Chow was exhibited in the United States, and in 1903 the American Kennel Club (AKC) officially recognized the breed, with the Chow Chow Club of America being admitted as an AKC member club in 1906. Since that time the Chow has become popular in the United States and internationally, particularly among the rich and famous. The psychoanalyst Sigmund Freud (1856–1939) had a fascinating relationship with his Chows. Freud was devoted to the dogs and believed that the presence of the dog in his psychotherapy sessions helped to calm the patients.

NORWEGIAN LUNDEHUND

ANCIENT — NORWAY — RARE

SIZE *Males 13–15 in./females 12–14 in.*	*high, carried trailing or arched over back*
APPEARANCE *Athletic, graceful, alert. Proportionate head, medium-length muzzle, black nose and lips. Almond-shaped eyes, pale brown preferred; triangular, erect, ears, very mobile, able to fold shut. Strong neck, straight front legs, feet turn slightly out, level back, slight tuck up, bushy tail set*	**COLOR** *White with red or dark markings, shades of fallow to reddish brown or tan with black hair tips and white markings. Double coat, dense, with soft, thick undercoat*
	APTITUDE *Originally hunting puffins, showing, companion*

THE NORWEGIAN LUNDEHUND is an extraordinary breed of dog with an abundance of unique characteristics. It has faced a very real threat of extinction several times, and although now stabilized, it is still rare. Given its remote and isolated place of origin, it is possibly one of the purest surviving dogs of ancient type.

The breed originates from the Lofoten Islands, a Norwegian archipelago that lies within the Arctic Circle, and which is home to large communities of puffins. The Lundehund takes its name from the puffin—*lunde* translates as "puffin"—and it is often referred to as the "puffin dog." The dogs were used by local hunters as an indispensable part of the puffin hunt. Typically the Lundehund has five fully developed, three-jointed toes—plus at least one two-jointed toe—that are fully muscled; in contrast, all other dog breeds have only four toes. This allows the Lundehund to be extremely surefooted across the sheer rock cliffs where the puffins live. The dogs are able to scramble up and across rock faces that appear largely unnavigable, and are then able to make their way back down, often carrying a heavy bird in their mouth.

The dog's unique morphology extends to its incredible flexibility. It is able to bend its head over its back until its forehead rests on its spine; it can also turn its head 180 degrees to either side. This allows the dog to twist, turn, and maneuver in tight, rocky gaps. It is further aided by the articulation of its front legs, which are able to turn sideways to a 90 degree horizontal angle from the body, thus enabling the dog to move rapidly over treacherous terrain. The Lundehund also has a premolar missing in its mouth, which allows it to carry birds without crushing them. Finally, the dog can close its ears by folding them forward or backward, which prevents water or dirt getting inside.

Early references to the dogs include one by Erik Hansen Schennebol who, in 1591, described the puffin population on Lovunden and the dogs that were needed to hunt them. In the early 1800s the Swedish zoologist Sven Nilsson (1787–1883) described how the Lundehund had been taken to Iceland and became known as the "Icelandic sheep dog."

Most households in the northern coastal areas of Norway kept Lundehunds. As the dogs' value increased, government taxes were levied against them, which made them expensive, and in the mid-1800s when hunting puffins with nets became popular, the breed population declined. It was not rediscovered until 1937, when breeder Eleanor Christie became interested in salvaging the Lundehund. She obtained four females and a male, and by 1943 she had built her Luxor Kennels in southern Norway, where she produced up to sixty of the purebred dogs. In 1943 the Norwegian Kennel Club recognized the breed.

A deadly distemper virus hit the island of Værøy in 1942, wiping out the entire population of Lundehunds on Værøy and many across Norway. Tragedy struck again in 1944 when all of Christie's dogs except her old male, Ask, died. Through much effort and dedication, the breed was saved, and the Norwegian Lundehund Club was established in 1962 to help preserve and promote the breed.

Lundehunds arrived in the United States in the late 1980s and there are now three breed clubs. The Norwegian Lundehund Association of America, formed in 2004, was made the parent club to the American Kennel Club (AKC) in 2007, and the AKC recognized the breed and placed it in the Non-Sporting Group in 2011.

NORWEGIAN ELKHOUND

ANCIENT – NORWAY – COMMON

SIZE
Males 20½ in./females 19½ in.
APPEARANCE
Powerful, close coupled, proud. Wedge-shaped head, oval dark eyes, dark nose and muzzle. Small, mobile, erect ears, very strong jaw. Neck is medium length and muscular, powerful body, deep and broad chest strong front and hindquarters with well laid back shoulders. Tail set high, tightly curled over middle of back and thickly and closely haired without brush
COLOR
Coat is gray with silver undercoat and legs. The coat is thick, hard and weather resistant
APTITUDE
Hunting big game, guard dog, showing, companion

THE NORWEGIAN ELKHOUND is a remarkable breed that is the perfect product of its environment and historical function. This dog is a superb hunting animal, bred to hunt big game in the rugged landscape of Scandinavia and used through time to capture moose, elk, bear, and reindeer. It has retained its impressive hunting skills and is still used, primarily in its native Norway, to track and hold big game. With its thick, double-coated coat, the Norwegian Elkhound is impervious to the bone-chilling temperatures of Scandinavian winters and is particularly noted for its "dogged" stamina; this dog will track and hunt all day in plummeting temperatures and be ready the next day to go all over again. Noted for its courage and heart, the Norwegian Elkhound is also incredibly loyal to its owners and highly affectionate to those it knows and loves.

Like nearly all of the spitz-type dogs, the Norwegian Elkhound is popularly believed to be of ancient origin, although a study in 2004 (HG Parker *et al*) of dog genomes in purebred domestic dogs indicated that it might be a more recently propagated breed. There is, however, irrefutable evidence for the existence of a large spitzlike dog in Norway since very early times, and it exhibited similar characteristics to the Elkhound. For centuries, the Elkhound has been described as the "dog of the Vikings," and it is this early culture, which flourished between the eighth and eleventh centuries, with which this large spitz type is most closely identified.

The Elkhound was an important part of Viking life: it was used as a guard dog, an all-important hunting aid, and also for watching over and herding livestock. Evidence of the dogs that far predates the Vikings has also been uncovered through excavations at the Viste Cave at Jaeren in western Norway. Stone implements, bones, and four dog skeletons have been discovered and loosely dated to between 5,000 and 4,000 B.C.E. Two of these dog skeletons have been described as being of Elkhound type—meaning that they are clearly spitzlike—by Professor Brinchmann of the Bergen Museum. In Scandinavia these early spitz-type dogs were often referred to as Torvemosehunden or Swamp Dogs. There are a number of spitz-type breeds that developed in Scandinavia; they all share some similar characteristics but developed specific traits according to their different geographic regions and their early usage. The Swedish Elkhound (Jamthund), for example, has much in common with its Norwegian neighbor, and it is clear that they shared similar relatives early in their history, although they are not recognized by either the American Kennel Club (AKC) or the Kennel Club. The Norwegian Elkhound Association (of Norway) recognizes nine different breeds within the umbrella of Elkhound, that is, dogs that are actively adapted to hunting big game.

For years the Norwegian Elkhound was prized as a rugged working dog rather than a show dog, and it was not until 1877 that the Norwegian Hunters Association held its first dog show. It was at this time, late in the nineteenth century, that the public became interested in these admirable dogs, and from this time onward there was a move toward maintaining pedigrees, a more selective breeding approach, and the establishment of stud books. The British Elkhound Society was formed in 1923 and changed to its current name, the Norwegian Elkhound Club of Great Britain, in 2003; the Norwegian Elkhound Association of America was established in 1930 and recognized by the AKC in 1935.

FINNISH SPITZ
ANCIENT – FINLAND – COMMON

SIZE	hindquarters; rounded compact
Males 17½–20 in./females	*feet. Plumed tail that curves over*
15½–18 in.	*back and rests pressing against*
APPEARANCE	*either thigh*
Compact, foxlike, strong, bold.	**COLOR**
Foxlike head, lively expression,	*Shades of red to gold. Double*
narrow muzzle, black nose and	*coat: top layer of coat harsh,*
lips. Almond-shaped, dark eyes;	*medium length; undercoat, soft*
small, erect ears; muscular neck;	*and short*
square, muscular body; straight,	**APTITUDE**
strong back; deep chest; powerful	*Hunting, showing, companion*

FINLAND IS ONE OF THE WORLD'S northernmost countries and it was here that the Finnish Spitz, or Finkie, developed its individual characteristics several thousand years ago. These dogs were an essential component of early settlers' lives and were used for hunting, chiefly birds but also larger game such as elk and even bear. They were, and still are, also kept as guard dogs, and although they are a nonaggressive breed, they will sound a vigorous alarm at the sight of intruders. Barking is something at which the Finkie excels. It is also a vital part of the dog's hunting role and is actively encouraged in its homeland.

Finkies were originally known as *Suomen-pystyykorva,* meaning literally "prick-eared dog," which is an accurate description. The Finnish Spitz is referenced frequently in the many national patriotic songs and since 1979 has been the national dog of Finland, where it is still bred in relatively large numbers. With its tremendous character, intelligence, and hunting abilities, in addition to its distinctive golden red coat, this dog is equally at home working for its living hunting or as a companion animal.

The Finnish Spitz excels at hunting, and this working character of the breed is encouraged in Scandinavia where the dog must have obtained a working or trials certificate before it can qualify for a Champion title. Its chief quarry is the capercaillie, which is the largest member of the grouse family. The dogs have a highly reasoned method of hunting. The capercaillie lives in forested areas and is a poor flyer because of its body weight and short, rounded wings. The dog will seek and find the bird and follow it until it flies up and settles in a tree, then the dog will run back and forth around the tree to hold the bird's attention. This perpetual motion appears to have a calming effect on the bird, and the dog then starts to bark quietly to alert the hunter to its whereabouts. Gradually the barking becomes louder and louder, which camouflages any noise the hunter might be making in his approach. The hunter is then able to take a shot at the bird in the tree. If the bird flies away, the dog will take up the hunt again and follow it to the next tree. The barking element is important, and Finkies are prized for the tone of their bark to such an extent that annual competitions are held in Scandinavia to crown the "King of the Barkers." The dogs' propensity to bark is the only downside to this breed, but it is possible to train them not to bark indiscriminately if lessons begin early.

Over time, the breed's bloodlines became diluted as people moved to or through Norway and brought their own dogs with them. By the late nineteenth century the breed was in danger of disappearing. Its salvation is attributed to two Finnish men, Hugo Sandberg and Hugo Roos, who were instrumental in encouraging the Finnish Kennel Club to take steps toward preserving the dogs, and in 1892 it accepted the breed for registration in the Stud Book.

The first known Finkie in the United States was imported from England in 1959, and the earliest breeding programs date to the 1960s. The breed was established quickly, and in 1975 the Finnish Spitz Club of America was formed. The first US breed standard was written in 1976. The American Kennel Club (AKC) accepted the breed into the Miscellaneous class in 1983, and approved it for showing the following year. In 1988 the Finnish Spitz was accepted into the AKC Non-Sporting Group, where it has remained ever since. Although breed numbers are relatively high in its homeland, in the United States and United Kingdom the Finnish Spitz remains moderate in number.

KEESHOND

ANCIENT/MODERN – NETHERLANDS – COMMON

SIZE *Males 17–19 in./females 16–18 in.*	*Tail set high and tightly curled over back, pale plume with black tip*
APPEARANCE *Compact, lively, intelligent, and outgoing. Wedge-shaped head, dark muzzle, and black nose. Almond-shaped dark eyes with spectacle markings; small, dark erect ears. Moderately long, arched neck; straight front legs; short, compact body; muscular hindquarters.*	**COLOR** *Mixture of gray and black. Thick double coat; undercoat pale gray or cream. Tips of the top coat hairs are black* **APTITUDE** *Originally guarding barges, showing, agility, search and rescue, companion*

THE KEESHOND IS ONE OF SEVERAL spitz-type dogs of Europe. The spitz type is universally recognized as one of the oldest types of dog; it evolved chiefly in northern Siberia or the Arctic and gave rise to large breeds such as the Alaskan Malamute and the Samoyed. The smaller spitz-type breeds of Europe count these among their ancestors. The origins of the Keeshond are complicated. The Fédération Cynologique Internationale groups the Keeshond together with four other breeds under the family heading of German Spitz, although the Keeshond is associated with the Netherlands throughout several hundred years of its history. It first appeared in Dutch history from the seventeenth century, and from this time onward the breed was bound to the Netherlands.

The Keeshond was never used for hunting. It was employed as a watchdog and still has a great ability to "sound the alarm" when intruders approach. It has also always been a companion animal and makes a perfect boating companion because of its small size. Indeed, it was widely used on riverboats and barges where security was an issue and is often referred to as a "Dutch barge dog." It was first registered as such in the United Kingdom in 1925.

The Keeshond plays a part in the history of the founding of Amsterdam and can be seen on the Great Seal of Amsterdam peering over the gunwales of a ship. According to legend, a fisherman and his Keeshond rescued the sole survivor of a Viking ship that had run into trouble on the Friesland coast near Stavoren. Having made the rescue, the fishing boat became caught in a storm before eventually running aground. In thanks for their deliverance, the two men built a chapel where the Amstel river flows into the sea. A fishing village developed there, and a dam was built across the river. The town became known as Amstelerdam, and later Amsterdam. Since then it has been considered a good omen to have a dog on board ship.

In the eighteenth century the Keeshond had an unfortunate association with the Dutch Patriot party when it was adopted as its mascot. A popular story recounts that a leading figure in the Patriot party, Cornelius de Gyzelaar, was always accompanied by his spitz-type dog. Cornelius's nickname was Kees, and it is said that the breed derived its name from this and *hond*, meaning dog. Sadly for the Keeshond, the Patriot party lost its battle with the Orangists, and many of the dogs were destroyed. However, the Keeshond was preserved by the riverboat people and farmers who valued it for its qualities, not its status. This rural Keeshond was bred chiefly for its character rather than its conformation, because it was important for owners to have a dog that was a loyal and excellent watchdog.

It was not until the end of the eighteenth century that specific breeding kennels were set up. Around the same time the first Keeshond arrived in the United Kingdom. The first Keeshonds in the United States are thought to have arrived in 1923, brought by Carl Hinderer who had been a breeder of Wolfspitz in Germany. The first Keeshond to be registered with the American Kennel Club was in fact a Wolfspitz and was entered in the Non-Sporting Group in 1930. The breed name was changed to Keeshond because of anti-German feelings after World War I. The Keeshond Club of America was formed in 1935, and although breed numbers were low at this time, after World War II the dogs became popular and they have remained so ever since.

AMERICAN ESKIMO DOG
MODERN – GERMANY/UNITED STATES – COMMON

SIZE

Standard 15–19 in./miniature 12–15 in./toy 9–12 in.

APPEARANCE

Compact, alert, white, or biscuit cream with lionlike ruff. Beautiful, softly wedge-shaped head, broad muzzle, black to dark brown nose, lips, eye rims. Intelligent expression; dark, oval eyes, set well apart. Erect, triangular, blunt-tipped ears, set well apart; medium, slightly arched neck; deep, wide chest;

compact, strong body with level topline; underline has slight tuck up. Tail set moderately high, carried loosely over back, though may fall when at rest

COLOR

White or white and biscuit cream preferred. Stand-off double coat, thick, dense, straight. Ruff at neck, feathering to back of legs, tail covered profusely with long hair

APTITUDE

Watchdog, herding, obedience, therapy, agility, show, companion

THE BEAUTIFUL AND INTELLIGENT American Eskimo Dog, colloquially referred to as an Eskie, did not originate in America, nor indeed have anything to do with Eskimos. The breed is descended from German spitz-type dogs, but it developed its uniformity and characteristics in the United States and has been produced as a US breed within the twentieth century. It is recognized by both the American Kennel Club (AKC) and the United Kennel Club (UKC), the latter of which is the second of the US breed registries and was established in 1898 with an emphasis on performance and working breeds. Eskies are also recognized by the Canadian Kennel Club, but not the Kennel Club in the United Kingdom.

There is a long tradition of different spitz-type dogs in northern Europe, where they developed individual characteristics dependent on geography and selective breeding. In Germany, the spitz types were employed on farms and were used for herding and guarding livestock, often remaining on their own to watch over the herds, and also hunting. Their protective instinct is strong, and as such, they were valued watchdogs of the home and were even used for babysitting children.

It is thought that small spitz types were favored by German gypsies, who are said to have been the first to use these small dogs for performing tricks. German immigrants began settling in North America in the late seventeenth century, primarily in New York and Pennsylvania, and in the nineteenth century large numbers of Germans continued to arrive. They brought their small, versatile, working spitz dogs with them, and it is these dogs from which the American Eskimo Dog derived; originally it was called the German Spitz. The UKC recognized the breed in 1913, but in 1917, with growing anti-German feelings, the name was changed to American Spitz, then American Eskimo Spitz in 1922. The following year "Spitz" was removed. This nomenclature was taken from the kennel name, American Eskimo Kennels, which belonged to Mr. and Mrs. Hall, who were the first to register the dogs in 1913.

In Germany the Eskie's ancestors exhibited a range of colors. The white dogs, however, became popular because of their distinctive color and the fact that they were easy for farmers to spot. The breed was specifically bred and the dogs became sought after as pets among the European aristocracy. In the United States the Eskie is only recognized in white or cream coloring. Although the UKC registered the first Eskies in 1913, no breed standard was written until 1958; this was then revised some years later. The National Eskimo Dog Club of America, formed in 1970, was the first breed club. In 1985 the American Eskimo Dog Club of America (AEDCA) was established by a group of owners and breeders who wanted AKC recognition for the breed. After collecting the pedigrees of 1,750 Eskies, the AEDCA achieved its aim, and the AKC recognized the breed in 1995. The AKC recognizes three height divisions whereas the UKC does not acknowledge the toy division.

An Eskie is a vivacious and intelligent dog that makes an excellent companion but also thrives when given a job to do. It excels at agility and any endeavor that requires thought and training.

BASENJI
ANCIENT – CENTRAL AFRICA – MODERATE

SIZE
Males 17 in./females 16 in.
APPEARANCE
Intelligent, dignified, athletic. Noble head with distinctive wrinkled brow; almond-shaped, "far-seeing," dark eyes; pointed, pricked, alert ears; muscular, slightly arched, elegant neck; legs long in relation to body; deep chest; short, level back; deep

brisket; defined waist. Muscular hindquarters, hocks well let down. Tail set high, curled over back
COLOR
Black, red, black and tan, brindle; all with white feet, chest, tail tips; white legs; blaze; collar optional. Short, smooth, fine coat
APTITUDE
Hunting small game, showing, lure coursing, companion

THE BASENJI IS AN EXTRAORDINARY breed and a precious link to ancient history. Through genetic testing, this highly intelligent dog has been placed among the oldest type of dog in the world. It exhibits a number of unusual characteristics that align it closely with the wolves from which it descends. The Basenji will generally only have one heat cycle a year, and it is also known for being "barkless." It is not silent and has a range of vocal communication that is best described as a yodel or crow. Another feature is its cleanliness and lack of odor; the Basenji grooms itself with care. It is also inquisitive, independent, and athletic.

The western translation of the word "Basenji" is "wild dog from the bush," although in Africa, the dogs are referred to as "dogs of the villagers," "wild dogs," and even "jumping up and down dogs." The dogs are most associated with Africa, and it is here where they developed their unique characteristics. The ancestor to the Basenji probably evolved in Central Asia before migrating into Africa. With its highly distinctive curled tail and erect ears, the Basenji type is easily identifiable and appears frequently in ancient artworks, often wearing a collar with a bell. Even today in Africa the Basenji wears a collar with a bell made from a shell with a small bone fixed inside. The bell is used to alert the owner to the dog's whereabouts.

There is little documented history of this breed until it was rediscovered by explorers in the nineteenth century. One of the first accurate descriptions of the dogs was made in around 1868 by the explorer Dr. Schweinfurth (1836–1925), who found the dogs within nomadic hunting communities. The dogs are believed to have lived on the fringes of these communities but many were tame and used for hunting. The ability to be independent is still a characteristic of the breed and was a necessity for its survival through the years. Basenjis were useful for hunting because of their silent approach and they were used to drive small game into nets positioned by hunters.

The first Basenji dogs taken from Africa to Europe arrived in the late nineteenth century, and were called African Bush Dogs or Congo Terriers. A pair was exhibited at Crufts in London in 1895 but died shortly afterward, having contracted distemper. This disease killed nearly all the early imports of the dogs.

The first Basenjis arrived in the United States in 1937, but they did not survive for long. In 1941 Alexander Phemister rescued a Basenji who had hidden in the hold of a ship from West Africa. Two further Basenji, Kindu and Kaseny, were imported in 1940 as part of a shipment of gorillas for American zoos. They are found in many of the British and American Basenji pedigrees. Kindu and Kaseny's son, Ch Kingolo, was also important in US breeding lines before he was exported to Ireland where he became influential in European pedigrees.

The AKC recognized the breed in 1944, and from the 1950s the popularity of the Basenji grew enormously. The gene pool of the Basenji in the West is small, because of the small number of foundation stock, and in 1990 the Basenji Club of America (BCA) persuaded the AKC to reopen the stud book to register fourteen dogs that had been sourced in Africa, including reds, tri-coloreds, and brindles. The AKC standard was changed to allow for the brindle color pattern, which had never been registered in the United States before these African imports arrived. The BCA was again instrumental in the stud book being reopened from 2009 to 2013 for Basenjis imported directly from Africa.

CHAPTER 3
POWER AND STRENGTH

The term "Mastiff" can be used to describe a type of dog—dogs that exhibit shared characteristics and some assumed heritage—but it is also the name of a specific breed that heralds from England, and this can cause confusion. In addition, some people refer to Mastiff-type dogs collectively as Molossers in order to avoid confusion with the specific English Mastiff breed, and the term "Molosser" is often used to describe the ancestors of Mastiff-type breeds. Ancient descriptions and numerous artworks characterize Molossers as large, heavy-boned dogs with powerful square jaws, blunt muzzles, and terrific courage: qualities that are seen in the modern Mastiff-type breeds. The name originates from the ferocious Molossi tribe of Epirus in the remote, rugged area of northwest Greece (modern-day Albania). The Molossi people were famed for their fighting dogs that were used in warfare, and consequently dogs from this area were widely sought after for their effectiveness in combat.

It is unknown where the Molosser originated, although it is speculated that the breed traces back to Central or Southeast Asia and is related to the ancient Tibetan Mastiff. Some of the earliest depictions were found in the area historically known as Babylonia, south of Baghdad, Iraq, and date to between 2500 and 2000 B.C.E. The earliest written reference to Molossians was recorded by the ancient Greek philosopher Aristotle (384–322 B.C.E.), who referred to them as two different types of dog—one for hunting and one for guarding livestock—in his *History of Animals* (350 B.C.E.). The hunting dog had a slightly lighter frame, whereas the livestock guardian was more massive and had to be more aggressive to ward off predators such as wolves and bears.

Massively framed dogs of basic similar type spread throughout the ancient world and developed different characteristics within their geographic location; over many centuries this resulted in specific breeds such as the English Mastiff and Bulldog, the French Dogue de Bordeaux, the Boxer and Great Dane of Germany, and the Chinese Shar-Pei. They were originally used primarily for guarding livestock, in warfare, for home protection, and for big game hunting (in conjunction with faster hound types); they were also used for animal baiting and dogfighting. Dogs of Mastiff type were widely used to bloody effect by the Spanish conquistadors against the Native Americans, and to a lesser extent by English colonists. The dogs were particularly favored for keeping large predators at bay and consequently were used for personal protection.

By the fifteenth century Mastiff types were particularly popular across Europe, where they were frequently used as diplomatic gifts. In 1461, for example, Edward IV (1442–83) sent Louis XI of France (1423–83) five Mastiff types as a gift to mark his accession to the French throne. By the sixteenth century the "sport" of animal baiting had become extremely popular, and dogs of Mastiff type were preferred for their tenacity and fearlessness. Animal baiting was considered appropriate, if not essential, royal entertainment and reached an apogee in England under the rule of Elizabeth I (1533–1603). A diverse range of animals was used, including exotics such as lions, tigers, and jaguars—even a polar bear in 1721—bulls, bears, horses, and asses. Animal baiting, and dogfighting in particular, was also popular in Asia during the same period.

Mastiff types were used by tradesmen through much of Europe, Asia, and the United States for hauling loads, making deliveries, and carrying packs: everything from meat to milk and post to medical supplies. Although they continued to be used for baiting and fighting until the nineteenth century, they were also in widespread use as guard dogs, for protecting properties and livestock, and for personal protection. It is said that the young Princess de Conti (1693–1775), while living at the court of Louis XV, decided to teach her jealous husband, Prince de Conti, a lesson. He used to make numerous nocturnal checks on his wife, so she trained a huge Mastiff to sleep in bed with her at night and attack intruders. When her husband arrived, instead of catching her with another man, he found the dog, which promptly bit him. Apparently he forgave the dog, but not his wife.

The enthusiasm for animal baiting gradually declined, but dogfighting, which was easier to stage, became increasingly popular through the eighteenth and first half of the nineteenth century. Invariably these events were held in "pits," such as the Westminster Pit, St. Matthew's Street, London, and it was this practice that gave rise to certain Mastiff types being referred to as pit dogs. Those that excelled were Bulldogs, often crossed with Terriers, Pit Bull Terriers, and eventually Staffordshire Bull Terriers. In the United States, the American Staffordshire Terrier and American Pit Bull Terrier developed from the English Staffordshire Bull Terrier. Baiting and fighting were not banned until 1835 in the United Kingdom but sadly still exist underground today. In the United States dogfighting was illegal in most states by the 1860s, but not in all states until 1976. After the various bans, these sports breeds assumed a new role as companion animals: a transition that they have made with ease. In fact, it is hard to imagine breeds such as the Bulldog or Mastiff as anything other than a loving family member.

The Mastiff type's natural instinct to guard and protect has been widely utilized for centuries by farmers, who have employed the dogs to guard livestock and property. Mastiff types are also attributed with being instrumental to the development of the mountain dog breeds, a generic grouping of livestock guardian breeds that typically (although not always) herald from the mountainous regions of Eurasia. These include the St. Bernard, Bernese Mountain Dog, Newfoundland (the only Canadian Molosser type), and many more. Some of these breeds exhibit not only a protective instinct but also an overwhelming instinct to "save" people. These dogs have been widely used in search and rescue in the mountains and, in the case of the Newfoundland, in water, too. They exhibit enormous natural intelligence and resources, are able to work on their own unsupervised, and are (in general) extraordinarily affectionate. Mastiff types are tremendously loyal dogs, and are also noted for their calm, quiet, and loving temperament.

MASTIFF

ANCIENT – ENGLAND – MODERATE

SIZE
Males minimum 30 in./females minimum 27½ in.

APPEARANCE
Powerful, grand, brave. Substantial head; broad between ears; short, blunt muzzle; black nose. Eyes brown, the darker the better, set wide apart. Small, thin ears that lie flat when resting; slightly arched, muscular neck; heavy, muscular shoulders; straight front legs; chest broad and deep; back moderately long, flat, level, broad, and very muscular. Broad, muscular hindquarters, legs set well apart. Long tail, set moderately high, wide at base and tapers to end

COLOR
Fawn, apricot, or brindle, with dark muzzle, nose, and ears, and dark extending up between eyes. Coat short and smooth

APTITUDE
Originally war dogs, bull/bear baiting, dogfighting, guarding, draft, watchdog, dog carting

THE MASTIFF'S LONG AND BLOOD-SMEARED history has been full of highs and lows. The breed was used for dreadful purposes for centuries; its sheer size and power was exploited for wicked human endeavors. Yet today these massive, noble dogs are recognized as being among the most gentle and quiet creatures, noted for their loyalty; their undemanding, calm nature; and their intelligence.

Mastiff-type dogs have existed for millennia, and some of the earliest actual depictions of them trace to Babylonia in approximately 2500 to 2000 B.C.E. A clay plaque from this period shows a dog in bas relief that is strikingly similar to the modern Mastiff. At King Ashurbanipal's (reigned 669–630 B.C.E.) palace at Nineveh, a great many Mastiffs appear on the wall reliefs forming part of a lion hunt and in a separate scene in which they are being used to hunt wild asses. Their dominance, along with sight hounds, in this area and throughout Egypt, Greece, and Rome is well recorded, but it is with England that the Mastiff is most associated. The Mastiff's ancestors probably evolved in Central or Southeast Asia or the Middle East and were widely dispersed with the movement of people and cultures in early prehistory. The first appearance of Mastiff-type dogs in England is undocumented, although it is speculated that the Phoenicians, with their great maritime trading culture, may have been responsible, possibly as early as 500 B.C.E.

Nevertheless, Mastiff-type dogs were thoroughly established in England by the time of the Roman invasion in 55 B.C.E. Julius Caesar (100–44 B.C.E.) was greatly impressed by the English dogs that fought alongside their owner soldiers and were bigger and more powerful than their Greek and Roman relatives. Such was the notoriety of the English Mastiff type that accounts indicate that the Roman emperors employed a Procurator Cynegii (Procurer of Dogs) at Winchester to source dogs suitable for shipping back to Rome for use in war and to fight in the arena. It was in this category of arena fighting that the dogs were perhaps most prized, and they were pitted against lions, bears, bulls, other dogs, horses, and asses. This barbaric form of entertainment continued in one form or another until the nineteenth century. Although an "international" sport, it was undertaken with particular relish in England, and it was the English Mastiff that had the dubious record of being the most proficient fighter.

The Mastiff was highly regarded as a guardian and was employed on farms to protect livestock against predators, such as bears or wolves, and to keep the homestead free from unwelcome human interlopers. It is still very efficient in this respect, and its size and power are often deterrent enough. The Mastiff was also used for hunting, at which it was so skilled that King Canute of England's (c. 985–1035) Forest Laws included stipulations that Mastiffs should have the middle toes of their front feet removed to prevent them from catching and killing any of the royal deer, because all forests were the hunting preserve of royalty.

One of the earliest references to a specific Mastiff dates to 1415 and the Battle of Agincourt, which saw an English victory over the French in northern France. One of the English, Sir Peers Legh (d. 1422), was seriously injured in combat, but his dog, a female Mastiff, stood guard over his prone body throughout the battle. She is attributed with saving his life and was returned to his family home, Lymes

Hall, where she is said to have been the foundation female of the Lymes Hall Mastiffs. This line of Mastiff pedigrees continued until the end of the nineteenth century. A stained-glass window depicting Sir Legh and his Mastiff can still be seen in the drawing room at Lymes Hall.

The first Mastiff types were taken to the United States with Christopher Columbus (1451–1506) in 1493, and classified as "weaponry." Columbus, subsequent conquistadores, and later colonists used Mastiff types against the Native Americans; they were even used in public executions of captives. In 1585, Sir Walter Raleigh (1552–1618) included English Mastiffs on his trip to colonize Virginia for the express purpose of killing bears, wolves, and "humans if necessary." At the same time, dogfights and pitting dogs against bears, bulls, badgers, or any other suitable opponent was popular on both sides of the Atlantic, and reached particularly barbaric proportions during the reign of Elizabeth I (1533–1603).

These types of fights were considered essential royal entertainment and were staged to entertain visiting dignitaries. On one such occasion in 1559, a French Ambassador visiting the court of Elizabeth I was so impressed with the skills of the Mastiff against bears and bulls at the Paris Gardens (Bankside, Southwark) that he took a number of the dogs back to France. The English Mastiff was greatly valued by royalty and the aristocracy, and was often given as a diplomatic gift. Elizabeth I frequently gave dogs of various types as gifts, including Mastiffs to Charles IX of France (1550–74). She also sent 100 Mastiffs from the royal kennels to the Earl of Essex for use in his battles against the Irish. Mastiffs were popular throughout Europe, as can be seen by their numerous appearances in works of art, most notably in *Las Meninas* (1656) by Diego Velasquez (1599–1660). They were also favored throughout Asia and North America.

One of the first "breed" descriptions of the Mastiff in English was written in 1631 by Barnaby Googe, who refers to the dog as "the Mastie that keepeth the house," thus highlighting its role as a guard dog. Although popular for its use in sporting events, the Mastiff was most valued for its role as a protector; the royal households and aristocracy kept the dogs to safeguard their properties and for use as personal bodyguards. Many of the large estates also kept sizable breeding kennels for the dogs.

It was not until 1835 that animal baiting was banned in England. Matching the demise of the "sport," the number of Mastiffs also began to decline. There were many outcrosses made to other breeds, which threatened the survival of the original Mastiff type. It would have disappeared altogether had it not been for the dedication of a group of breeders, including Commissioner Thompson of Halifax, John Crabtree, T. H. Lukey, and the Marquis of Hereford. By the second half of the nineteenth century, emphasis was being placed on producing a more consistent type within the breed. It was also at this time that the Mastiff began to be bred as a show dog. At one of the first dog shows in 1859 only six Mastiffs were entered; by 1871 there were sixty-four exhibited. The Kennel Club was established in 1873, and the Old English Mastiff Club was formed in 1883; in 1885 the American Kennel Club (AKC) recognized the breed.

The ascendance of the "modern" breed was relatively short lived because World War I had a devastating effect on breed numbers on both sides of the Atlantic, and in both pre- and postwar years there was some damaging crossbreeding to Bullmastiffs. Mastiff breeding picked up again in England through kennels such as the Gorings, Havengores, and Miss Bell's Withybush line during the 1920s and 1930s. In the United States the breed had virtually died out by this time but was restored by a number of imports. The situation was even worse in England, where food rationing during World War II meant that feeding, let alone breeding, Mastiffs became virtually impossible. Only one female of breeding age remained, Sally of Coldblow, who was bred to a dog named Templecomb Taurus, who had no papers. Only one of their puppies, Nydia of Frithend, born in 1947, survived. Breeders in North America and Canada helped by sending over three closely related puppies and a male, Valiant Diadem. Valiant and Nydia eventually produced more than thirty puppies, which was instrumental in saving the breed. Given the tiny gene pool, considerable inbreeding had to occur, but it resulted in the preservation of the breed, which has since rapidly increased in numbers in the United Kingdom, North America, and Canada. Today, although the Mastiff is still fairly conservative in numbers in the United Kingdom, it has bloomed in the United States and is regularly within the top thirty most popular dog breeds according to AKC registration figures.

BULLDOG

ANCIENT – BRITAIN – COMMON

SIZE
*Males 12–15 in., about 50 lbs/
females 12–15 in., about 40 lbs*

APPEARANCE
*Broad, low, short-legged,
dignified, resolute. Low-slung,
heavy, very deep body; massive
head; short face; broad, blunt,
turned-up muzzle; large, black
nose. Broad, massive, square,
undershot jaws; projecting lower
jaw. Dark, round, wide-set eyes;
small, thin ears set high on head.
Short, thick, powerful neck.
Topline falls slightly behind*
*shoulders, rises to loins, which are
higher than shoulders, curves to
tail, forming arch. Underline
shows tuck up at belly. Short tail
hangs low, thick at base, fine at
tip, straight or screwed. Muscular,
short, stout forelegs, set apart.
Hind legs longer than front legs*

COLOR
*White, red, fawn, brindle, any of
these and white. Smooth, fine,
short coat*

APTITUDE
*Originally bull baiting, dogfighting;
now showing, companion*

THE BULLDOG IS A QUINTESSENTIALLY British breed and has frequently been used as the nation's symbol to project the qualities of courage, power, and tenacity. Since the early 1700s, the Bulldog has often been depicted alongside John Bull, a fictitious character who served as a personification of Britain in political cartoons and graphic works. Despite its inherently British heritage, the breed has been adopted and promoted in North America, where it is also used as the official mascot of the United States Marine Corps and a number of American universities. Quite at odds with the breed's early history, Bulldogs are now universally loved for their affectionate, loyal, and often comic nature. The modern Bulldog is a breed that has been carefully and selectively bred to fix its affable characteristics and is only still in existence thanks to the efforts of dedicated breeders on both sides of the Atlantic.

The origins of the Bulldog are unknown although it is closely related to the Mastiff. Some sources, such as author and illustrator Sydenham Edwards (1768–1819), suggest that it originally arose through Mastiff crossed with Pug. Traditionally all dogs of clear Mastiff type were referred to as Mastiffs, and it was not until 1631 that written reference was made to specific dogs as "Bulldogs." This was in a letter from the Englishman Prestwich Eaton to his friend

George Wellingham of London, in which Eaton requested he be sent a "good Mastive dog" and "some good bulldoggs." This underlines that there was a clear difference by this time between the Mastiff and the Bulldog. In the previous century references were made to Bondogge, Boldogge, or Bandog as an aggressive dog that was kept chained up and used as a guard dog.

The Bulldog takes its name from bull baiting, for which the dogs were specifically bred and adapted as early as the thirteenth century. Mastiff types were used in this capacity, and it is likely that as the "sport" developed people began to breed their Mastiff types to be better suited for use on bulls. Bull baiting was not entirely sport driven; butchers believed that the bull's meat was greatly improved if the animal was baited before being slaughtered.

Bull baiting was ferocious, and in order to excel in this endeavor the dogs had to be aggressive, brave, and largely insensitive to pain. The bull would usually be tethered and either one or several dogs were set on it. The dogs instinctively attacked the weakest part of the bull, its nose, clamping down until the bull was brought to its knees. The dogs were certainly not always victorious and, like the bull, suffered horrendous injuries. However, the Bulldog was noted for continuing its attack with relentless viciousness often while seriously injured itself. The fighting Bulldog of history was different physically to the modern, re-created Bulldog: it was more athletic, slightly longer in the leg, and somewhat lighter in the body, although still relatively low to the ground. Its jaws became modified for bullfighting: the lower jaw projects beyond the upper jaw (still seen today), which allowed the dog to clamp its mouth shut with tremendous strength. It is said that a Bulldog's jaw was so strong that it would remain fastened shut on the bull's nose even if the dog itself had lost consciousness.

The practice of bull baiting and other similar blood sports was not made illegal until 1835 in England, at which point the Bulldog began to decline in numbers. It was still

POWER AND STRENGTH

POWER AND STRENGTH

used for the popular sport of dogfighting, which, although illegal, was widely practiced and still continues. Bulldogs began to be crossed with Terriers to produce the Bull and Terrier, which was considered better in dogfights. By the mid-nineteenth century the Bulldog was out of a job.

A London dog dealer called Bill George (1802–81) is partially attributed with the "remarketing" of the Bulldog as a pet. George had bred and dealt in Bulldogs as fighting animals prior to 1835, and had run his business from Canine Castle in Kensal New Town, London. After the ban on baiting and fighting, he began to sell his dogs as pets— breeding the Bulldogs in three different sizes—and also dealt in Mastiffs. A number of other Bulldog enthusiasts set about preserving the breed and adapting them to be companion animals. The Bulldog Club was established in 1875, and held its meetings at the Blue Post pub on Oxford Street, London. A breed standard was drawn up, and in 1894 the Club was incorporated. The London Bulldog Society was established in 1891.

It is unclear when the first Bulldogs arrived in the United States, although they were there by the mid seventeenth century when Richard Nicholls (1624–72), the governor of New York province, ordered a roundup of stray bulls using Bulldogs. The breed became popular in the nineteenth century when many dogs were imported from England. The first Bulldog to be shown in the United States was Donald, in New York in 1880, and in 1886 Bulldogs were recognized by the Amercian Kennel Club (AKC) and entered into the Non-Sporting Group. At the first Westminster Kennel Club Dog Show in 1877, ten Bulldogs were exhibited, and the first AKC champion was Robinson Crusoe who earned his title in 1888. The Bulldog Club of America was established in 1890.

Both world wars took their toll on Bulldog numbers. An important English breeder between the wars was Mrs. Pearson, who became the first lady president of the Bulldog Club in 1936. At the same time, in the United States, Edna Glass was one of the leading breeders and produced many champion dogs. After World War II, Bulldog numbers increased, and the breed is now supported by dedicated breeders and enthusiasts; in the United States it is within the top ten breeds based on AKC registration statistics. The Bulldog of today is a singularly charismatic and gentle dog, who bears little relation to its historic ancestors.

AMERICAN STAFFORDSHIRE TERRIER

MODERN – UNITED STATES – COMMON

SIZE
Males 18–19 in./females 17–18 in.

APPEARANCE
Great strength for their size, muscular but agile. Broad skull; pronounced cheek muscles; medium-length muzzle with well-defined jaws; black nose; round, dark eyes set far apart. Ears set high, can be cropped in US, uncropped preferred. Strong, slightly arched neck; muscular, sloping shoulders. Back fairly short, slopes slightly from withers

to rump. Broad, deep chest; front legs set wide apart. Hindquarters well muscled; tail set low, relatively short, tapers to point

COLOR
Any solid color, parti, or patched permissible. All white, more than 80% white, black/tan; liver not encouraged. Coat short, stiff, glossy

APTITUDE
Originally bullbaiting, dogfighting, guarding; now agility, obedience, showing, companion

LIKE MANY OF THE BREEDS formerly used for animal baiting and dogfighting, the modern American Staffordshire Terrier is now noted for its loyal, quiet nature and often comic character. Although it is not always welcoming of other dogs, the American Staffordshire Terrier is a dedicated and affectionate family dog and typically good with children. Sadly, it has had poor press in recent years that has associated it with aggression and (illegal) dogfighting. This is not a true reflection of the breed in general but of a minority of irresponsible owners.

There is also confusion between the American Staffordshire Terrier and the American Pit Bull Terrier, which has received similar media attention. The United Kennel Club only recognizes the latter breed. In the past it accepted American Staffordshire Terriers through its single registration process and included them as Pit Bull Terriers, but the ruling was changed in 2010. Most breeders feel that these two breeds have been bred along separate bloodlines for long enough to warrant this clear difference. The American Kennel Club (AKC) does not recognize the American Pit Bull Terrier and only registers American Staffordshire Terriers.

The history of the American Staffordshire Terrier traces back to the early nineteenth century in England and has its origins with the Bulldog and various types of terrier.

Bulldogs were more athletic at that time, although they were still of relatively massive build, and had been bred for their strength and courage. During the nineteenth century breeders began to cross these dogs with lighter weight, faster terrier types, with the aim of combining the strength and tenacity of the Bulldog and the lively gameness of the terrier. Terrier types used included the now extinct English White Terrier, the Black and Tan Terrier (now known as the Patterdale), and the Fox Terrier. The results were called Bull and Terrier Dogs, Half and Halfs, Pit Dogs, or Pit Bullterriers. The reference to "pit" came from dogfighting, which was held in pits. The dogs would be thrown into a pit and the last one fighting or surviving was pronounced the winner. Later these dogs became known as Staffordshire Bull Terriers in England.

The English Staffordshire Bull Terrier arrived in the United States in the late nineteenth century, and developed into a bigger and more powerful breed than its English relative. It was used by farmers and ranchers as a general purpose dog for hunting and guarding, as well as a companion dog, and it was still used by some for fighting. Illegal dogfighting was popular and attracted serious gambling. The dogs were first known as Pit Dogs, Pit Bull Terriers, or American Bull Terriers. It was common during fights for the handlers to be in the pit with the dogs, which were bred to be biddable to humans while maintaining their tenacity toward other dogs. It is this gentleness around people that makes these dogs so popular today.

The breed was accepted into the AKC stud book in 1936, listed as Staffordshire Terrier, and the same year the Staffordshire Terrier Club of America was established. The breed's name was changed to American Staffordshire Terrier in 1976. In 1975 the British Staffordshire Bull Terrier was recognized by the AKC. One of the best known American Staffordshire Terriers to be registered by the AKC was Pete the Pup (Petey), who was a canine star in the hit comedy show, *Our Gang,* which aired in the 1920s and 1930s.

POWER AND STRENGTH

BOXER

MODERN – GERMANY – COMMON

SIZE
Males 23–25 in./females 21½–23½ in.

APPEARANCE
Strong, muscular dog of character. Square body profile. Distinctive head; muzzle broad and blunt; lower jaw protrudes slightly beyond upper jaw. Dark, intelligent eyes. Ears set at the highest point of the skull and may be cropped to be long and tapering in the US. Strong, arched, elegant neck; short, straight back that slopes slightly to the hindquarters when Boxer is at attention, levels out when moving. Chest is deep and fairly wide and underline shows clear tuck up. Very muscular hindquarters; tail set and carried high and can be docked in the US

COLOR
Any shade of fawn or brindle; face should have black "mask" markings, but limited white may replace part of the otherwise essential black mask. White on flanks or back undesirable and more than 1/3 body markings in white not allowed. Short, shiny smooth coat

APTITUDE
Originally bull baiting; watchdog, military, police, agility, showing, companion

THE MODERN BOXER DOG, with its exuberant personality and regal bearing, was developed toward the end of the nineteenth century in Germany but is based on dogs of far older heritage. These were ancient war dogs of relatively heavy build, which were in existence by at least the time of the ancient Assyrians in c. 2000 B.C.E. These dogs of Mastiff-like characteristics were termed "Molossian" after the city of Molossis in Epirus, a remote area of modern-day Albania. Molossian dogs were prized for their ferocious nature and were used as guardians and in battle. The dogs spread throughout the continent and eventually gave rise to a number of variations in type. In Spain these became what is now recognized as the Spanish Alano, or Spanish bulldog; in Britain they gave rise to the Mastiff and Bulldog; and in France to the Dogue de Bordeaux and the little-known Bouldogue du Mida, all of which share characteristics with the modern Boxer.

Organized animal fights that pitted dogs against bulls, bears, and large game were popular in Ancient Rome and became very popular in Britain from the time of the Roman invasion (43 C.E.). The barbaric practice led to the selective breeding of courageous, powerful, and aggressive dogs, which were also used for hunting game. The popularity of the "sport" spread across Europe and gave rise to three main types of dog: the large Bullenbeisser (Mastiff-like dog), the Great Dane (massive hound-type dog achieved through Bullenbeisser and Deerhound), and the small Bullenbeisser (Bullenbeisser with British Bulldog). The small Bullenbeisser, bred in Brabant, northeast Belgium, is considered to be the direct ancestor of the modern Boxer.

In Germany the most extensive selective dog breeding took place at the vast kennels of noble estates, where the dogs were bred specifically for their hunting and/or fighting prowess. Later, the dogs were used by cattle dealers for moving cattle and more frequently by butchers for moving cattle around the slaughterhouse yards. The small Bullenbeisser was also popular as a domestic pet because of its affable nature and superlative guarding skills. During the 1830s, however, there were large imports of British Bulldogs to Germany, and these were bred to the Bullenbeissers. At that time the British Bulldog was a much leggier, more athletically framed dog than the modern type and was often white or had white markings. The modern Boxer also carries white markings and is sometimes completely white in color, which is not accepted by the Kennel Club, the American Kennel Club (AKC), or the German Kennel Club. By 1895, a Boxer Club had been established in Munich, and the first Boxer breed standard was drawn up. The foundation dogs of the breed, which included a white Bulldog as well as Boxers, were all initially heavily interbred to "fix" the genetic characteristics.

Boxers were one of the first dogs to be employed by the police and military in Germany and excelled in both respects on account of their versatility, intelligence, and strength. The first registration of a Boxer by the AKC was in 1904, and in 1935 the American Boxer Club was established. The breed became popular in the early 1940s and has for many years ranked within the top ten most popular dog breeds.

POWER AND STRENGTH

DOGUE DE BORDEAUX
ANCIENT – FRANCE – MODERATE

SIZE
Males 23–27 in./females 23–26 in., at least 99 lbs
APPEARANCE
Muscular, athletic, powerful. Large, broad head; characterful look with wrinkles; short, broad muzzle; powerful jaws, lower jaw projects. Oval, wide-set, brown eyes; small high-set ears; powerful muscular neck, broad at base, blending smoothly into powerful shoulders. Deep, long, broad chest; solid, broad, muscular back. Hind legs powerful with strong bone. Tail very thick at base, tip reaches hock, carried low when resting, carried up when moving, never over back or curled
COLOR
Any shade of fawn, can have dark mask. Coat short, fine, soft
APTITUDE
Originally animal baiting, fighting, guardian; now guardian, showing, companion

THE DOGUE DE BORDEAUX, or French Mastiff, is an immensely powerful breed that was used by the French in a range of roles from early times. The dog is a clear Mastiff type and as such its ancestors are among those that developed in Central or Southeast Asia, spreading outward from there as early cultures migrated. It was probably used as an ancient war dog by the Molossian people who lived in the mountainous regions of ancient Greece. The Molossus dogs are believed to have been instrumental in the development of a range of large dog "breeds" across Europe, including the Spanish Alano and the Neapolitan Mastiff. These massive, powerful dogs have existed across Europe since prehistory and developed into different types (that eventually gave rise to breeds centuries later) in their different regions. Further sources claim that the Dogue de Bordeaux derived from crosses between (English) Mastiffs and native French dogs and that Mastiff, Bulldog, and Bullmastiff also run in its blood.

The strong and talented Dogue de Bordeaux was universally a war dog and capable of extreme ferocity. It was also noted for its guarding skills, aided by its natural protectiveness, which is still seen in the breed today. The Dogue de Bordeaux was used for guarding livestock from predators and for big-game hunting, too. It was prized for animal fighting and was pitted against bears, bulls, and exotic animals such as lions and jaguars, and set on other dogs. The dog was greatly valued across the social classes; it was bred and kept by the aristocracy for fighting and guarding their estates, and also by the working classes, in particular butchers, who used it for guarding their stock and for "tenderizing" the meat through bullbaiting prior to slaughter. Often the dog had its ears cropped for fighting in order to minimize the risk of the ears ripping.

The Dogue de Bordeaux's association with both the ruling and working classes in large part saved the breed from disappearing, certainly during the years of the French Revolution (1789–99) when many of the dogs belonging to the aristocracy were slaughtered. The Dogue de Bordeaux suffered again during both world wars, when breeding slowed down considerably, and it saw active service during World War II when it was used for hauling carts, which often carried stretchers. The French Resistance favored the breed for protection, although its effectiveness in this respect nearly resulted in its demise when Hitler ordered that these dogs be slaughtered in their hundreds.

The Dogue de Bordeaux was relatively unknown outside its homeland until the nineteenth century, and it was not until 1863 that it was given its current name, based on the area of its greatest association. That same year a dog exhibition was held at the Jardin d'Acclimatation in Paris, which was won by Magentas, a female Dogue de Bordeaux. At this time there were three different types: the Toulouse, the Paris, and the Bordeaux. In 1896 the first breed standard was put together for the Dogue de Bordeaux. This has since been updated several times.

Although the first of the breed arrived in the United States in the 1890s, few of the dogs were seen there until the 1980s when their fortunes turned. A Dogue de Bordeaux starred in the Hollywood hit film, *Turner and Hooch* (1989), which immediately sparked interest in the breed. The Dogue de Bordeaux Society of America was formed in 1997, and in 2008 the American Kennel Club entered the breed into the Working Group category.

GREAT DANE
ANCIENT – GERMANY – MODERATE

SIZE
Males minimum 30 in./females minimum 28 in.

APPEARANCE
Noble, athletic, dignified. Refined, long head; deep muzzle; broad through bridge of nose; deep-set dark eyes; triangular ears, set high and can be cropped in the US. Long, arched neck; sloping shoulders; long, straight front legs. Deep chest; withers slope smoothly to short, level back; muscular hindquarters, hocks set low. Tail thick at root and tapers to point, carried level with back but never curled over back

COLOR
Brindle, fawn, blue, black, harlequin (white with black torn patches), mantle (black with white collar and markings). Coat short and smooth

APTITUDE
Originally guarding, large game hunting; now showing, companion

THE MAJESTIC GREAT DANE is a most distinctive dog breed, not least on account of its great size. It is one of the world's tallest dogs yet it is also extraordinarily elegant. It lacks the bulky frame of many Mastiff types and has the appearance of all the best parts of both the Mastiff and the Hound types. Despite the athleticism of its frame, the Great Dane is an extremely powerful dog and was historically renowned for its ferocity, which was channeled toward its use as a big game hunter and guardian. There is little comparison in terms of this to the modern Great Dane, which is noted for its affectionate, calm, and loving temperament. Great Danes are particularly good with children and other animals—provided that they are properly introduced—but still make good watchdogs, with their size rather than their temperament being the deterrent.

The Great Dane may be great, but it is not Danish and it has no links with Denmark. It is most commonly cited as a German dog, and it is in Germany that the breed developed, although some sources argue that its real heritage is English and Irish. Great Danes are also referred to as Deutsche Dogge, or German Mastiff, and were not termed "Great Danes" (in English) until the 1700s when the French naturalist Comte de Buffon (1707–88) saw them in Denmark and described them as such. It is, however, unclear why his description was adopted by the English. The dogs continue to be called Deutsche Doggen in Germany, and the breed club—the Deutsche Doggen Club—was established in 1888. The Great Dane was recognized as the national dog of Germany in 1876.

The ancestors of this charismatic breed can be traced back to the ancient Egyptians and Babylonians, whose depictions of dogs of this stature frequently appear on monuments and tombs. They are identifiable by their size in relation to the people also featured and are taller and finer than other Mastiff types that appear in images. The Great Dane, which was referred to as the "king of dogs" on account of its size and noble bearing, probably descended from the original Mastiff types that came from Central Asia early in prehistory. These gave rise to a number of different types that shared similar characteristics and were universally used for warfare, animal baiting, and fighting, as well as guarding and hunting. With the constant movement of people throughout Europe, particularly during the Roman invasions, different types of dog were brought into contact with each other, resulting in crosses. Some sources for the Great Dane, given its slightly different morphology from the heavier Mastiff breeds, are suggested to include the English Mastiff and the German Bullenbeisser (extinct), along with Irish Wolfhound, Scottish Deerhound, and/or Greyhound influences. These latter breeds could account for the height and frame of the Great Dane, but their true impact can only be speculated.

Great Danes were widely used for hunting wild boar in Germany and were at first called Boar Hounds. The huge hounds were kept and bred by the aristocracy (who could afford to feed such large animals) and were often singled out for particular attention: favorite hunting dogs were kept in the house, greatly pampered, and given expensive collars. One such dog was a Great Dane that was given by the poet Alexander Pope (1688–1744) to Frederick, Prince of Wales (1707–51) of the House of Hanover in 1738. This dog's collar was inscribed with the words, "I am His Highness' dog at Kew, Pray, tell me sir, whose dog are you?"

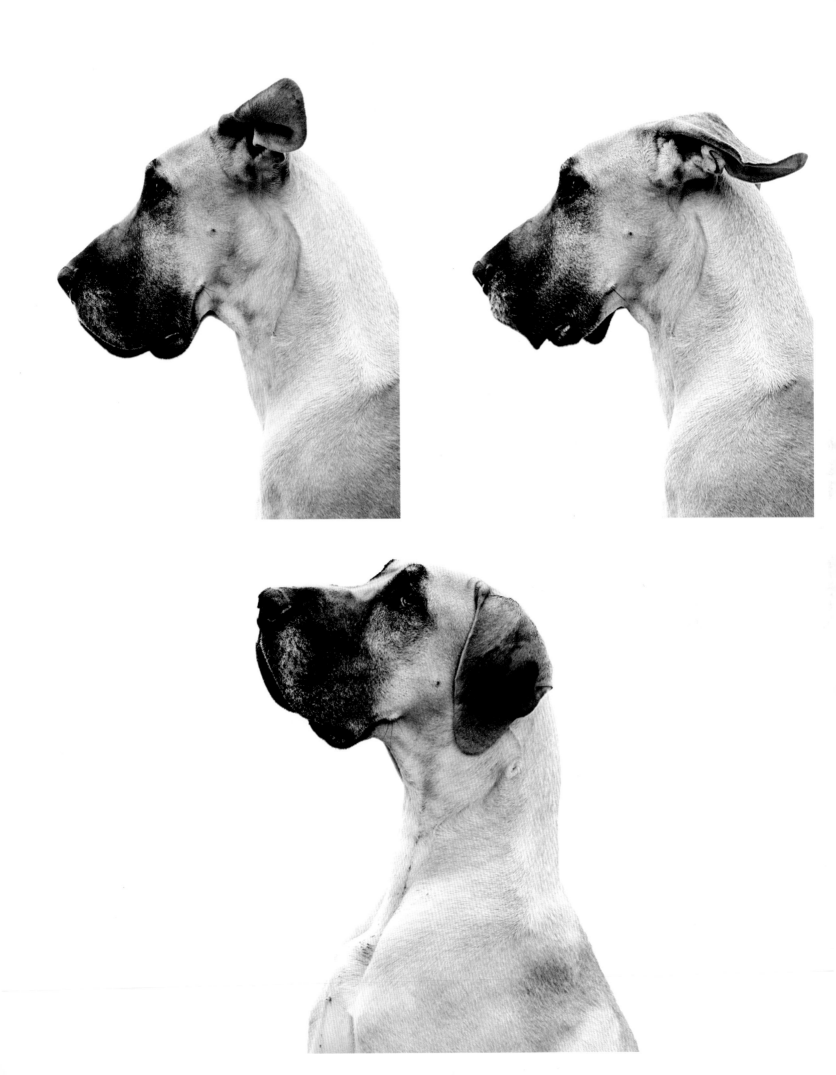

The Great Dane continued to be used for hunting large game in Germany, and for guarding, where efforts were made to preserve the size, frame, and disposition that made the breed easy to handle and affectionate with loved ones, as well as brave watchdogs. In 1880 it was decided that the dogs exhibited characteristics that set them apart from the English Mastiff. In 1883 the Great Dane Club was formed in England and shortly afterward Prince Albert Solmes (1798–1869) of Germany wrote to the *Kennel Club Gazette* to express his support for the English club, and also, delicately, to ask for the name to be changed to the Great German Doggen Club; this did not happen. The German club, the Deutsche Doggen Club, drew up its breed standard in 1891.

In 1894 Edward Prince of Wales (1841–1910) proposed the banning of ear cropping, which had until then been commonly practiced on Great Danes in England, Europe, and the United States; although contested, the ban was adopted in England. In the twentieth century, the Great Dane Club of Great Britain made big strides in popularizing the breed, and numbers increased significantly. Although breeding programs slowed down during World War I, the Great Dane remained popular, and two important kennels— the Send and Ouborough—were established during the 1920s and 1930s. World War II had a more profound effect, and many smaller kennels closed. After the war, however, the situation improved, and in 1953 a Great Dane won Best in Show at Crufts, which popularized the breed.

The American Kennel Club (AKC) recognized the breed in 1887, later adding it to the Working Group category, and the Great Dane Club of America was founded in Chicago in 1889. Since then the breed has gradually gained in favor and now ranks within the top twenty breeds based on registration statistics with the AKC.

With their beautiful appearance and lovely, slightly humorous nature, Great Danes have often appeared in films and books and made their name in history. One of the most charming true-life characters is the Great Dane Just Nuisance, who was the only dog ever to be officially enlisted by the Royal Navy. He made his mark in Simon's Town, South Africa, where he ingratiated himself with naval sailors, and was eventually officially enrolled as a morale booster during World War II. When he died in 1944, he was buried with full military honors.

POWER AND STRENGTH

CHINESE SHAR-PEI
ANCIENT – CHINA – MODERATE

SIZE
Males/females 18–20 in.

APPEARANCE
Compact, solid, square, distinctive "hippopotamus" head. Relatively large head, with wrinkled forehead and cheeks; broad, full muzzle; large, preferably black nose. Dark, small, almond-shaped eyes; very small, thick ears set high, wide apart, forward on skull, lying flat to head. Strong, medium-length neck with loose folds of skin about the throat and neck.

Muscular shoulders; straight front legs; deep, broad chest; short, close-coupled back; muscular hindquarters. Topline dips slightly over withers, rises slightly over loins. Tail set, carried high, curved over back

COLOR
Any solid color including sable. Coat short, extremely harsh and off standing

APTITUDE
Originally dogfighting, herding, hunting; now watchdog, showing, companion, agility

THERE IS NO MISTAKING the wrinkled brow of the Chinese Shar-Pei, whose frown it was said was enough to ward off evil spirits; whether true or not, it was certainly efficient at keeping human interlopers at bay. This solid, muscular, and dignified dog was originally bred and used as a general purpose farm dog, whose particular skill was guarding. The Shar-Pei is fiercely loyal and protective of loved ones, and characteristically it remains aloof and standoffish with strangers. Providing it is carefully introduced to children and other pets, it makes a wonderful and affectionate companion that is as happy lying in front of the fire as it is racing around an agility course.

Its history is believed to trace back to at least the Chinese Han period (206 B.C. E.–220 C.E.), when pottery and jade figurines of dogs with Shar-Pei characteristics began to appear with frequency. Many of these were used for placing in tombs to watch over and protect the dead, and to ward off evil spirits. A great many statuettes and figurines exist from this period and are particularly important because they indicate differences between dogs' appearances. As such, although no specific documents survive, it is possible to appreciate clear dog types that resemble the Shar-Pei, the Chow Chow, a large Mastiff type, the Shih Tzu, and others. The Shar-Pei and the Chow Chow

both exhibit blue-black tongues, and some sources suggest that they were closely related. The Shar-Pei also shares some similarities with the Tibetan Mastiff; undoubtedly there was much interbreeding among native dog types.

The Shar-Pei is most associated with southern China, where it is said to have developed. It was bred as a universal peasant farmer's dog, able to herd and guard livestock, protect the home, hunt, track, and eventually fight. The diverse nature of the Shar-Pei's early roles meant that it developed into an intelligent and adaptable dog, capable of exhibiting great aggression while being equally loyal and trustworthy with its owners and with livestock. The Shar-Pei is also noted for its bravery and tenacity, and during fierce wild boar hunts or dogfights it would continue an attack even when severely injured. Physically it is well adapted to hunting and fighting. Its solid, muscular body, with its low center of gravity, gives it great thrust and strength, but it is its tremendous coat and wrinkles that serve it best in these grisly endeavors. The Shar-Pei has a distinctive and unique coat that is short, bristly, and harsh, and to bite it is particularly unpleasant for an aggressor. The wrinkles provide protection for the eyes but also allow the Shar-Pei to turn around to face an aggressor even when being bitten. This gives it a great range of deadly movement, which made it an excellent fighting dog. The village of Tai Leh, near Canton in southern China, was known for dogfighting, and the Shar-Pei is often said to have originated from there.

Like other dogs, the Shar-Pei was a consumable in its homeland, particularly during times of famine and war when food sources were scarce. The breed was almost obliterated during the Communist Revolution (1911) and the subsequent establishment of the People's Republic of China in 1949, when dogs in general were considered a luxury and associated with the wealthy, although this was not the case for poor rural farmers. Heavy taxes and subsequent fines were imposed on dog ownership, and

dogs were slaughtered in great numbers. It was a dark period for Chinese dogs, and the Shar-Pei in particular seems to have suffered. Some of the dogs were smuggled from the mainland and survived in small numbers on Hong Kong, Macao, and Taiwan during the 1950s, when they were still being used for dogfighting. The Hong Kong Kennel Club recognized the breed in the late 1960s, and a dog registry was established.

Around the same time a few Shar-Pei were imported to the United States. By this time the Shar-Pei had become virtually extinct and would almost certainly have disappeared had it not been for the efforts of two breeders, C. M. Chung and Matgo Law. They tried to increase their foundation stock through searching for dogs, but the biggest breakthrough came when Law wrote an article that was published in the American *Dogs Magazine* in 1973, in which he asked dog enthusiasts to help save the breed. The response was overwhelming, and in the same year Law was able to send around twelve dogs to the United States from his Down-Homes Kennels, including Down-Homes Little Pea, who was the first Shar-Pei from his stock to have puppies in the United States. The early US owners of Shar-Pei dogs kept in touch with each other, and it was because of their efforts that a national dog club and registry, the Chinese Shar-Pei Club of America, was formed in 1974. Its first Annual National Specialty Show was held in 1978 and it has been held every year since. It was also in 1978 that *The Guinness Book of World Records* listed the Shar-Pei as the world's rarest dog breed.

The first of the breed in England was imported in 1981 from the United States, and more arrived the following year, including a female that came directly from Law's kennels in Hong Kong. Within only four years, there were more than 350 Shar-Pei registered with the Kennel Club, and a number of imported US champions influenced the British development of the breed. The Shar-Pei Club of Great Britain was founded in 1983 by a group of breed enthusiasts and was the first Shar-Pei breed club to be recognized by the Kennel Club. In the United States the American Kennel Club accepted the Shar-Pei into the Miscellaneous Group category in 1988, and in 1992 it was moved to the Non-Sporting Group. The Shar-Pei has since been exported around the world and is popular in Australia, New Zealand, Europe, South Africa, and Russia.

NEWFOUNDLAND
ANCIENT – CANADA – MODERATE

SIZE

Males average 28 in./females average 26 in.

APPEARANCE

Balanced, powerful, alert. Broad, large head; short, square muzzle; black nose. Small, wide-set, dark eyes; small ears lying close to head; strong neck of moderate length; straight front legs; deep, broad chest; broad, level back; very muscular hindquarters;

strong webbing between pads on feet. Tail moderately long, carried slightly elevated when moving, but never curled over back

COLOR

Black, brown, or gray, minimal white on chin, chest, toes, tail tip, or white with black markings

APTITUDE

Originally fisherman's helper, draft, water rescue, showing, companion

THERE ARE FEW BREEDS of dog that can lay claim to such an honorable history as the magnificent Newfoundland: a breed that has an inherent instinct to protect and save people from danger, and from water-related incidents in particular. This dog will rush to save anyone whom it sees struggling and has earned itself many recorded tales of heroism. This natural protective instinct is combined with a lovely temperament: affectionate, loyal, devoted, and calm.

Given these qualities the Newfoundland became extremely popular, particularly in the United States, the United Kingdom, and much of Continental Europe from the early nineteenth century onward, and it appears alongside many well-known names from history including presidents, royalty, explorers, composers, poets, and artists. Dog painting gained ascendency during this period, and the Newfoundland appears with frequency; the British artist Sir Edwin Landseer (1802–73) honored the breed so often in paint that a variety of the Newfoundland was named after him. The Landseer is white with black markings, and although it is recognized as a color variant by the American Kennel Club and the Kennel Club, the Fédération Cynologique Internationale categorizes it as a separate breed.

The origins of the breed are largely speculated. The huge dogs derive from the Canadian island of Newfoundland, where the Beothuk—a tribe of Native Americans—lived from at least 50 B.C.E. One theory suggests that the Beothuk

had large, black, primitive dogs, and that these lie at the foundation of the Newfoundland. The Viking explorer Leif Ericson (c. 970–1020) established a Norse settlement on Newfoundland in around 1001, and it is probable that the Vikings brought their large dogs with them and that they would have crossbred with the indigenous dogs of the Beothuks. The island was rediscovered at the end of the fifteenth century by European fishermen, and from this time many Europeans sailed to the island in search of fish. The Newfoundland shares some characteristics with Mastiff breeds taken by the British and Portuguese and with mountain dog breeds such as the Great Pyrenees.

Colonization of the island was granted in 1610, and by this period a dog of fairly fixed characteristics had developed, referred to as a St. John's Dog. The dog exhibited two general types: the Greater, which was a heavier-bodied, long-haired dog; and the Lesser, a smooth-coated, slighter, and smaller animal. The former developed into the Newfoundland, whereas the latter gave rise to the Labrador Retriever. St. John's Dogs were used in the foundation of the German Leonberger breed and in the restoration of the St. Bernard breed in the nineteenth century, whereas dogs from Newfoundland were also used in the development of the Flat Coated and Curly Coated Retriever.

The dogs on Newfoundland were used extensively in the fishing industry, and they remain enthusiastic water dogs. They were used for hauling boats, loads, and nets, for swimming out into the water to tow boats back in, for search and rescue (for which they are still used), and as companions. The dogs have exceptionally waterproof coats and webbed feet that aid in their swimming, and a highly refined natural desire to "save" people.

The dogs on Newfoundland earned their name in 1775 when a man referred to his dog as such, and the title stuck. The dogs were taken in large numbers back to the United Kingdom, Continental Europe, and North America, and it was in the United Kingdom that the breed developed into

its present form. The Newfoundland Dog Club was formed there in 1886, and the breed was recognized by the American Kennel Club in 1886. By the turn of the century the fashion for Newfoundlands had waned slightly, although the dogs remained popular in the United Kingdom until World War I, when their numbers were diminished by the cessation of breeding programs. World War II had a similarly devastating effect; after the war, the breed in the United Kingdom was helped by the introduction of American Newfoundland stock.

There have been many well-known Newfoundland dogs throughout history, including Seaman, who was bought for $20 in the US in 1803 by explorer Meriwether Lewis (1774–1809) on his way to meet William Clark (1770–1838) before embarking on their expedition across the United States (1804–06). At the same time, the English poet Lord Byron acquired his Newfoundland, Boatswain, to whom he was devoted. On the dog's death in 1808 he erected a memorial at Newstead Abbey, Nottingham, inscribed with a poem to his faithful friend. The German composer Richard Wagner (1813–83) was adopted by a Newfoundland called Robber, whom he befriended in a shop in Riga, Latvia. Later, Wagner owned another Newfoundland called Russ, who saved his daughter, Eva, from drowning after she fell into a river. Today Newfoundlands are used for life-saving on beaches and they form part of search and rescue teams.

ST. BERNARD

ANCIENT – SWITZERLAND – MODERATE

SIZE

Males minimum 27½ in./females minimum 25 in.

APPEARANCE

Substantial, friendly, noble. Large head with kind expression. Short muzzle; large, black nose. Dark eyes; medium-sized ears that lie close to head. Long, muscular neck; sloping shoulders; straight front legs; deep and wide chest; broad and level back; powerful hindquarters. Tail set high and carried low, should never curl over the back

COLOR

White with red, or red or brindle with white. Must have white on muzzle, chest, feet, tail tip, and collar. Can have dark mask and ears. Coats can be either short haired or long haired, and layered

APTITUDE

Draft, search and rescue, showing, companion

THE GREAT ST. BERNARD PASS in the Swiss Alps, which connects Switzerland to Italy, is the oldest known pass through the Western Alps and one of the highest passes in Switzerland. Although a road is now in place, for centuries this route was isolated and treacherous, and was snowbound for much of the year. At its highest point is the Great St. Bernard Hospice, established in c. 1050 by (Saint) Bernard de Menthon to offer shelter and refuge to weary travelers, and it is here that the St. Bernard dog developed.

It is likely that the Hospice dogs had Mastiff types at their foundation, brought to the area by Roman legions during the first two centuries C.E. Much crossbreeding occurred between the Mastiff types and native dogs from the surrounding mountains and valleys of Switzerland, and the dogs were widely used on farms. Despite crossbreeding, the Mastiff-type foundation remained strong.

The Hospice was largely destroyed by fire in the sixteenth century, and most of its archives were lost. The first mention of the Hospice dogs was in the early 1700s, and the earliest paintings of dogs exhibiting characteristics in line with the St. Bernard are those attributed to Italian artist Salvator Rosa (1615–73) in the late 1600s.

The Hospice dogs were best known as search and rescue dogs. Given the difficult passage through the Alps, travelers were frequently lost and injured. Surviving records indicate that the Hospice dogs began to exhibit search and rescue skills around the beginning of the eighteenth century, when they accompanied monks who would sweep the area after storms to check for lost travelers. At some point the dogs' inherent skills took over, and they were sent out, unsupervised and in pairs, to locate people in difficulties. Once someone had been found, the dogs would either guide that person back to the Hospice, or one dog would lie beside the injured person to provide warmth, while the other would fetch help. It is estimated that the dogs have saved around 2,000 lives.

The height of their fame as rescue dogs was between the 1790s and 1814, and much of this success was attributed to one dog, Barry (1800–14), who is said to have saved forty people during his lifetime. In his honor a dog is now always named Barry at the Hospice.

The winters of 1816 to 1818 were particularly harsh and featured deadly avalanches. Many of the Hospice's dogs died during rescue attempts, and to such an extent that valuable breeding stock was lost and the breed was in danger of dying out. The monks replenished numbers using local dogs, and, some claim, through the introduction of Great Danes and English Mastiffs. From the 1850s breeding began outside the Hospice, spearheaded by Heinrich Schumacher who was instrumental in establishing the first stud book for the breed. He bred the dogs to supply back to the Hospice and also sold a number to the English. The Swiss Kennel Club was formed in 1883, and in 1884 adopted the first Swiss breed standard. It was also in the early 1880s that the dogs, which had until then been referred to as Hospice, Barry, Mountain, or Swiss Alpine Dogs, were given the name St. Bernard.

The breed was recognized by the American Kennel Club (AKC) in 1885 and entered into the Working Group category; in 1888 the Saint Bernard Club of America was established. Despite its massive size, the St. Bernard is popular in the United States and is regularly within the top fifty dogs based on AKC registration statistics.

CHAPTER 4
NOBLE AND FAITHFUL

As domestic dogs evolved within human cultures, they developed along different lines, which gave rise to dogs that naturally excelled as war dogs and hunters, as haulage animals, guardians, and herders. Although some ancient breeds were diverse enough to fulfill a number of these roles, some became more specialized, and this is seen in the livestock herding dogs. This role requires very specific and highly honed skills from the dog, as well as great obedience, intelligence, and the ability to work in synchronization with humans, and on their own. The wealth and livelihood of many ancient cultures depended on their herds of animals, and as such it was vital that they had dogs that could be relied on, that worked quietly, and most importantly were nonaggressive toward the stock.

Although there are a number of breeds that excel at livestock herding, one of the best is the Border Collie, a dog of almost unequaled intelligence and phenomenal working abilities. Hailing from the country along the borders of Scotland and England, the Border Collie is a true product of definitive breeding for a very specific role. They, like virtually all working livestock breeds, excel at agility competitions; they are also one of the top breeds to compete in sheepdog trials.

These competitions test the working ability of the herding dog, which is required to move groups of sheep through a set course. The dogs are commanded chiefly through whistles and hand signals and demonstrate total obedience and an inherent affinity for the sheep. The sport developed in New Zealand from 1867 and the first British event was held in Bala, Wales, in 1873. The following year Scotland held its first trials, and by the 1880s the sport had reached the United States.

Within the scope of pastoral work, there is a demand for dogs to perform a number of different roles, and these are invariably filled most successfully by different types. Dogs that excel at working sheep might not necessarily be as adept at working cattle, and vica versa. Herding sheep requires a dog with a special skill set, and often involves dogs working at the head end of the sheep to turn them and move them; they must work quietly and subtly for the best results. Cattle react and work differently and are best suited to dogs that move them from the tail end. Breeds such as the Australian Cattle Dog, also known as the Blue or Red Heeler, are just one of many stock dog breeds that are particularly suited to cattle work and excel at both gathering herds on open range and close-quarters corral work. Cattle can react violently and are prone to kicking out, so cattle herding demands dogs that are tenacious, bold, agile, and wholly unafraid. Although it is rarely seen in this capacity today, the Corgi was traditionally a cattle dog, and with its low but stocky frame was perfectly adapted to ducking away from kicking heels. Rottweilers and Giant Schnauzers were also traditionally used for cattle work in Germany, particularly for moving cattle to and from market and for use within the butchers' yards. Both these and a number of other breeds were often referred to as "Butcher's dogs."

A further role for the pastoral dog is that of livestock guardian, and this is most successfully filled by certain breeds that have inherent protective characteristics. Whereas the herding dog works around the outside of the flock or herd, the livestock guardian dog lives within the flock. These dogs, such as the Komondor, Briard, or Great Pyrenees, provide unsupervised round-the-clock predator protection. Some, such as the Briard, fulfill a dual role and will also work as herding dogs when required. As guardians, the dogs have to be very aggressive to predators, but utterly reliable with their charges. Most guardian dogs blend well within the flock and are hard to distinguish because they are often white and distinctly "woolly" in appearance. The herding dogs by contrast are most often a darker color, which makes it easier for the handler to see them.

An important aspect of farming life was guardianship of property, and many dogs that were used for livestock guarding would also have been used for general protection, although other breeds are specifically used for this purpose. The Doberman breed traces its origins to a tax collector who deliberately set about establishing a breed of dog that would provide him with protection at work, and would also be useful for "encouraging" people to part with their money. The ancient Canaan dog of Israel worked as a property and livestock guardian, and the Briard was also noted for its effective guarding skills. Even the Standard Schnauzer, most often viewed as a "lap dog," was a formidable farmyard alarm system. These plucky dogs were versatile farm animals that were used for vermin control, property guarding, and droving cattle and were also happy to curl up with the farmer in the evening.

As the emphasis and nature of farming changed through the twentieth century, there was a decline in the need for purely working farm dogs. This has seen many of the livestock and guardian breeds being utilized in different areas that require the same intelligence, agility, stamina, bravery, loyalty, and protective instinct. The use of dogs in war predates the Romans, but from the end of the nineteenth century highly specialized dogs were trained for a variety of roles. These include messenger dogs, guard and patrol dogs, search and rescue, dogs for packing supplies, dogs trained to detect landmines and trip wires, dogs for tracking, scout dogs for detecting snipers and booby traps, and "anti-tank" dogs. German Shepherds were favored because they were easy to train, but virtually any dog breed was considered for military use, including mongrels. Throughout the twentieth century, hundreds of thousands of dogs met dreadful ends performing military roles, and dogs continue to be used in active service in the Middle East in the twenty-first century. Without doubt, the qualities of the livestock and guardian breeds—faithfulness, bravery, intelligence, and tenaciousness, for example—and their versatility are quite extraordinary.

BEARDED COLLIE
ANCIENT – SCOTLAND – MODERATE

SIZE
Males 21–22 in./females 20–21 in.

APPEARANCE
Hardy and active, intelligent, stable, and self-confident. Medium-sized, broad head; strong muzzle; square nose; large, soft affectionate eyes—toning with coat color. Shoulders well laid back; deep chest; body longer than tall; muscular hindquarters; legs and body covered with abundant hair

COLOR
Black, brown, blue, and fawn. At maturity, the coat color lightens to any shade of these colors. White may appear on the foreface, blaze on skull, tip of tail, chest, legs, and feet, and around the neck. Double coat with soft furry undercoat, outercoat harsh, flat, and shaggy

APTITUDE
Sheep herding, trials, agility, showing, companion

THE BEARDED COLLIE, or Beardie as it is affectionately known, is a superb sheepdog that is also adept at working cattle. This lovely dog hails from Scotland, where it was also referred to as Scotch Sheepdog, Mountain Collie, Highland Collie, or Hairy Mou'ed Collie. The Beardie developed as a farmer's dog, a constant companion, and an essential working tool on rural Scottish farms. The dog remained largely unknown outside Scotland for centuries and was mostly associated with working people.

The Beardie was developed specifically for herding sheep and is thought to have developed from similar long-haired herding breeds of Continental Europe. One of the earliest mentions of outside influence on the Scottish herding dog dates to 1514 when a Polish shipowner, Kazimiez Grabski, sailed from Gdansk to Scotland to trade grain for Scottish sheep and brought six Polish Lowland Sheepdogs with him. The Scottish shepherd traded a horned ram and a ewe in exchange for two females and one male.

There are no records to indicate how the dogs were bred with the native Scottish stock, or how the Beardie was developing at this point. The Beardie's long coat, which includes shaggy facial hair, was well suited to the harsh Scottish climate, so although there was no unilateral breeding standard, the best dogs for the job were the ones that developed, and these in turn shared similarities.

Some sources suggest that the Beardie began to appear in the arts in the eighteenth century, and was first seen in a portrait by Thomas Gainsborough (1727–88) of the 3rd Duke of Buccleuch who is accompanied by a small, shaggy dog. Joshua Reynolds (1723–92) later painted the Duchess of Buccleuch with, allegedly, the same dog. One of the earliest descriptions of the dogs appeared in *British Dogs* (1879) by Hugh Dalziel, who referred to the "Bearded Colley" of west Scotland as a shaggy-coated dog that he believed was crossed to a hound. In the second edition, he changed the spelling to "Collie" and suggested that the dog derived from English Sheepdogs and Collie crosses.

By this time the sport of sheepdog trialing had started, and the first British event was held in Bala, Wales, in 1873. Since then the sport has rapidly grown in popularity and is practiced across the world, particularly in the United States, Australia, and New Zealand. Beardies excel in this event and continue to make their mark.

Despite increasing interest in the breed, the first proper standard was not drawn up until 1898; for the most part this is the standard that continues for the breed today. Beardie numbers remained relatively conservative through the start of the twentieth century, and steps toward forming a breed club were halted by the outbreak of World War I. After the war, breeders again began to promote their Beardies. Mrs. Miller became a leading figure through her Beardie breeding efforts, managing to register fifty-five dogs between 1929 and 1934, until the outbreak of World War II stopped breeding activities.

The Bearded Collie Club was established in 1955; since then Beardies have steadily increased in popularity in Britain, Continental Europe, the United States, South Africa, and Australia. The Bearded Collie Club of America was established in 1969, and in 1977 the breed was recognized by the American Kennel Club. One of the most important Beardies in the United States was Brambledale Blue Bonnet, who became the first American Champion.

BORDER COLLIE
MODERN – BRITAIN – COMMON

SIZE	*moderately long tail set low, may*
Males 20–22 in./females 18–21 in.	*be raised when excited, but never*
APPEARANCE	*over back*
Graceful, athletic, intelligent,	**COLOR**
smooth outline in perfect balance.	*Solid, bicolor, tricolor, merle,*
Relatively flat skull with tapering	*sable. Solid white not allowed.*
muzzle; oval, wide-set eyes, brown	*Rough coats have flat or*
or blue in merles; medium-sized,	*moderately wavy, medium-length*
erect, or semierect, responsive	*hair; smooth coats slightly coarser*
ears. Good length neck; rather	*in texture and short haired*
broad, deep chest; athletic frame;	**APTITUDE**
slightly arched, muscular loins	*Sheepherding, trials, obedience,*
leading into gently sloping croup.	*search and rescue, agility,*
Hindquarters muscular;	*showing, companion*

THE BORDER COLLIE is the world's premier sheepherding dog and it is regularly listed within the top ten most intelligent dog breeds. It is extremely sensitive to vocal commands and gestures, and demonstrates exceptional problem-solving skills. The Border Collie is a very loyal and affectionate dog with those it knows, but it requires a high level of exercise and mental stimulation; those that are not working dogs excel at agility competitions.

In Britain from c. 600 B.C.E. to 50 C.E. the different Celtic clans established agricultural and pastoral farming traditions, including sheep farming. Various types of sheepdog developed to work the flocks in their specific area, which gave rise to the Welsh Sheepdog, Black and Tan, Welsh Hillman, Shetland Sheepdog, Bearded Collie, Old English Sheepdog, Scotch Collie, and others. The Border Collie developed along the Scottish and English borders, emerging from this foundation of working dogs but not formally "developed" until the nineteenth century, when it was called a Working Sheepdog. It was given its present name in 1915 in order to differentiate the dog from other collie breeds.

During the 1840s Queen Victoria (1819–1901) had two working collies, which were kept at the royal kennels, but it was not until the 1860s that she really began to patronize the breed. Her first pet Border Collie, named Sharp, was photographed with the queen for a series of images in 1866. Another of her Borders, a female named Nanny, was white; this color is not accepted within Kennel Club (KC) or American Kennel Club (AKC) breed standards. The first British sheepdog trials were held in Wales in 1873. The Border Collie excels at trials, and the public was astonished at the skills of the dogs, which responded to only the whistles and hand signals from their handlers.

There are several individual dogs that were particularly important in the development of the modern Border Collie, including Old Hemp (born 1893) who is said to have sired more than 200 male dogs and an unrecorded amount of females. The breeder and trainer J. M. Wilson also contributed to the quality of the Border Collie, especially through his dog, Wilson Cap (born 1937), who fathered 188 registered puppies. It is to him that the legendary Wiston Cap (born 1963) can be traced. Wiston Cap is portrayed on the International Sheep Dog Society badge, and his bloodline is seen in most modern Border Collies.

In Border Collie breeding the emphasis has always been on the dog's working ability rather than its physical appearance. This has led to friction between those who show Border Collies and those who have working Border Collies. The KC, which accepted the breed for showing in 1976, has introduced a working test to safeguard the future development of Border Collies and to maintain their essentially working nature. Only dogs that have passed this test and have three Challenge Certificates can take a full Champion title. In the United States there is some conflict between the AKC, which registers dogs based purely on their physical appearance, and owners of working Borders, who do not wish the breed to lose its integrity. The AKC recognized the Border Collie in 1995, but many breeders of working dogs are greatly opposed to this because it is felt that the emphasis will now be moved to appearance and not ability. The breed in the United States is split into working and showing lines, with the latter less numerous.

NOBLE AND FAITHFUL

COLLIE

MODERN – SCOTLAND – MODERATE

SIZE
Males 24–26 in./females 22–24 in.

APPEARANCE
Beautiful, dignified, alert. Head resembles blunt, lean wedge from profile/front views; nose always black; almond-shaped, dark, kind eyes. Merle-colored dogs can have blue eyes. Small, velvety ears carried semierect when alert, with tips tipping forward. Muscular, long, arched neck; deep chest; straight front legs with feathering; long body; strong back;

powerful hindquarters; legs feathered to hock. Tail long, carried low, may be carried higher when alert. Heavily feathered

COLOR
Sable/white, tricolor, blue merle, white, preferably with markings. Double-coated, thick coat. Top layer straight, harsh, long, undercoat thick, soft. Smooth coated, coat is hard and short

APTITUDE
Sheepherding, trials, agility, showing, companion

THIS ELEGANT AND BEAUTIFUL DOG is referred to by a number of names, ranging from Collie, or Rough Collie, to English Collie, Scottish Collie, and sometimes the Long Haired Collie. There are also two types of Collie: the rough coat or long-haired variety, and a smooth, short-haired type. The former has become more popular during the last century partly based on its looks but also because of its appearance in the novels of Eric Knight (1897–1943), who immortalized the Rough Collie in the fictional character of Lassie, and of Albert Payson Terhune (1872–1942), who championed the dogs.

The Rough Collie developed from working and herding stock in the Scottish Highlands and upland and moorland areas of the British Isles. Its basic qualities were its nonaggressive behavior, obedience, intelligence, endurance, and a good turn of speed when needed. Today, although the breed is not widely used in farming, it is still used in a working capacity. The Rough Collie is intelligent and does best when it has a job to do. It makes a good agility and obedience candidate and a wonderful family pet. It is also noted for its extremely kind temperament and individual loyalty, but it can have a propensity to bark.

Some sources theorize that the Rough Collie was infiltrated with Borzoi blood during its development and that this contributed to its distinctive "wedge"-shaped head. In fact, Rough Collie and Borzoi were crossed a number of times and in particular at the request of the czar of Russia. However, the Rough Collie's distinctive head is probably attributed to early drovers crossing their Collies with Deerhound or Greyhound. In the early twentieth century the Rough Collie contributed toward the development of the Shetland Sheepdog, and this vivacious, little dog has more than a passing resemblance to the larger Rough Collie. The Rough Collie made its first appearance in the public forum in 1860 when the first show classes for "Sheepdogs, Colleys, Yard, or Keepers' Dogs" were held at the Birmingham Dog Society show. Shortly afterward, Queen Victoria (1819–1901) became an enthusiastic owner and supporter of the Rough Collie.

The Colley Club was established in 1881 and set out a breed standard that has changed little since that time. The Scottish Collie Club was formed in 1885 and is still in existence; it was granted Kennel Club recognition in 1939.

The first Rough Collie to arrive in the United States was imported in 1879. The breed rapidly escalated in popularity and numbers showed a great increase between 1900 and 1920, based largely on British imports. The Collie Club of America Inc. was established in 1886 and was the second parent club to join the American Kennel Club (AKC) after its formation in 1884. US President Calvin Coolidge (1872–1933) and his wife, Grace, were devoted pet owners and had several Rough Collies. They gave the breed great press, and their first official photograph after Coolidge was sworn in was taken in 1924 on the steps of the White House and included their family and their white Rough Collie, Rob Roy. Grace also had another beloved white Collie named Prudence Prim, who slept alongside her bed and was often dressed in bonnets to attend tea parties.

The Rough Collie regularly ranks among the top forty most popular breeds in the United States, based on AKC registration statistics, and is also an enthusiastically supported breed in England.

OLD ENGLISH SHEEPDOG
MODERN – ENGLAND – MODERATE

SIZE

Males minimum 22 in./females minimum 21 in.

APPEARANCE

Strong, intelligent, abundantly hairy. Skull quite broad; head reasonably squarish, covered with long hair; square muzzle; large, black nose. Dark or wall eyes; small ears carried flat to head; long, strong, arched neck; sloping shoulders; short, compact body; deep chest; muscular hindquarters. Topline rises from withers to loins. Tail traditionally docked (not in UK)

COLOR

Any shade of gray, grizzle, blue, blue merle with or without white markings. Coat long, shaggy, harsh

APTITUDE

Livestock work, agility, showing, companion

IN 1961 A WELL-KNOWN BRITISH paint company called Dulux introduced an Old English Sheepdog as its mascot and the "face" of its advertising campaign. The first dog to appear on the televised commercials was Shepton Dash, from the well-known Shepton Kennels at Shepton Mallet, Dorset. These kennels were of great influence in the breed's modern history. Dulux continued to use a variety of Old English Sheepdogs until 1996 when they were removed from the campaign. They were reintroduced in 2011. The use of this breed for advertising brought it firmly into the public forum, and it remains a popular breed, which is in large part due to the dogs' lovely temperaments. The Old English Sheepdog has also appeared in numerous films, including *Chitty Chitty Bang Bang* (1968) and *The The Little Mermaid* (1989).

The origins of the breed are unknown but are commonly attributed to the influence of Bearded Collies and the Russian Ovcharka—there are definite physical similarities discernible in both—and occasionally the French Briard is also cited. It is speculated that the Russian Ovcharka arrived in Scotland on board Baltic ships and crossbred with the Bearded Collie. By the nineteenth century the Old English Sheepdog had developed into its clear type and was closely associated with the South Downs region in Sussex. It was used primarily as a droving dog to move cattle and sheep to market but was also used for moving New Forest ponies. Sometimes it was called a "Smithfield dog" after the London Smithfield market. In the eighteenth century a tax was introduced for pet dogs, but working dogs were exempt. In order to differentiate the pet from the working sheepdog, the sheepdog had its tail docked. This led to the dog being referred to as "Bobtail," a name that is still sometimes used. In England, tail docking was banned in 2007, but the dogs can still be docked in the United States.

An early reference to the qualities of the Bobtail was made in 1810 in R. Parkinson's *Treatise on the Breeding and Management of Livestock,* in which he describes the breed in detail and cites Dorset as its county of origin. The dog became noted for its working abilities, and because only the best of the best were bred—those that were hardiest, most intelligent, and obedient—they developed their distinctive characteristics. In 1877 two dogs described as "sheepdog, short tailed English" were registered with the Kennel Club, and in 1881 the influential Shepton Kennel of Old English Sheepdogs was founded by two brothers, William and Henry Tilley. These kennels produced numerous champion dogs and provided stock for the foundation of a number of different kennels. Henry Tilley served as president of the Old English Sheepdog Club in England and was also instrumental in introducing many excellent Old English Sheepdogs to the United States. The UK breed standard was written in 1888, and Henry Tilley and Freeman Lloyd wrote the first US standard in 1904; the Old English Sheepdog Club of America was established in the same year.

The Old English Sheepdog had begun to become popular in the United States by the late 1880s, partly due to the enthusiasm of industrialist William Wade of Pittsburgh, and the breed rapidly became supported by America's wealthiest families, including the Guggenheims and Vanderbilts. Although numbers decreased on both sides of the Atlantic during both world wars, they were quick to recover, and today the Old English Sheepdog remains a much loved and greatly supported breed.

GREAT PYRENEES

ANCIENT – FRANCE – MODERATE

SIZE
Males 27–32 in./females 25–29 in.

APPEARANCE
Beautiful, imposing, noble. Wedge-shaped head with rather rounded crown; medium-length muzzle; black nose. Almond-shaped, dark eyes; fairly small triangular ears that lie flat when resting. Strong neck; powerful shoulders; straight front legs; broad, deep chest; moderately long, broad, muscular back.

Strong hindquarters; double dew claws on back legs; hind feet might turn out slightly. Long tail with long, feathered hair, carried low when resting, curled over back when alert

COLOR
White, may have patches of gray, badger, reddish brown, or tan. Thick double-coated coat

APTITUDE
Guarding, livestock guardian, military use, showing, companion

THE MAJESTIC PYRENEES MOUNTAIN RANGE of southwest Europe is home to the Great Pyrenees dog. This beautiful white dog has lived in relative geographic isolation in these mountains for millennia, and traces its roots back to the large dogs that evolved in Central or Southeast Asia in prehistory. As dogs migrated from there, they developed their own characteristics, shaped by environment and circumstance. It is speculated that the Great Pyrenees ancestors were in the region by around 3000 B.C.E.

These dogs developed to be perfectly adapted to their environment and their role of guardian; they are superlative in this capacity and are highly effective guardians of both the home and family, as well as livestock. For centuries they have been used for looking after sheep in particular and will watch over a flock unsupervised. One of the earliest written accounts of the dogs dates to 1407 when the historian of the Chateau of Lourdes described the merits of the "Great Dogs of the Mountains." However, it was in the seventeenth century that the breed came to the wider public's notice, and this was when Louis XIV (1638–1715) selected it as the Royal Dog of France. The dogs were sought after by the aristocracy and used for guarding their large estates. Within the same time frame they accompanied Basque fishermen and whalers on their journeys to Newfoundland, where they contributed to the Newfoundland breed.

The French aristocrat and military leader General Lafayette (1757–1834) is credited with introducing the first of the great white dogs to the United States in 1824. In England the first account of the dogs dates to 1844 when King Louis Philippe I (1773–1850) of France gifted one to Queen Victoria (1819–1901). Unusually for a Great Pyrenees, the dog became aggressive and bit the queen badly on the arm, for which he was banished to the Zoological Society. The dogs were first exhibited in England at Crystal Palace in 1885, and in the same year they were registered with the Kennel Club. They were still considered a working animal, and attempts to breed them in the United Kingdom were slow to start. It was not until the 1930s that the breed became established.

Breed numbers also suffered in France, despite the formation of two separate breed clubs; these were combined in 1920 to form the Réunion des Amateurs de Chiens Pyrénéens, which still exists. In 1927 it drew up the breed standard that has formed the basis for standards in other countries. The breed was greatly reduced by both world wars, and Great Pyrenees were drafted into active service for carrying messages for the French military.

The Great Pyrenees dog was reintroduced to the United States in 1931. In 1933 the American Kennel Club recognized the breed and placed it in the Working Group category. The dogs are called Great Pyrenees in the United States but are known as Pyrenean Mountain Dogs in England and Continental Europe. In 1936 the Pyrenean Mountain Dog Club of Great Britain was established.

At the end of the twentieth century, several brown bears were brought to the Pyrenees to boost the dwindling bear population. Concerned local shepherds were given grants by the European Union to purchase extra Great Pyrenees dogs to guard their flocks. Consequently, most flocks of sheep now have around four or five of these dogs with them working as flock guardians. The Great Pyrenees also make exceptional family dogs and companions.

AUSTRALIAN CATTLE DOG
MODERN — AUSTRALIA — COMMON

SIZE
Males 18–20 in./females 17–19 in.

APPEARANCE
*Solid, compact, athletic.
Proportionate head; medium-
length muzzle. Dark, oval eyes;
ears broad at base, pricked, set
wide apart. Very strong neck;
muscular, sloping shoulders; dense,
strong leg bones. Deep chest; strong
back; broad, muscular*

*hindquarters; sloping croup.
Tail set low, hangs in slight curve*

COLOR
*Blue or blue mottled, with or
without other markings, or red
speckled. Coat short and hard,
double coated with dense
undercoat*

APTITUDE
*Cattle herding, agility, showing,
companion*

THE AUSTRALIAN CATTLE DOG (ACD), also referred to as the Blue Heeler, Queensland Heeler, or Australian Heeler, is one of the world's leading cattle dogs. The breed was specifically developed in the early nineteenth century to work cattle. It is a job at which the dog still excels, particularly in Australia and North America. Despite the deliberate production of this master worker, the ACD also makes an excellent, although lively, family pet.

The breed's ancestors trace to the end of the eighteenth century during Australia's colonization by Europeans, and to Sydney and the surrounding area. European settlers brought their working dogs with them, specifically a type called the Smithfield, which is a large, shaggy, collie type that was influential to the foundation of the ACD. This dog took its name from the well-known London meat market, Smithfield, to where it drove cattle from all over the southeast of England. In Australia, the Smithfield was used to move the relatively docile cattle in the Sydney area in much the same way. Gradually people began to move farther away from Sydney in search of better, more extensive grazing. This was greatly helped by the discovery in 1813 of a route westward from Sydney through the Blue Mountains of the Great Dividing Range. Suddenly the vast interior of New South Wales (NSW) was accessible and with it thousands of acres of grazing for cattle. These new enormous pastures, where livestock had little contact with humans, produced wild cattle, and the slow English

Smithfield was neither able to keep up with them nor to cope with the vast terrain and extreme weather.

The Smithfield and other working collie breeds from England were very adept at herding sheep, and for this they tended to work at the head of the sheep, often barking. This method was unsuitable for the wild Australian cattle, because they were agitated by the noise and dispersed by the "heading" tactics. Ranchers realized that they would need to develop a specific type of Australian dog that was able to withstand the heat, cover huge distances, and work quietly at the heels of the cattle. One of the first breeding attempts was made by a rancher called Timmins in the 1830s, who crossed the Smithfield with the barkless Australian Dingo to produce a quiet, tenacious working dog. Although these dogs worked efficiently, they tended to be independent and aggressive biters, thus earning themselves the name Timmins' Biters. Other breeds were also tried, including the Rough Coated Collie, which proved to be too excitable, and the Bullterrier, which tended to go for the cattle's nose and hang on.

One of the first successful crosses was made by the rancher Thomas Hall of Hunter Valley, NSW, who imported two blue merle, smooth-coated Highland Collies from Scotland and crossed them with Dingo to produce good, silent cattle dogs. Known as Hall's Heelers, these dogs gained a glowing reputation among ranchers. Meanwhile, others were undertaking similar breeding programs, including George Elliott in Queensland who continued to cross the blue merle Highland Collie with Dingo. The reputation of these dogs spread, instigated by a butcher named Fred Davis who used them at the sale yards in Canterbury, Sydney. Soon cattlemen were inquiring about the dogs, and their popularity increased.

Jack and Harry Bagust, brothers and cattlemen from the Canterbury area, bought a number of dogs from Davis and began their own breeding program. They crossed the dogs to an imported Dalmatian in order to improve the Heeler's attitude to horses and to further its watchdog instincts. Unfortunately the cross diminished the working effectiveness of the dogs, but it did add interesting color, including the red and blue speckled coloration that is now seen regularly in the breed. In an effort to restore the dogs' working abilities, the Bagusts crossed them to black and tan Kelpies. The result was the foundation of the modern ACD: a compact, superlative worker, with great stamina, and a look of the Dingo; it also exhibited unique coloring. Blue dogs had black eye markings and ears; tan legs, chest, and head markings; and a small white patch in the middle of the forehead, whereas the body was dark blue with even blue speckling. The red dogs showed dark red markings instead of the black and were covered all over with an even red speckle.

Robert Kaleski began breeding and showing Blue Heelers in 1893. In 1902 he drew up a standard for the breed, basing it on the Dingo type in an effort to try to preserve the type that had proved the best worker. The standard was accepted the following year by the Cattle and Sheep Dog Club of Australia and the original Kennel Club of NSW. It was at this time that the breed became known as the Australian Heeler, then finally the Australian Cattle Dog.

The ACD is a popular working breed in the United States and is still widely used by ranchers. It was not until the 1960s, though, that the Australian Cattle Dog Club of America was established. The American Kennel Club (AKC) insisted that all dogs entered into the stud book must have pedigrees that traced back to registered dogs in Australia. Many of the dogs in the United States at that time were not purebred and so were ineligible. The AKC took over the stud book in 1979, and the following year the Australian Cattle Dog was entered into the Working Group category, before being transferred to Herding in 1983.

The first ACD to arrive in England was imported from the Landmaster Kennels in Australia by John and Mary Holmes in 1979 to their Formakin Kennels. Around the same time Malcolm Dudding from Kent imported a pair of blue puppies to his Swordstone Kennels. Dogs from these two kennels were bred together to form the foundation stock of the breed in England, and at the same time more ACDs were imported annually. The Australian Cattle Dog Society of Great Britain was formed in 1985 to promote and preserve the breed.

BRIARD

ANCIENT – FRANCE – MODERATE

SIZE
Males 23–27 in./females 22–25½ in.

APPEARANCE
Rugged, muscular, attractive with extrovert nature. Noble head; powerful jaws; square, black nose; dark brown eyes. Ears set high and lifted when alert. Muscular neck; broad chest; level, strong back with slight slope at croup. Slightly longer in frame length than height at shoulder. Long-haired coat; long tail covered with long hair, carried low but with upward curve at tip called a crochet

COLOR
All uniform colors including black, tawny, and gray, not white

APTITUDE
Originally guarding and protecting herds, herding, military use, showing, companion

THIS ANCIENT FRENCH BREED of working dog has a long, but little-documented history and has only come to the public's attention within the last couple of centuries. It is believed to have developed into a distinctive type by the eighth century and is said to have been favored by the Frankish King Charlemagne (742–814), appearing alongside him in tapestries. Charlemagne was a keen hunter and horseman, and it is surprising that he would choose to keep company with a breed of dog that is most associated with herding sheep. However, the Briard was originally used for guarding herds and was valued for its fiercely protective nature and tremendous bravery, making it a suitable companion for a king. Many centuries later, Napoleon Bonaparte (1769–1821), who was reputedly not unduly fond of dogs and barred his wife Josephine's pugs from the bedroom, had two Briards, possibly as guard dogs.

The name "Briard" was not coined until the late nineteenth or early twentieth century; prior to this the dogs were referred to as French sheepdogs. They are also known as Chien Berger de Brie, a name that has two plausible origins and one that was not applied to the dogs until the nineteenth century. The dogs are associated with the area of Brie in northern France, between the Seine and Marne Valleys. Famous for its cheese, this beautiful rugged area is home to rich farmlands and herds of cattle and sheep. There is no evidence to prove that the Briard

developed in this specific area, but the dogs were used here and across the country in an agricultural role. The second explanation for the name centers on a fourteenth-century tale of murder and bravery that was recorded in a letter by Julius Caesar Scaliger (1484–1558). According to legend, a French courtier called Aubry de Montdidier was murdered in c. 1371 in the forest of Bondy, north of Paris. The only witness was his dog, who relentlessly pursued the perpetrator, Robert Macaire, until he was captured. The king ordered that Macaire and the dog should fight a duel, which took place on the Isle de Notre Dame. The dog won, and Macaire confessed and was hanged. The name "de Brie" derives from d'Aubry, and the two words clearly sound similar. The dog's description in the tale resembles a Briard, and a statue depicting the fight can be found in the town of Montargis.

It is unusual for working breeds to excel at both guarding and herding, but these dual talents of the shaggy French Briard made it indispensable to French farmers. The dogs were originally used for guarding livestock and would live out with the herds, unsupervised, to protect them from predators such as wolves, foxes, and even human intruders. The dogs formed an important part of the rural French farmer's family, looking after invaluable livestock and protecting the homestead. The Briard's natural herding skills were also important, and the dogs were routinely used to move livestock between pastures and to prevent the herds spreading onto neighboring land; they are still used for working livestock today.

Before becoming the third president of the United States, Thomas Jefferson (1743–1826) served as a foreign diplomat in France and in 1785 was made the United States Minister to France. During his time in Paris (1784–89) Jefferson became friendly with the Marquis de Lafayette, who introduced the American to the Briard. Jefferson was so impressed by the rustic French sheepdogs that he returned to the United States in 1789 with three of them. Jefferson

imported another female Briard in 1790, and in 1806 and 1809 Lafayette sourced three more and sent them to Jefferson's home at Monticello. The president bred the dogs and gave them to his friends as gifts. Although Jefferson admired the dogs' skills, he was not especially fond of them, and they were never allowed into his house.

The long-haired French sheepdog were first termed Chien de Brie in 1809 by Abbot Rozier in his *Course of Agriculture*. In 1863 the first French dog show was held in Paris, and a Briard won the Sheepdog class. The Club du Chien de Berger, the Sheepdog Club, was formed in 1896, and in 1897 it drew up the first breed standard. The society Les Amis du Briard was founded in 1909, and although it disbanded during the war years, it reformed in 1923 and in 1925 produced a more precise breed standard.

Briards were widely deployed by the French military during World War I and suffered devastating losses. They were used for packing urgent supplies to the front line and as sentries. They have very acute hearing, and their most heartrending job was to scour the battlefields and find fallen soldiers who were clinging to life. During the 1920s Briards began to be imported to the United States, and in 1922 the first litter of Briard puppies was registered with the American Kennel Club. The Briard Club of America was established in 1928; it adopted the French breed standard, with slight changes.

CANAAN DOG
ANCIENT – ISRAEL – RARE

SIZE
Males 20–24 in./females 19–23 in.

APPEARANCE
Square, balanced, alert.
Wedge-shaped head appearing
broader because of low-set ears.
Black nose; almond-shaped, dark
eyes; medium-sized ears;
muscular neck of medium length;
muscular shoulders; straight front
legs. Square, strong body; level
back; powerful hindquarters,
hocks well let down. High-set tail

with thick brush, carried curled
over back when excited

COLOR
Either mostly white with mask,
with or without color patches, or
solid color with or without white
trim. Color from black through
shades of brown, or solid white.
Gray and/or brindle not allowed.
Coat straight, short, harsh

APTITUDE
Herding, guarding, agility,
showing, companion

THE MODERN CANAAN DOG descends from ancient pariah dogs of the Middle East and dates back to prehistory. There are numerous depictions of dogs that exhibit similar characteristics to the Canaan, including the striking drawings of dogs at the Beni-Hassan tombs that date from 2200 to 2000 B.C.E.

The Canaan is believed to have been used by the ancient Israelites for guarding and herding their camps and flocks. They were widespread throughout the ancient land of Canaan, from where they derive their name, but when the Israelites were dispersed by the Romans more than 2,000 years ago, the dogs were set loose and largely made their way to the Negev Desert, a natural refuge. Here they became mostly feral, and as a result of the process of natural selection developed their hardiness, tenacity, and self-sufficiency. Some were adopted by the nomadic Bedouin people living in the same region and used for guarding their herds and camps, whereas others were taken in by Druze people who inhabit a region farther north. The Bedouin and Druze people still keep these dogs today.

The dogs lived here largely unknown to the outside world and mostly undomesticated until the twentieth century. Their history was changed in 1934 when Dr. Menzel, a noted dog authority, and her husband emigrated from Vienna to Israel. Shortly afterward Dr. Menzel was recruited by Haganah, part of the Israel Defense Forces, to establish a dog section and oversee the procurement and training of special service dogs. These were needed to protect Hebrew settlements and perform a number of roles including tracking and mine detection. Dr. Menzel realized that if it were possible to train the local pariah dogs (Canaans) they would be the perfect candidates. She began by luring some of the feral dogs into her camp to gain their trust and was amazed at how quickly they reverted to domestication and at the speed of their learning.

After the establishment of a number of feral dogs, she then implemented domestic breeding programs. These dogs proved to be extremely intelligent, obedient, and agile, which, together with their highly developed senses, made them ideal military dogs. They were among the first dogs to be trained to detect land mines, and more than 400 were used in World War II with great success. After the war, Dr. Menzel became involved with training Canaan dogs as guide dogs for the blind. She had some limited success, but the dogs were too independent and also too small to be suitable. Menzel based her Canaan breeding program at the Institute for Orientation and Mobility of the Blind and established the B'nei HaBitachon Kennels. In order to preserve the original characteristics of the Canaan, she frequently reintroduced feral dogs back into her breeding program.

The breed was recognized by the Palestine Kennel Club, and by 1948 there were around 150 Canaan dogs registered. The Israel Kennel Club recognized them in 1953, and in 1966 they gained international recognition through the Fédération Cynologique Internationale. During the same period the first Canaan dogs arrived in the United States and the United Kingdom. In 1965 the Canaan Dog Club of America was established and a stud book opened. The Canaan was entered into the Miscellaneous Group category by the American Kennel Club in 1989, and in 1997 it was moved to the Herding Group category.

KOMONDOR
ANCIENT – HUNGARY – RARE

SIZE
Males minimum 27½ in./females minimum 25½ in.
APPEARANCE
Powerful, striking, brave. Moderate head; broad muzzle. Dark eyes; medium-sized ears hang close to head. Strong neck; muscular forequarters; deep, broad chest; level back; very
powerful hindquarters. Tail quite long, curves at the end, held raised in line with body when excited
COLOR
White. Double-coated: outer layer coarse, wavy, falls in cords; woolly undercoat
APTITUDE
Sheep guardian, showing, companion

THERE IS NO MISTAKING A KOMONDOR because it is one of the more unusual and imposing of the many dog breeds. It is an interesting and powerful dog, magnificent to look at and an absolute master in its field of protection; it is a foolish predator that takes on a Komondor. This grand dog is considered a national treasure in Hungary, its country of origin, and is frequently referred to as the "king" of livestock guardian dogs. Its protective instincts are absolute, and a Komondor will protect a flock of sheep with the same enthusiasm as it protects its home and owner. Such is its skill in this respect that it is reputed to have cleared Hungary of its wolf population.

The Komondor is a fiercely territorial dog over property and individuals, which makes it a superb livestock guardian. It has been bred for centuries to be an independent thinker and decision maker, to work on its own, and to be self-sufficient: qualities that have greatly endeared it to the farming and ranching communities. However, despite its charming, sometimes comical appearance, this is not a suitable dog for a novice dog owner. It requires consistent and firm obedience training from a young age, is happiest when working outside, and has a high maintenance coat. For the well informed, the Komondor can be a devoted and loyal companion.

Some scholars claim that the Komondor is the dog of the Magyar tribes, who moved westward to settle in the Carpathian Basin in the ninth century. This huge area once formed the kingdom of Hungary, which was a much larger geographic mass than modern Hungary. A second and more plausible theory, and one supported by archeological evidence, is that the Komondor is associated with the ancient Cumans who originally came from near the Yellow river in China and were gradually forced westward by the expansion of the Mongols from the end of the tenth century. By the thirteenth century, they had reached Hungary via the Ural Mountains and were granted asylum by the Hungarian king Béla IV (1206–70). Despite this, the leader of the Cumans, Köten Khan, was murdered by Hungarian soldiers, and in retaliation the Cumans ransacked their way south through Hungary and settled in Bulgaria.

An alliance was later formed by the Hungarians and Cumans, which was cemented by the marriage of Köten Khan's daughter, Elizabeth, to King Béla's oldest son, Stephen. Following Mongol attacks on Hungary between 1241 and 1242, King Béla asked the Cumans to return to bolster their defenses, and they were given the area between the rivers Danube and Tisza to settle. Excavations of ancient Cuman grave sites in Hungary have revealed dog and horse skeletons positioned in clearly ritualistic formations, which indicates the importance of both animals to the Cuman belief system. In one grave the deceased was buried with his head resting on a dog; in another a series of dogs was buried around the grave. These remains have been identified as resembling the Komondor. It is also theorized that the name "Komondor" originates from the dogs' association with the Cumans, that is, "Koman dor," or "dog of the Cumans."

The Komondor is thought to owe some of its development to the influence of the Russian Ovcharka, a sheepdog breed that the Cumans may have come into contact with as they traveled from the Ural Mountains down through southern Russia. It also exhibits some similarities to the Bergamasco Sheepdog of the Italian Alps, particularly in the nature of its corded coat, although the Bergamasco is normally black and the Komondor is

always white. The Komondor and the Hungarian Puli also share many characteristics, and it is widely held that these two breeds were commonly used in conjunction with each other. The Komondor's chief role was that of livestock guardian, whereas the much smaller Puli was more suited to herding livestock. The two dogs together provided the shepherd with a formidable working team.

The Komondor, which is still used in its original role, has a highly specialized coat that allows the dog to blend in easily with the herd and provides it with enormous protection from both predators and weather. The dog would live out with the flocks of sheep, in and among them to provide full-time defense against wolves, coyotes, bear, and human threats. Such is the Komondor's protective instinct that it is not unknown for it to attempt to care for orphaned lambs. Historically, it was only a shepherd's dog and was not used by the aristocracy. Given the isolated nature of the sheep farms, the Komondor never came into contact with other breeds, so it has remained essentially very pure throughout its history, simply being bred to perform its working duties.

The breed is utterly fearless and will take on any perceived predator or threat, both in the working livestock environment or in the domestic forum. For this reason it must be socialized with other dogs and people from a very young age; if this is done correctly, it can make a loving and calm pet. It was first introduced to the United States in 1933, and the American Kennel Club recognized the breed in 1937. Breed numbers dropped dramatically during World War II but have since picked up. More recently this efficient dog has been reintroduced as a livestock guardian in the United States with great success.

The first Komondor in the United Kingdom was a female that was imported from Hungary by Mrs. Lanz in the early 1970s. She was followed by another female and a male who were both imported from the United States. The first litter was born in 1976, giving rise to three puppies, one of which went back to the United States. These first few dogs formed the foundation of the breed in the United Kingdom and were followed by more imports and successful breeding. The Komondor Club of Great Britain was established in 1978 and is supported by a core group of dedicated enthusiasts, although numbers of the breed remain low in the United Kingdom.

STANDARD SCHNAUZER
ANCIENT – GERMANY – COMMON

SIZE
Males 18½–19½ in./females 17½–18½ in.

APPEARANCE
Intelligent, robust, lively. Head of good length; blunt-ending muzzle; chin whiskers; black nose; dark, oval eyes; ears set high, V-shaped, dropping forward or cropped to stand upright (US only). Long, slightly arched neck; compact body; straight front legs; deep chest; strong, straight back; powerful hindquarters. Tail carried erect, docked (US only) or of moderate length, carried erect, undocked

COLOR
Pepper/salt, each hair banded, unique to the breed, or pure black. Coat harsh, wiry, medium length, dense, weatherproof undercoat

APTITUDE
Ratting, livestock guardian, guardian, military service, agility, showing, companion

ALTHOUGH TODAY THE SCHNAUZER is chiefly known as a delightful companion animal, in its past it was one of Germany's most versatile working breeds. It is noted for its lovely temperament and intelligence; it also often exhibits a high level of intuition and has been successfully used as a therapy animal. There are three types of Schnauzer: the Standard, often referred to as the Schnauzer and the propagator of the other two: the Giant Schnauzer and the Miniature Schnauzer. These charming dogs derive their name from the German word for "moustache," in reference to their characteristic facial whiskers, although the name was not used officially until the early twentieth century.

The Standard Schnauzer is the oldest of the three and is believed to trace back to at least the fourteenth century and to Germany. Many resources indicate that Schnauzers appeared frequently in European works of art from the fifteenth century onward and in particular in works by Albrecht Dürer (1471–1528). This German artist often depicted small to medium-sized dogs in his works, although it has not been proved that these were Schnauzers. Similarly, the statue of the "Night Watchman" in Stuttgart (1620) features a small dog of possible Schnauzer heritage that accompanies the watchman.

The Schnauzer is thought to have originated in Württemberg and Bavaria in the southwest and southeast of Germany, possibly based on terrier, livestock guardian, and hunting dogs, and the dogs exhibit inherent skills from all three of these types. The earliest Schnauzers differed considerably in appearance from the modern breed, which was properly established during the nineteenth century. However, these early Schnauzers were highly valued as all-around farm dogs. They were excellent at vermin control and were enthusiastic ratters; they provided companionship in the homestead and were vigilant guardians of their property and of livestock. The Giant and the Standard Schnauzer were also used for droving—moving livestock chiefly to market—and both types would guard the farmers' carts as they waited for the sales. The Giant Schnauzer was often referred to as a "butcher dog" and was used in and around butchers' yards. Both the Standard and the Giant were also used for hauling light loads, and although the Standard is only a medium-sized dog, it is exceptionally robust and strong for its size. The Miniature was developed toward the end of the nineteenth century, and was initially a working dog used for ratting and other forms of vermin control on German farms.

Although the Schnauzer had existed for centuries as a rugged farm dog and loyal companion, it was not until the mid nineteenth century that there was a considered move toward producing this valuable dog as a specific type. At this point in its history, black German Poodle and gray Wolfspitz were introduced to fix their typology. These crosses resulted in the two coat colorings that are now recognized: black and salt and pepper. Although black Schnauzers are fairly common in Germany, they are less typical in the United Kingdom and the United States. At first these dogs were referred to as Wire Haired Pinschers, and this was the name under which they were shown in Germany in the 1870s; "Pinscher" is often used to describe a type of dog that is specifically adept at vermin control (of terrier type). At the third German International Show in 1879, Hanover, the winning Wire Haired Pinscher was called "Schnauzer," and from then on this name was

NOBLE AND FAITHFUL

adopted by many to describe the dogs. The first breed standard was published in 1880, and the dogs suddenly became sought after as show dogs and pets. The Pinscher Club was established in Cologne in 1895, and in 1907 the Bavarian Schnauzer Club at Munich was formed. These two clubs were united in 1918 and became the official representative of the breed in the German Kennel Club, known as the Pinscher-Schnauzer Club.

In addition to their other skilled roles, the Standard and Giant Schnauzers were also used by the police force and later by the military. As a breed, the Schnauzer is highly intelligent, and this, combined with its obedience, made it an exceptional service dog that was used as a dispatch carrier and aide during World War I, as well as a guard dog.

The first Standard Schnauzers arrived in the United States at the beginning of the twentieth century and they were recognized by the American Kennel Club (AKC) in 1904 and placed in the Working Group category, although they were not imported in significant numbers until after World War I. The Schnauzer Club of America was formed in 1925, and in 1933 this club was split to form the Standard Schnauzer Club of America and the American Miniature Schnauzer Club. The Miniature Schnauzer was recognized by the AKC in 1926 and placed in the Terrier Group category; the Giant Schnauzer was recognized in 1930 and placed in the Working Group.

Schnauzers gained media attention during the 1940s thanks to the fondness of Hollywood actor Errol Flynn for the breed. Flynn owned several Schnauzers but his favorite was Arno, who was the actor's near constant companion and who accompanied him on movie sets. Arno was also a frequent guest on Flynn's yacht, *Sirocco,* where the dog would chase flying fish. One evening Arno drowned while apparently leaping into the water after a fish. Flynn was inconsolable, and later gave Arno a naval burial at sea.

Schnauzers also began arriving in the United Kingdom early in the twentieth century, and one of the first was a German champion dog nicknamed Bruno, who arrived in 1928. He went on to win Best in Breed in 1930, which was when the first class for the breed was held at Crufts. The Schnauzer Club of Great Britain was established in 1929, and the Kennel Club recognizes the Standard and Miniature Schnauzers within the Utility Group category and the Giant in the Working Group.

PEMBROKE WELSH CORGI

ANCIENT – WALES – COMMON

SIZE
Males/females 10–12 in.

APPEARANCE
Low-set, robust, alert. Head foxlike in appearance; slightly tapering muzzle; black nose. Brown, oval eyes; pricked, medium-sized ears. Longish neck; short legs with good bone; broad, deep chest; medium-length back; strong hindquarters. Tail short naturally or docked in the US

COLOR
Red, sable, fawn, black and tan, with or without white markings. Double coated; top layer medium length, hard; undercoat soft

APTITUDE
Cattle droving, showing, companion

CORGIS ARE BIG DOGS IN EVERY WAY, apart from their height. They have tremendous character, stamina, and working skills, as well as a powerful body that is carried on very short legs. They developed many centuries ago for their role as a drover's dog. The Corgi is able to move livestock, including cattle, pigs, and geese, with great dexterity and is low enough to the ground to avoid kicking heels. Although the Corgi might look like a nonworking lap dog—a job at which it can also excel—it is a driven worker and likes nothing better than having a job to do. It is a plucky, fearless dog that has been used until recently as a versatile farm dog that is just as capable of droving livestock to market as guarding the farmyard, killing vermin, and providing companionship to its family.

Since the twentieth century the Corgi has become synonymous with the British royal family. Her Majesty Queen Elizabeth II is a Corgi enthusiast and has bred the dogs for many years; she has also crossbred her Corgis to her sister's Dachshund, Pipkin, creating what is affectionately termed a "Dorgi." The queen still owns several Corgis and Dorgis, although the Dorgi is not a recognized breed.

There are two types of Corgi, the Cardigan and the Pembroke, named after the respective areas of Wales—Cardiganshire and Pembrokeshire—where they originate. The Cardigan is considered to be the older of the two breeds, and there are distinct differences between the Cardigan and the Pembroke, although they were often bred together. They were not officially divided by the Kennel Club until 1934 after strong protest from breeders of the respective types. The main differences between the two are that the Cardigan has a much longer body with a heavy, full tail; the ears are slightly larger and more rounded; the feet are rounder; and the fur can be any color as long as white does not dominate. The Pembroke looks more foxlike and is smaller, with sharper features, and characteristically has no tail.

There are a number of possible breeds behind the Pembroke Corgi's development, such as the Swedish Vallhund, the Norwegian Buhund, the Schipperke, and the early Pomeranian, which are all spitz-type dogs. The older Cardigan Corgis, on the other hand, descended from the Teckel, which is similar to the German Dachshund.

The British royal affiliation with Corgis began in 1933 when the Duke of York (later King George VI; 1895–1952) procured a puppy for his daughters, Elizabeth and Margaret. The puppy was sent to be housetrained by a kennelman, who referred to the puppy as Duke at first, then Dukie, and finally with his Yorkshire accent, Dookie. Dookie was quickly followed by Jane, and the two produced two puppies, of which one, Crackers, lived to be fourteen years old. It is said that the Queen Mother had a special bath chair crafted for him, in which she could push him around when he was no longer able to walk. Her Majesty Queen Elizabeth II was given a Corgi puppy called Susan on her eighteenth birthday, and all subsequent Corgis in the royal household now trace back to Susan.

Corgis began to be imported to the United States in the 1930s; the American Kennel Club (AKC) recognized the Pembroke Corgi in 1934 and the Cardigan in 1935. The Pembroke Welsh Corgi Club of America was established in 1936, and today the Pembroke Corgi regularly ranks within the top thirty most popular breeds in the United States, based on AKC registration statistics. Both breeds have thriving national and regional breed clubs. In fact, Corgi enthusiasts are active in many countries across the world.

ROTTWEILER

ANCIENT – GERMANY – COMMON

SIZE
Males 24–27 in./females 22–25 in.
APPEARANCE
*Imposing, powerful, athletic.
Medium-length head, broad
between ears; broad muzzle,
tapers slightly to end. Almond-
shaped, dark eyes; triangular,
pendant ears set well apart.
Moderately long, slightly arched,
very muscular neck; straight front
legs with good bone; broad, deep
chest; compact body; straight,
powerful back. Muscular*
*hindquarters; strong, well-
angulated hocks. Tail docked at
first or second joint in US. When
natural tail is long, carried
horizontally in movement,
can be higher when excited*
COLOR
*Black with rust to mahogany
markings. Coat coarse, dense,
straight*
APTITUDE
*Watchdog, livestock guardian,
cattle drover, drafting, police dog,
agility, showing, companion*

THE ANCIENT AND NOBLE ROTTWEILER is one of the
powerhouses of the canine world and a truly magnificent
breed that has sadly suffered from poor press because of
irresponsible dog ownership. It is a big, powerful animal
that requires a knowledgeable owner who is prepared to
provide it with consistent training, socialization, exercise,
and mental stimulation. In return, the Rottie can be a
wonderful companion animal: loyal, obedient, intelligent,
and protective of its loved ones.

The Rottweiler's history is thought to trace back to the
Romans and the expansion of their empire. They had huge
armies of men mobilized, and following these legions were
herds of cattle to provide the troops with food. Their
tenacious Mastiff-type dogs were used to move the cattle
along and to guard livestock and the camps at night. The
modern Rottweiler owes its heritage to the dogs that
accompanied the Romans as they traveled through
Switzerland, which had been subjugated by Julius Caesar in
58 B.C.E., into southern Germany. This area near the Black
Forest was settled by the Romans in 73 C.E. as Arae Flaviae.
Through their journey and in their new region, the dogs
came into contact with the projected ancestors of breeds
such as the Bernese Mountain Dog, Greater Swiss
Mountain Dog, Appenzeller Mountain Dog, and the
Entlebucher, all of which share some physical similarities.

At some point in medieval times the area became known
as "das Rote wil," based on the red roof tiles of the
preexisting Roman villas. From this the name "Rottweil"
emerged, and the dogs of the area were similarly named. As
the cattle trade boomed, the dogs became increasingly
essential and most associated with the area's butchers,
being called "butcher's dogs" (Rottweiler Metzgerhund).

As the railways developed in the nineteenth century, the
dog's draft role became unnecessary. At the same time,
cattle droving was outlawed, and suddenly the dogs were
redundant. At the end of the nineteenth century the
short-lived International Club for Leonbergers and
Rottweiler Dogs was formed in Germany, and in 1901 the
first breed standard for the Rottweiler was drawn up. Prior
to World War I the Rottweiler had been used by the
German police, a role in which it excelled. During the war
it was used as a messenger dog and for packing supplies, as
well as guarding, protection, and in the ambulance service.

In 1921 the Allgemeiner Deutscher Rottweiler Klub
(ADRK) was formed, and in 1924 it published its first stud
book. The Rottweiler was recognized by the American
Kennel Club (AKC) in 1931 and placed in the Working
Group category. The first Rottie in the United Kingdom
was imported in 1936 by Mrs. Thelma Gray. She continued
to import until World War II when she sent her dogs over
to Ireland for their safety. Another important breeder
whose dogs were influential in establishing the breed in
the United Kingdom was Captain Roy Smith, who began
to import Rotties in 1953. He became chairman of the
Rottweiler Club in 1960, and from this time onward, a
number of people imported the breed, and it eventually
became established. The Kennel Club recognized the
Rottweiler in 1965, placing it in the Working Group
category. Since then the Rottweiler has become very
popular in the United Kingdom and the United States and
is regularly within the top fifteen most popular US dog
breeds based on AKC breed registration statistics.

NOBLE AND FAITHFUL

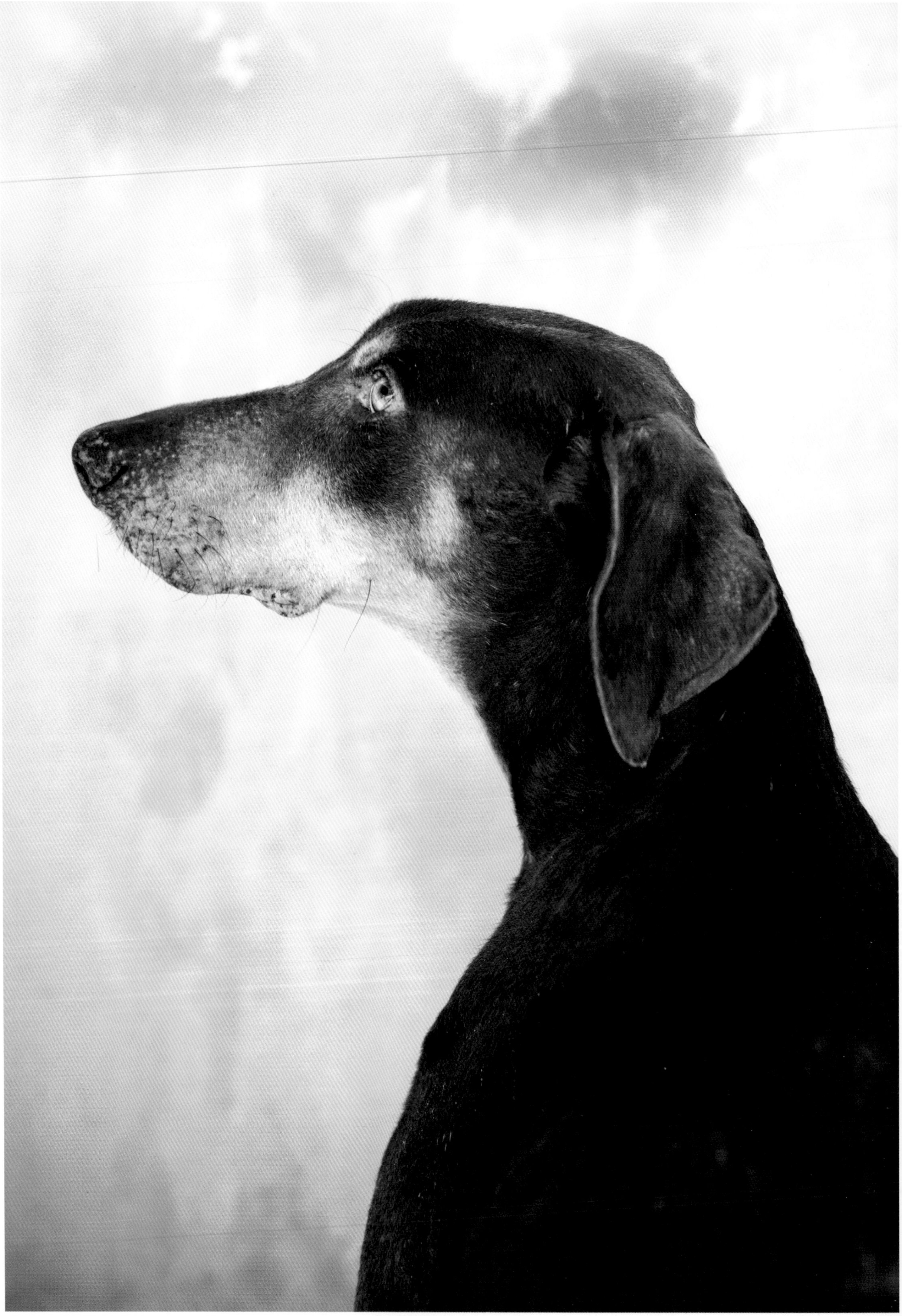

DOBERMAN PINSCHER
MODERN – GERMANY – COMMON

SIZE
Males 26–28 in./ females 24–26 in.

APPEARANCE
Elegant, noble, athletic. Head long and wedge shaped; black, brown, dark tan, or gray nose depending on body color. Almond-shaped brown eyes with lively expression; soft dropped ears set high on head in the UK, ears are usually cropped in the US to stand erect. Muscular, arched neck; smooth sleek outline; square body with short, compact, muscular back; stomach well tucked up; hindquarters well developed and powerful. Tail is docked at the second joint in the US, left naturally it can be raised and carried freely

COLOR
Black, red, blue, fawn (Isabella) all with tan markings. Coat smooth and short

APTITUDE
Guardian, police work, military, agility, showing, companion

THE DISTINCTIVE DOBERMAN, which dates to the late nineteenth century, owes its existence chiefly to one man, a German tax collector called Friedrich Louis Dobermann (1834–94), who set about creating a dog that was suited to helping him with his work. He wanted a dog that would protect him in adverse situations but that would also be a useful tool in "encouraging" people to pay their money. In addition, he wanted a loyal and affectionate companion. Unfortunately, Herr Dobermann did not keep records of the dogs that he crossbred to achieve the Doberman, and his efforts have become the subject of much speculation.

Herr Dobermann lived in the German town of Apolda where his other jobs were dogcatcher and "skinner," which gave him access to a wide variety of dogs. Initially, his criteria was to produce a dog based on character rather than physical conformity, but surprisingly his dog appears to have become a "type" with amazing speed. His breeding experiments began in the last decades of the nineteenth century, and from early on his dogs were known as Dobermann's Hunde. The foundations of the breed were from a dog named Schnupp, described only as clever and fearless, and a female guardian type named Bisart; their puppies were black puppies with rust-colored markings. From the 1890s onward, there have been conflicting accounts of the breeds that contributed toward the Doberman, but the most common are the "butchers dog" (ancestor to the modern Rottweiler), German Pinscher, Beauceron, German Shepherd, Weimaraner, German Short Haired Pointer, Great Dane, Black and Tan Terrier, Manchester Terrier, and Greyhound. The extent and ratio to which these different breeds were used are not known.

In 1863 Herr Dobermann introduced his Doberman Pinschers to the Apolda Dog Market, where they proved to be an instant success. Herr Dobermann died in 1894, but his breeding efforts were taken over by Otto Goeller and Goswin Tischler, both of whom were key in promoting the breed. Goeller went on to found the National Doberman Pinscher Club in 1899. In c. 1900 the German Kennel Club approved the first breed standard, which meant that the breed had developed in a phenomenally short period of time.

The first Doberman was registered with the American Kennel Club in 1908 and entered into the Working Group category, and in 1921 the Doberman Pinscher Club of America was established. The dogs were popular with the police and were often used as tracking dogs, given their excellent sense of smell. Later they were used by the military, and during World War II they were adopted as the official war dog of the US Marine Corps, serving as sentries, messengers, scouts, and trackers. In 1994 a memorial to the Dobermans who lost their lives during combat was installed in Guam, where many of them had perished.

In the United Kingdom the Doberman Club was established in 1948. It was around this time that the Germans dropped the "Pinscher" from the breed name, because this referred to the German terrier type and was considered no longer necessary; the United States has retained "Pinscher" in the nomenclature. Today, because of greater emphasis on breeding for temperament, the Doberman has emerged as a versatile and multitalented dog that excels when given a job to do but also makes a valuable companion. It is noted for its intelligence, agility, loyalty, and protective nature.

GERMAN SHEPHERD
MODERN – GERMANY – COMMON

SIZE
Males 24–26 in./females 22–24 in.

APPEARANCE
Noble, intelligent, powerful. Chiseled head; powerful, wedge-shaped muzzle; almond-shaped eyes, preferably dark; medium-sized, pointed, erect ears; strong, muscular neck; strong shoulders; straight front legs with good, oval bone; body slightly longer than height at withers. Deep chest, not too broad; slightly sloping croup; powerful hindquarters; bushy tail, quite long, hangs low with slight curve at rest, carried higher when moving but not over back

COLOR
Most colors allowed, strong colors preferred, white not acceptable. Coat straight, harsh, relatively short undercoat

APTITUDE
Livestock guardian, sheepherding, watchdog, police, military, guide dog, tracker, agility, showing, companion

THE GERMAN SHEPHERD is an extraordinary feat of modern breeding, and despite its relatively short history, it has become one of the world's most popular dogs. The German Shepherd is also one of the most versatile dog breeds and has been used to serve humans across a great range of roles. The breed is noted for its intelligence, which has allowed the dog to be trained in innumerable ways; it is no coincidence that the early breeding of these dogs was based on intelligence and working abilities rather than on physical appearance. A particularly charming story that underlines the German Shepherd's intellect is that of Wolf, a German Shepherd who belonged to renowned dog lover and psychoanalyst Sigmund Freud (1856–1939). Freud had bought Wolf chiefly as a companion for his daughter, Anna, who was living with him at the time. One day Anna and Wolf went out for a walk and came across some soldiers who began shooting blank rounds into the air. The noise startled Wolf, who ran away and eventually leaped into a taxi as the door was opened. According to the taxi driver, the dog then kept lifting its head and leaning toward the driver until he realized that the dog's address was written on the collar. Wolf was given a taxi ride home and the driver a large tip from Freud. It should be noted that German Shepherds are generally associated with tremendous acts of heroism rather than for taking taxis!

Germany had a tradition of strong, dependable, working dogs that were used for herding or guarding livestock. These sheepdog types had developed over many centuries and acquired different characteristics depending on their region, environmental factors, and specific breeding within areas; this had given rise to a variety of coat types, colorations, physiques, and skills. In the nineteenth century there was a move to formalize these different types of dog and to categorize them by breed names, thus creating standards and clubs to promote their different qualities. An early club in Germany was the Phylax Society, which was established in 1891 to organize the native German breeds. There was infighting between the committee members, however, who were divided on breeding for appearance or working abilities, and the club disbanded several years later. One member was Captain Max von Stephanitz (1864–1936), and it is to his efforts that the modern German Shepherd owes its existence.

Stephanitz was interested in using local, native German dogs to produce a distinct working type. While visiting a dog show in Karlsruhe, western Germany, in 1899, he came across a working sheepherding dog of wolfish appearance that was exactly what he wanted to achieve. He purchased the dog, named him Horand von Grafrath, and used him as the foundation of his breeding program. Stephanitz founded the Verein für Deutsche Schäferhunde, the Society for the German Shepherd Dog, and Horand von Grafrath was named the first German Shepherd dog and was the first to be added to the breed registry. Stephanitz acquired Horand's brother, Luchs, and bred the two to suitable females; the progeny were then intensively inbred to fix characteristics, with some outside sheepherding blood also being introduced. Horand's most successful son was Hektor von Schwaben; together with another relative, Beowolf, they feature heavily in the founding bloodlines. Stephanitz's motto for the breed became "utility and intelligence" and a breed standard was formulated.

NOBLE AND FAITHFUL

As demand for working sheepherders and livestock guardians began to dwindle in the early twentieth century, Stephanitz began to market the German Shepherd specifically toward the police force. The dog had already demonstrated its great intelligence, combined with a propensity for training in any number of roles, and its loyal and protective instincts. These qualities made it one of the foremost police dogs in the world. The German Shepherd was then adopted by the military, and in World War I in Germany alone many thousands of these dogs were enlisted, which gives an indication of the rapidity with which this breed had grown from its inception only decades previously. The dogs were used as messengers, rescue dogs, sentries, and as personal guards, and exhibited great courage that impressed soldiers of all nations.

The first German Shepherd to be exhibited in the United States was a dog called Mira von Offingen, in 1907, and the following year the American Kennel Club recognized the breed and placed it in the Herding Group category. The German Shepherd Dog Club of America was formed in 1913, but in 1917, when the United States entered into World War I and all things German were shunned, the name was changed to the Shepherd Dog Club of America. In England at around the same time, the breed name was changed to Alsatian, after the German–French border area of Alsace-Lorraine, and remained as such until 1977.

After the war, many of the dogs were taken back to the United States and England by returning troops who had been won over by their bravery and loyalty in action. One such dog was a puppy who had been rescued from an abandoned German war dog station in Lorraine, France, by army corporal Lee Duncan. Duncan originally found two puppies whom he named Rin Tin Tin and Nanette; Nanette sadly died but he was able to return to the United States with Rin Tin Tin. Duncan taught the dog numerous tricks and high jumping and, in 1922, after reputedly seeing a wolf refuse to perform on a movie set, he decided to put Rin Tin Tin forward as a canine actor. The dog performed in twenty-three Hollywood films, and earned large amounts of money before his death in 1932. His heirs continued to perform in Hollywood, and in the 1950s *The Adventures of Rin Tin Tin*, a children's television series that underlined the relationship between a boy and his German Shepherd dog, was aired. German Shepherds have since featured in a number of other screen productions, all of which have added to the breed's international popularity.

In 1919 in the United Kingdom the breed was officially recognized by the Kennel Club, when it was called the Alsatian, and fifty-four dogs were registered. In the 1920s the Prince of Wales, later Edward VIII, entered his Alsatian, Claus of Seale, in Crufts; his grandmother, the Duchess of Teck, had kept a breeding kennel for the breed in Germany prior to the war. By 1926 registrations of Alsatians had risen to around 8,000 in the United Kingdom, and in the United States in the same year the breed accounted for thirty-six percent of total breed registrations.

At this time the German Shepherd embarked on another important role, as a guide dog. The dogs had first been trained as guide dogs in 1917 by the Germans to guide soldiers who had been blinded by mustard gas. The French set up similar programs shortly afterward. In 1925 the first German-trained guide dog, called Lux, was sent to the United States as a gift for Senator Thomas D. Schall of Minnesota, who had been blinded in 1907 by a shock from a cigar lighter. During the same period Helen Keller acquired a privately trained guide dog, which was the first to be trained in the United States. In 1929 Dorothy Harrison Eustis and Morris Frank established the Seeing Eye Foundation. The dogs came from Eustis's kennels in Switzerland where she felt the quality of the German Shepherd was superior.

German Shepherds were again widely used by both sides in World War II; in addition to their customary roles, the dogs were also trained to detect land mines and trip wires. In the United States the company Dogs for Defense was established to provide dogs, chiefly German Shepherds, to the military. Despite the close and obvious association of the German Shepherd with the Germans, including with Adolf Hitler who was very fond of the breed, the reputation of the German Shepherd was undamaged. It has continued to be an exceedingly popular breed, although the dogs have also suffered the effects of indiscriminate and poor breeding, which has resulted in conformational, health, and temperament issues. However, the dedicated work and support of the breed's many clubs and enthusiasts have been instrumental in correcting this and striving for the preservation of all the qualities that make the German Shepherd such an unrivaled dog.

CHAPTER 5
DETERMINED AND BRAVE

Scent hounds rely on their highly developed sense of smell to find and track prey and are specialized in this endeavor. Unlike the sight hound breeds that hunt by sight and at great speed, the scent hound breeds work more slowly, but with tremendous endurance. Within the scent hound breeds, there are two loose types of hunters: the hot nosed and the cold nosed. Hot-nosed hunters, typified by the English and American Foxhounds, follow fresh trails at some speed. These hounds are best followed on horseback and will provide a fast-paced and exhilarating chase, providing that they find a fresh scent. Cold-nosed hunters are able to pick up an old scent and trail it; some such as the rare Otterhound are able to follow a scent through water. Others such as the Bloodhound are such excellent cold-nosed hunters that they are frequently used for tracking missing persons and even cadavers. Beagles and other breeds are often used for drug and bomb detection.

Scent hounds are believed to trace their origins back to the ancient Mastiff types of prehistory that were used primarily in warfare and for hunting. The ancient Celts are thought to have selectively bred their Mastiff types for hunting as did the Alani tribes of Sarmatian Indo-Iranian ancestry. Records do not exist, but it is thought that dogs exhibiting certain skills, such as hunting, guarding, or herding for example, were bred together to try to fix characteristics. Breeding was geared toward working ability, not appearance, and different types of dog that showed the same skills were bred together. Over the centuries, types began to emerge: war dogs and guardians retained the heavy muscular frame of the Mastiff type, whereas scent hounds became lighter and more athletic.

One of the earliest known examples of specific scent hound breeding dates to around the eighth century and to the monastery of St. Hubert in Belgium. The monks bred the St. Hubert Hound and gifted these skilled scenting hounds to the kings of France. The St. Hubert Hound was at the foundation of several other scent hound types, including the Talbot and Southern Hound (both extinct) and the

British Bloodhound. The monks are also credited with developing short-legged scent hounds, possibly through a genetic mutation. A number of short-legged scent hound breeds are recognized in France and these gave rise to the exceedingly popular Bassett Hound. Both Bassett and Bloodhound have characteristically long, hanging ears and long, sensitive noses. As these hounds track, their ears stir up the ground, which helps to release the scent.

During the Middle Ages in France and in Britain formal hunting by royalty and the aristocracy became extremely popular, with enormous emphasis placed on the pomp and ceremony of the occasion. The English throne supported great numbers of different types of hunting dogs, including scent hounds. In the eleventh century the forests of England were designated for royal hunting only under the Forest Laws, and the chief quarry was hart, red deer, wild boar, hare, and wolf.

The earliest account of foxhunting with dogs in Britain is thought to date to the sixteenth century and was initially undertaken by farmers as a form of vermin control; it is not known what type of dogs were used. The first instance of specific scent hounds used for foxhunting dates to 1668, and the practice became increasingly popular during the seventeenth century as stag hunting declined; in line with this the Foxhound was developed. Foxhounds varied quite considerably based on their location and the type of terrain they needed to cover, although at their foundation they are thought to combine Greyhound, Terrier, and Mastiff-type lines. Hugo Meynell (1735–1808) is regarded as one of the most influential figures in the development of the modern Foxhound and he used highly selective breeding to increase the speed and athleticism of the hounds.

The American Foxhound and all types of Coon Hound developed from English, French, German, and Irish hounds imported by early colonists, with the exception of the Plott Hound, which derived from Hanoverian hounds. The earliest record of a pack of hounds being imported to the United States dates to 1650 when a wealthy British man, Robert Brooke, moved to Southern Maryland taking his British Foxhounds with him. Foxhunting rapidly became popular in the southern states, and a specifically American Foxhound began to develop through crossbreeding English Foxhounds with other types of hound. The resulting hound is larger, more athletic, and better suited to its various terrains than the English Foxhound.

Alongside the fast-paced nature of foxhunting, other types of hunting developed that required cold-nosed hounds able to pick up an old trail and follow it with dedication; these are collectively called Coon Hounds. The quarry varied according to location but included gray fox, squirrel, lion, bear, bobcat, and perhaps most popularly raccoon. These hounds, which include the Bluetick Coonhound, Plott Hound, and Catahoula Leopard Dog, share similar characteristics such as courage, stamina, scenting ability, and obedience. The hunters unleash the hounds and allow them to pick up the scent and give chase to the quarry. They will "tree" the quarry and then remain under the tree, vocalizing. The voice of the hound is very important to the hunter because it alerts him to the "stage" of the hunt. Usually the hound will bay as it is giving chase, but when it trees the prey its vocalization changes to a "chop" sound, which allows the hunter to locate the dog.

Scent hounds come in all shapes and sizes and have developed specifically to their location and quarry. They include the speedy Foxhound varieties, the short-legged Dachshund, the enduring and rare Otterhound, the steady Bloodhound, and the courageous American Coon Hounds. Although these hounds are highly specialized hunters— originally providing food, vermin control, and now more commonly sporting entertainment—their scenting abilities have also been put to human service in other areas. These hounds are widely used in search and rescue, tracking, the detection of illegal and dangerous substances, and much more. Many scent hound breeds hunt and work in packs and as such are particularly cooperative with each other and good with other dogs. Generally they have exceptionally affable temperaments and are easily trained, providing that they are given time and consistency.

BLOODHOUND
ANCIENT – BELGIUM/ENGLAND – MODERATE

SIZE
Males 25–27 in./females 23–25 in.

APPEARANCE
Imposing, dignified, wise. Proportionately long, narrow head with pendant folds of loose skin around jowls and neck. Dark brown or hazel eyes, oval-shaped; thin, long ears, set low, hanging low. Long neck; powerful body; shoulders very muscular; front legs straight with good bone. Deep chest; strong back, loins, hindquarters. Hocks well let down. Long tail set high, thick at base, tapers to tip, carried high when moving or excited

COLOR
Black/tan, liver/tan, red. Coat short, weatherproof, smooth

APTITUDE
Tracking, police, show, companion

IN THE 1930S IN THE UNITED STATES a Bloodhound called Nick Carter is alleged to have tracked more than 600 criminals, leading to their arrest. Such is the renown of the Bloodhound's skills in this respect that their evidence is admissible in the US courts. The Nick Carter story may have been exaggerated over the years, but it is nonetheless testament to the extraordinary olfactory powers of the Bloodhound. Although it was originally developed for hunting game, throughout its history the Bloodhound has also been used for tracking humans, and it is still widely used by law enforcement agencies in this capacity, particularly in the United States. The Bloodhound's abilities allow it to track a human scent through virtually any countryside, sometimes across water, and even when the scent is very old. Such is the emphasis placed on the use of the Bloodhound by US law enforcement that several specific organizations have been established, including the National Police Bloodhound Association, founded in 1966, and the Law Enforcement Bloodhound Association, founded in 1998. Although Bloodhounds are found across the world, their greatest numbers are in the United States.

Two possible explanations are given for the breed's name. Firstly, that it derives from the dog's ability to follow a blood trail, or that it is a "blood seeker," and secondly, that it derives from being "pure of noble blood" (Blooded Hound). The modern Bloodhound is believed to be related to hounds that were bred at the monastery of St. Hubert in Belgium, dating to around the eighth century. Here, according to legend, the monks bred a specific type of scent hound that became known as the St. Hubert Hound, and it is thought to be the ancestor of the Bloodhound. The monks are said to have sent the kings of France several pairs of their purebred hounds annually in order to curry favor and to publicize the qualities of their hounds among the aristocracy and the elite. Prior to the efforts of these Belgium monks, scent hounds are believed to have descended originally from the Mastiff types that came from Central or Southeast Asia and the Middle East. As these dogs were spread across Europe, they began to be developed along specific lines for certain roles. Long before the Christian era, the Celts in Gaul (France) are attributed with having large Mastiff-type dogs with impressive scent-tracking abilities. It is believed that these formed the basis for the St. Hubert Hound, which went on to feature in the development of a number of different types of scent hound in France and Belgium, namely, the now extinct Talbot Hound and the white Southern Hound.

As a result of the foresight of the monks, the St. Hubert Hound spread rapidly throughout Europe and was a feature of many of the noble kennels. Its tracking powers became legendary, and although this hound was not fast it was efficient and suitable for following on foot rather than on horseback. It had a deep, distinctive, and mellifluous baying bark, which is characteristic today of the Bloodhound. Its skills at tracking people and animal prey were quickly recognized.

The St. Hubert Hound may have been taken to England by William the Conqueror (1028–87), although there is no evidence to support this. Undoubtedly hounds of some kind were brought over, and images on the Bayeaux Tapestry (eleventh century) that depict the Norman conquest of England confirm this, although it is not clear what type of hounds are featured. Scent hounds were also known by a number of different names, and were commonly referred to

DETERMINED AND BRAVE

as "Sleuth Hounds" in Scotland and as "Lyam Hounds" in the Middle Ages. This referenced dogs that were hunted on "lyams" or leashes; these scent hounds were used to pick up the trail of wild boar or harts, after which faster hounds in packs would be used to hunt down the quarry.

An account, which is probably part historical and part embellished, relates how in 1306 Robert the Bruce (1274–1329) was almost killed and then saved by his bloodhound, Donnchadh. Bruce, who became king of Scotland in 1306, was retreating from the English king Edward I (1239–1307) after a defeat in battle. His hound fell into enemy hands and was used to track him. The hound, delighted at picking up the scent of his lost master, led the forces straight to Bruce. However, when the English soldiers ambushed Bruce, the dog realized that his master was under attack and in turn set on the enemy. Bruce and Donnchadh eventually escaped.

One of the earliest and most informative accounts of a specific Bloodhound is found in the work of John Caius, *Of Englishe Dogges* (1570). Caius describes the dogs in great detail, indicating characteristics that have changed little over the centuries. Interestingly, he also refers to the dogs as being used for tracking cattle thieves along the border country of Scotland and England, which provides a link to the "Sleuth Hound" of the same area. *The Noble Art of Venerie or Hunting* (1575), ascribed to George Turbervile, provides further accounts of Bloodhounds. This work was heavily based on a French book on the art of hunting written by Jacques du Fouilloux and published in 1561. Both of these books mention the St. Hubert Hound but indicate that by this period these dogs had been widely crossbred and were no longer pure. It is tempting to simplify the development of breeds and attribute the Bloodhound purely to the St. Hubert Hound, but it is unlikely to be the case. It is only within the last few centuries that a move has been made toward keeping breeds "pure," and historically it was simply that the best dogs at the job were bred together. Although this gradually established certain characteristics that were pertinent to a particular job, it did not mean that these dogs were kept pure, and crossbreeding occurred on a large scale.

Accounts indicate that Spanish conquistadores took "bloodhounds" to the Americas with them during the fifteenth and sixteenth centuries, but it is possible that they were simply Mastiff types with scent hound abilities. They were used for tracking and "terrorizing" the native population, although Bloodhounds as they are known today are characterized by their soft temperaments, which makes this account seem unlikely. Specific reference was made to "bloodhounds" at the Virginia Assembly in 1619, when it was made illegal to sell the dogs to the Native Americans. Again it is likely that these were generic types of scent hound. The first significant import of Bloodhounds to the United States began in the mid 1800s, after the American Civil War (1861–65). They became particularly popular after 1888 when the English breeder Edwin Brough exhibited three of his hounds at the Westminster Kennel Club Dog Show in New York City. The American Kennel Club first registered Bloodhounds in 1885, but by 1889 they were still low in numbers, with only fourteen registered.

By the end of the eighteenth century in France, accounts indicate that the St. Hubert Hound had degenerated, presumably through poor crossbreeding, and that the dogs were no longer favored by the aristocracy. By the nineteenth century they had almost completely died out in France, but by this time the Bloodhound was established in England. However, it was not as widespread as it had been centuries earlier because hunting with faster Foxhounds had started to become popular. The revival of the breed in Continental Europe is ascribed to the British Bloodhound in the United Kingdom, which was imported into France during the nineteenth century in fairly large numbers. The breed in much of Continental Europe is now called the Chien de Saint Hubert and is recognized as such by the Fédération Cynologique Internationale. Queen Victoria's enthusiasm for Bloodhounds helped to popularize the breed in Britain, and by the late nineteenth century they were being exhibited at dog shows; they also proved a popular subject with British artists including Sir Edwin Landseer (1802–73).

The Bloodhound is generally typified by its superb temperament, which makes it an excellent family dog. It tends to be patient, good with children and other dogs, sociable, and affectionate. It can also be noisy if excited and not as easy as some breeds to obedience train; however, if its owner gets lost, a Bloodhound is almost certainly able to find them.

BASSET HOUND
ANCIENT – FRANCE/ENGLAND – COMMON

SIZE
Males/females preferably less than 14 in.

APPEARANCE
Low to ground, solid, calm, charismatic. Dome-shaped skull; deep, heavy muzzle. Loose lips; loose skin forming wrinkles on forehead. Dark, kind eyes; long, inward curling ears, set low. Muscular, moderately long neck; long body in proportion to low height. Short front legs, heavy in bone and wrinkled skin; upper forearm inclines inward and forechest fits neatly into crook when seen from front. Broad, strong, straight back; large, round feet. Some loose skin on legs. Long tail, thick at base, tapers to tip

COLOR
Any recognized hound color. Coat smooth, short, no feathering

APTITUDE
Trailing rabbits, hare, showing, companion

THE BASSET HOUND is a charismatic, endearing, intelligent breed with a slightly comical appearance; long, droopy ears; and soulful eyes. It has won the hearts of many and is often seen in advertising campaigns, films, television programs, and perhaps most famously in the cartoon strip *Fred Basset*. However, this adorable-looking dog is also a highly skilled hunting animal and was originally developed for hunting small game such as rabbit and hare in packs.

The Basset Hound seen most frequently in the United Kingdom and the United States developed in the late nineteenth century based on various different types of French Basset Hound. The word *bas* translates as "low" in French and is applied to a variety of different hound types of low height. This dog is believed to trace back to at least the eighth century and probably originally emerged as a genetic mutation. In the United Kingdom four types are seen: the Bleu de Gascoigne, the Griffon Vendeen (petite or grand), the Fauvre de Bretagne, and the Artesian-Normand; the (English or American) Basset Hound evolved primarily through the Artesian-Normand and the Griffon Vendeen. In the United States the American Kennel Club (AKC) only acknowledges the Petit Basset Griffon Vendeen in addition to the (English or American) Basset Hound.

There is no straight line of development of this short-limbed hunting dog in France. A popular theory is that it was originally developed by the monks at the monastery of St. Hubert in Belgium. St. Hubert (c. 656–727) was the patron saint of hunting, and special hounds were bred at his monastery to supply the French aristocracy. It is thought that a genetic mutation resulted in a short-legged Bloodhound type and that this mutation was then specifically bred. Short-legged hounds with Bloodhound-type features appear in the French arts dating to the fourteenth century and are also associated with Gaston Phoebus (1331–91), author of *Livre de Chasse* (c. 1387), an important medieval treatise on hunting. He kept a pack of short-legged hounds for hunting wild boar.

Short-legged hounds have several advantages for hunting, the main one being that their noses are closer to the ground. The Basset Hound is credited with having the keenest scenting abilities, second only to the Bloodhound; also its long ears stir up the ground and the trail, which helps with tracking a scent. Basset Hounds hunt at a slower pace than longer-legged hounds, which makes them ideal for hunting on foot rather than on horseback. Hunting on horseback had historically been the preserve of the aristocracy, which made the Basset Hound popular with the working classes. Typically these hounds hunt in packs and are used to drive small prey out of dense undergrowth. Basset Hounds are still used for hunting in France, England, and the United States.

The French Basset Hounds became popular among the wider general public during the reign of Emperor Napoleon III (1808–73), who owned a pack. One of the leading animaliers of the time was Emmanuel Fremiet, who exhibited a number of bronze sculptures of Napoleon's Basset Hounds at the Paris Salon in 1853, sparking immediate public interest. In 1863 Basset Hounds were exhibited at the first Paris Dog Show and gained an international audience. Shortly after this, the first two Artesian-Normand Basset Hounds were imported to the United Kingdom (by Lord Galway), although it was not until the 1870s that real interest in the breed in the United

DETERMINED AND BRAVE

DETERMINED AND BRAVE

Kingdom began. At this time Lord Onslow, Everett Millais, and George Krehl began to import Artesian-Norman Basset Hounds from two leading kennels in France. These Basset Hounds developed into different types. Those from the Lane Kennels were known as "Lanes," and were mostly lemon and white and heavy boned with knuckled-over front legs. The Le Couteulx Kennels had two types: a heavier, lower build, often tricolor type, and a lighter framed type that possibly included Beagle influence.

In 1884 the Basset Hound Club was formed with Millais, Krehl, Lord Onslow, and Lord Galway at the helm, along with Count le Couteulx de Canteleu. Not long afterward they were joined by Princess Alexandra (later Queen Alexandra), who kept a large kennel of Basset Hounds at Sandringham and was a great supporter of the breed. Today the majority of Basset Hounds in the United Kingdom trace back to her stock.

Consistent inbreeding meant that Basset Hounds began to exhibit a deterioration of quality, so in 1892 Millais bred his male Basset, Nicholas, to a female Bloodhound. The three surviving puppies were crossed back to purebred Basset Hounds and the progeny from this cross again bred back to Bassets. Millais's experiment resulted in a heavier-boned, better quality Basset of fixed characteristics. At the turn of the century, a number of French dogs were again imported, and this, combined with the influence of the Bloodhound outcross, gave way to the Basset Hound of today. While these dogs were popular in the show ring, the breed was also being worked in the United Kingdom, and three Basset Hound hunting packs were established.

The first Basset Hounds arrived in the United States in around 1883, and in 1884 the first Basset Hound was seen at the Westminster Kennel Club Show, causing an instant sensation. In 1885 the AKC registered the first Basset Hound in the Hound Group category, and in 1935 the Basset Hound Club of America was formed. In the United States the Basset Hound is regularly within the top thirty-five most popular dog breeds, based on AKC registration statistics, and this is no doubt due to its appealing temperament. The Basset Hound makes a wonderful family dog, and is very patient with children and extremely loving. It is not, however, noted for being a very effective guard dog and does tend to love everyone without discrimination—particularly if food is involved.

DETERMINED AND BRAVE

OTTERHOUND
ANCIENT – BRITAIN – RARE

SIZE
Males 27 in./females 24 in.

APPEARANCE
Imposing, shaggy, full of character. Noble head with domed skull; strong, deep muzzle; alert expression; lively, intelligent eyes. Low-set, long ears with leading edge rolled inward. Long, muscular neck; powerful body with deep chest; well-sprung ribs; level back; short, strong loins. Muscular hindquarters;

hocks well let down; large, rounded feet with webbing between toes. Tail set high, carried high when active, but never curled over back

COLOR
Any. Double coated, medium length, rough, dense, waterproof

APTITUDE
Originally hunting otters, tracking, agility, obedience, rally, showing, companion

THE OTTERHOUND IS A LARGE, powerful, and delightful dog with tremendous character, which is amplified by its appealing "shaggy" appearance. It is also extremely rare and only preserved through the great efforts of a small but enthusiastic group of supporters. It is found chiefly in the United Kingdom, its country of origin, but also in the United States, Canada, New Zealand, and in a few European countries.

This dog was originally bred and used for the purpose of otter hunting and is highly equipped for this endeavor, with its oily double-coated and largely waterproof coat and webbing between its pads to aid swimming. The Otterhound has a natural love of water and is an excellent swimmer. It is also able to follow a scent both on land and in water and has been known to swim for several hours while tracking its prey. Otter hunting was established centuries ago to combat the problem of otters preying on fish. It eventually became popular as a sport but has always remained less popular than other forms of hunting. Otter populations dwindled through the twentieth century, and otter hunting was eventually banned in the United Kingdom in 1978. This led to a great decline in the breed numbers of the Otterhound.

It is thought that Otterhounds were mostly smooth coated until at least the seventeenth century when the first suggestion of a rough coat was inferred by the writer

Gervase Markham (c. 1568–1637), who described them in 1611 as "a grizzl'd . . . shag hair'd" hound. The earliest mention of a private pack of Otterhounds was made in Isaac Walton's *Compleat Angler* (1653), in which he referred to Ralph Sadler of Hertforshire owning a pack. By the eighteenth century, otter hunting had become a relatively popular sport in Britain. In the nineteenth century a number of French hound breeds were introduced to the British Otterhound, including the Griffon Nivernais, Griffon de Bresse, and Griffon Vendeen. Toward the end of the century, there was even the introduction of wolf through the French kennels of Count le Couteulx de Canteleu, who crossed a Griffon de Bresse with a gray wolf.

During the same period in the late 1800s the Otterhound began to increasingly resemble the rough-coated French hounds. The Dumfriesshire pack, the best known of all Otterhound packs, was established in 1889 using foundation stock from the best packs throughout Britain. A Bloodhound named Baxter and a Griffon Vendeen Nivernais named Frivole were introduced to the pack and were highly influential on its subsequent development. Since this pack placed its chief emphasis on working abilities, other types of hound were frequently introduced in efforts to improve the breed. When otter hunting was banned in England in 1978, and in 1980 in Scotland, the Masters of the Dumfriesshire Otter Hunt and the Kendal and District Otter Hunt worked with breeders and the Kennel Club to register the remaining Otterhounds.

The Otterhound was first imported to the United States in the early 1900s and was first exhibited at an American Kennel Club (AKC) show in 1907 in Claremont, Oklahoma. In 1909 the AKC recognized the breed. In the 1930s a veterinary surgeon, Dr. Hugh Mouat, became interested in the breed and later established a breeding kennel called Adriucha, which produced the first champion Otterhounds in 1941. The Otterhound Club of America was established in 1960.

BEAGLE

ANCIENT – ENGLAND – COMMON

SIZE
Males/females, two types, either up to 13 in. or over 13 in. but under 15 in.

APPEARANCE
Small, sturdy hunting dog with cheerful demeanor. The skull is fairly long and slightly domed, with medium-length strong, square-cut muzzle. Large brown or hazel eyes with kind, appealing expression; long ears set moderately low, rounded at tip. Medium-length neck; short, muscular back and broad slightly arched loin. Straight front legs with plenty of bone and rounded feet. Tail set moderately high and carried gaily but not curled over back; good hair cover on tail especially underside

COLOR
Any true hound color. Coat hard, smooth, short

APTITUDE
Trailing rabbits, tracking, therapy dogs, agility, showing, companion

THE BEAGLE WAS DEVELOPED as a small hunting hound many centuries ago and is still widely used in this capacity. It is a scent hound and excels at hunting small game in packs. It is normally hunted on foot rather than on horseback and has a distinguished hunting cry. The Beagle has also become a popular companion dog, particularly in the United States. It is noted for being affectionate, charismatic, lively, and entertaining, although sometimes it can be a noisy pet. It is often used as a therapy dog and is also used by law enforcement agencies for tracking and drug and bomb detection.

The breed's early history is not proven. Small hounds of similar character to the Beagle trace to Ancient Greece and were described by the Greek writer Xenophon (c. 430–354 B.C.E.) in his treatise *On Hunting*, in which he referred to diminutive hounds used for tracking hare. It is also believed that the Romans took these small hounds with them during their conquests of Europe, including into England, where the Beagle eventually developed into a specific type. French hounds were introduced to England during the Norman Conquest in 1066 and were influential on British scent hound development. By the Middle Ages there were several different types of scent hound. Accounts indicate that Edward II (1284–1327) and Henry VII (1457–1509) kept packs of the small scent hounds, which were first referred to as Beagles in the fifteenth century by Edward, 2nd Duke of York, in his treatise on hunting, *The Master of the Game* (1406–13).

Early in its history there were several types of Beagle; one that was much smaller than the rest was called a Glove Beagle or Pocket Beagle. This was a tiny hound that could fit in a saddlebag or into the cuff of a gauntlet and be transported to a hunt on horseback before being turned loose to pick up a trail through dense undergrowth. Elizabeth I (1533–1603) kept a pack of Pocket Beagles. She also had her portrait drawn by the artist Frederico Zuccaro (c. 1540–1609) in 1575 and it includes one of her tiny Beagles. There are still two sizes of Beagle recognized in the United States: a large and small version.

Beagles were favored by the aristocracy who could afford to keep large packs of dogs. Through the eighteenth century, foxhunting become very popular, which led to a decline in Beagle packs that were more suited to rabbit and hare. The dogs were, however, maintained by a few enthusiasts, including Reverend Phillip Honeywood, who established a pack of Beagles in Essex in the 1830s, which were small and typically white. The Beagle Club in England was established in 1890; the Association of Masters of Harriers and Beagles was formed in 1891. The objective of both clubs was the promotion and preservation of Beagles.

In the United States, small hounds were used in the Southern states prior to the Civil War (1861–65) for hunting mainly fox and hare. General Rowlett of Illinois is credited with importing the first hunting Beagles from England in the early 1860s. The first Beagle to be registered by the American Kennel Club was entered into the stud book in 1885. In 1888 the National Beagle Club of America was established. The popularity of Beagles continued to grow, indicated by the large number of entries at the Westminster Kennel Club Show in 1917. It was here that the breed was divided into two separate height distinctions for the first time.

DETERMINED AND BRAVE

DETERMINED AND BRAVE

AMERICAN FOXHOUND

MODERN – UNITED STATES – RARE

SIZE
Males ideal 22–25 in./females ideal 21–24 in.

APPEARANCE
Powerful, athletic, and lively. Overall impression of balance. Head is fairly long and slightly domed; muzzle of fair length, square in profile; hazel or brown eyes with gentle expression; ears set fairly low, broad with rounded tip, and carried close to head; strong neck of medium length; muscular back; broad loins; straight front legs; deep chest that is not too wide; powerful hindquarters; rounded feet. Tail set moderately high and carried gaily, but ideally not curled over the back

COLOR
Any recognized hound color and markings. Coat, smooth, short, and dense

APTITUDE
Trailing fox, showing

THE AMERICAN FOXHOUND TRACES its roots to the seventeenth century and to the influence of English Foxhounds. It has developed into a swift and agile hound, typically hunting in a pack and able to cover vast tracts of countryside with speed and great tenacity. Once it has picked up a trail, it will continue unabated until either the fox runs to ground or the scent is lost. This hound is a specialist in the field of fox and coyote hunting. As it gives chase, it bays with great enthusiasm, as do many scent hound breeds. The American Foxhound also has an affectionate temperament and can make a good pet. However, it can be difficult to train, and it requires a lot of exercise. It is also used to being a pack animal and is not happy living on its own.

The earliest record of hounds imported to the United States dates to June 30, 1650, when a wealthy landowner, Robert Brooke, moved with his family and a pack of hounds from England to Maryland. He established his huge estate, De La Brooke Manor, in southern Maryland along the west banks of the Patuxent river. The Brooke hounds are attributed with being significant to the subsequent development of the American Foxhound and other types of American-bred hound.

By the 1700s foxhunting was becoming increasingly popular in the colonial states of Maryland and Virginia and provided an opportunity for colonists to meet, socialize, and enjoy the chase. An important early figure in the sport and in the development of the hounds was Thomas, Sixth Lord Fairfax (1693–1781), who established a pack of Foxhounds in northern Virginia in 1747. They are thought to be the first pack that was maintained for the enjoyment of a group of individuals.

It was during the same period that George Washington (1732–99), who would become the first president of the United States in 1789, became involved with foxhunting and breeding hounds. His diaries indicate his interest in creating a "perfect pack of hounds" using a mix of English Foxhound with Irish, French, and German hounds to produce a more athletic, stronger, and faster type suitable for the Virginia countryside. He built extensive kennels at his Mount Vernon Estate and hunted frequently; it was on the hunting field that he won many supporters in the government. Washington's hounds were of significant influence in the development of the American Foxhound.

As foxhunting became more and more popular, hunt clubs were established, and the first was the Piedmont Foxhound Club in Virginia in 1840. The early hunts were located in Maryland, Virginia, and Tennessee; each hunt kept its own kennels where the best hounds were bred together. This resulted in a number of different types of American Foxhound developing in specific areas because of prominent breeding lines, and these produced strains such as the Trigg, Walker, Goodman, and July. These strains exhibit different characteristics but are recognized as one breed, the American Foxhound. The hounds were used for four main purposes: field trials, foxhunting with a single huntsman, following a trail, and hunting in packs, although they were increasingly used for hunting in packs, and this is what they are chiefly known for today. They were recognized by the American Kennel Club in 1886 but are not typically registered by it. Instead they are generally registered with the International Foxhunter's Studbook, or similar specialty Foxhound registers.

CATAHOULA LEOPARD DOG

ANCIENT – UNITED STATES – RARE

SIZE

Males ideal 24 in./females ideal 22 in.

APPEARANCE

Powerful, alert, athletic. Broad head can have slight furrow between eyes; strong, deep muzzle; round, wide-set eyes, any color or part color; short- to medium-length, triangular-shaped, drop ears. Good length, muscular neck; body slightly longer than height at withers; front legs 50 to 60% of height at withers. Legs straight with good bone substance. Broad, muscular back; well-sprung ribs; deep, moderately broad chest. Oval-shaped feet with long, well-webbed toes. Tail moderately long, may be carried upright, may curve forward at tip. Natural bob tails can occur but are faulty

COLOR

Varied; spots, brindles, patchwork, solid colors except solid or mostly white. Coat short to medium, flat, can range from smooth to coarse

APTITUDE

Cattle/pig herding, hunting, companion

MUCH SPECULATION SURROUNDS the development of the Catahoula Leopard Dog, although it is commonly traced to Louisiana and to the Spanish conquistadores in the sixteenth century, specifically to Hernando De Soto (c. 1496–1542). Accounts indicate that the Native Americans in this area kept dogs that were wolflike in appearance, but instead of howling they barked. It is thought that these native dogs crossbred with De Soto's dogs that were left behind after a disastrous expedition that ended with De Soto's death in 1542. These dogs included Greyhounds and Mastiff types that were referred to as "war dogs" and were actively used against the native population.

Again, the native dogs and these remnant dogs bred and were used by the Native Americans, particularly in north central Louisiana around Catahoula Lake, from where the breed takes its name. Early settlers in the vicinity used the dogs for hunting and rounding up wild boar. It was quickly established that the local dogs displayed an inherent ability to both hunt and round up these animals, and the Catahoula Leopard Dog remains to this day an all-around ranch animal. It is noted for its working livestock abilities and it works in an unusual manner, moving cattle from the head end rather than in the traditional heel fashion. Catahoulas will also work as a group and will surround an animal to "hold" it until the hunter is able to dispatch it. This shows great cooperation among the dogs and a "reasoning" type of intelligence.

French settlers began to arrive in Louisiana in the early 1700s, accompanied by their Beauceron dogs. Crossbreeding between the native dogs and the Beauceron provided the foundation of the modern Catahoula. An important characteristic of the breed is its versatility; it is unusual for a dog to work livestock and be a great hunter. This dog is used for hunting a variety of wild game and is fearless when in pursuit. It will also trail and "tree" game, trapping prey up a tree until the hunter arrives, and has a loud, baying vocalization when hunting. The Catahoula is known for its great scenting abilities; in addition to being used for hunting for sport, it has also been used for search and rescue and for law enforcement. The breed is naturally territorial and will act as an efficient property guardian.

The Catahoula developed along three lines that showed variation in color and size. The largest was the Preston Wright line, which was most influenced by the dogs of De Soto. The second was Mr. Fairbanks's line of brindle or yellow-colored dogs, and the third was Mr. McMillin's line, which exhibited mostly blue leopard coloring with "glass" (blue) eyes and was the smallest of the three. As a result there is a wide variation in the appearance of the breed, because the dogs were bred for working abilities, temperament, and intelligence, and their appearance was secondary. In the early days of settlement, dogs needed to work, and there was rarely a place for a pet. As such, only the best dogs were bred, and those that were weak were dispatched. This has resulted in the excellent working qualities of the breed, which also makes a great companion dog, provided that its exercise requirements are met.

In 1979 the Catahoula Leopard Dog was made the official State Dog of Louisiana, and in 1995 it was recognized by the United Kennel Club; as yet it has not been recognized by the American Kennel Club.

BLUETICK COONHOUND
MODERN – UNITED STATES – MODERATE

SIZE
Males 22–27 in./females 21–25 in.

APPEARANCE
Compact, muscular, athletic. Head broad between ears and slightly domed. Deep muzzle, square in profile. Large, wide-set, dark brown eyes with "pleading" expression; ears set low and moderately long. Muscular neck of moderate length carried high but not vertical; body should be square or slightly longer than height at shoulder. Strong back; slightly higher at withers than hips. Deep chest, not too wide.

Well-sprung ribs, underline shows moderate tuck up. Tail thick at base, tapers to point, moderately long, carried high with a slight curve but not curled over back

COLOR
Dark blue mottled body with black spots on back, ears, and sides. Head and ears mostly black, can have tan markings over eyes, cheeks, chest, and underside of tail, red ticking on feet and lower legs. Coat smooth and glossy

APTITUDE
Trailing raccoons, hunting, showing, companion

THE DISTINCTIVE-LOOKING Bluetick Coonhound originally developed in the southern states from English Foxhounds that were brought to America during colonial times. These Foxhounds were bred with other types of hound to produce specifically American hound types that were suited to their varying terrain and prey. The Bluetick's distinguishing blue-mottled coat with dark patches indicates that it owes much of its heritage to the introduction of the French staghound, the Grand Bleu de Gascogne, to the English Foxhounds. Even today the Bluetick and the Grand Bleu de Gascogne share some striking similarities in their appearance. These French hounds were, and still are, known for being "cold nosed," which means that they are able to pick up an old (cold) scent and follow it. The English Foxhound is a "hot-nosed" hunter and is most skilled at following a fresh trail, which it does at great speed. The Bluetick is more cold nosed than hot; it will pick up and follow a scent with great deliberation and tenacity, generally at a slower pace than its Foxhound ancestors.

George Washington (1732–99), who was a great breeder of various types of hound, had a number of French hounds at his Mount Vernon Estate kennels, seven of which were given to him by the Marquis de Lafayette. Washington is recorded as describing their baying like the "bells of Moscow." Like the French hounds, the Bluetick has a distinctive voice and is valued for having a "bawl" mouth, meaning a drawn-out bay. Its vocalization has different pitches depending on the stage of the hunt, and it will change between following the scent and when it has tracked the prey to a tree, or "treed" the prey. This vocalization is an important part of the breed's skill set because it informs the hunter. Blueticks are also noted for their stamina and will hunt over any terrain.

Blueticks excel at hunting a variety of game including mountain lion, bobcat, and bear, but are most commonly used for hunting raccoon. Once they have picked up a trail they will follow it with determination until they find the raccoon. They will then hunt it until the raccoon goes up a tree. The dogs will characteristically attempt to climb the tree after the raccoon, and some Blueticks have an inherent tree-climbing ability, like many of the Coonhound breeds. Raccoon hunting is most often done at night, and night trials are a popular sport. The dog is given between one and two hours to find, trail, and tree a raccoon; if they tree any animal other than a raccoon they have points deducted in the lowest levels of competition, while in the advanced competitions they are eliminated for this misdemeanor.

Originally Blueticks were called English Coonhounds, but in 1946 breeders of true Blueticks broke away from the English Coonhound breeders who required faster, hot-nosed hounds; these breeders also wanted to preserve the characteristic Bluetick coloring. A group of Bluetick breeders gathered in Greenville, Illinois, and formed the Bluetick Breeders Association in 1946 and drew up a breed standard at the same time. Also in 1946 the United Kennel Club began to register the Bluetick Coonhound separately from the English Coonhound. In 1959 the Bluetick Breeders of America was formed, replacing the earlier association, and in 2009 the Bluetick Coonhound was recognized by the American Kennel Club.

PLOTT HOUND
MODERN – UNITED STATES – MODERATE

SIZE
Males 20–25 in./females 20–23 in.

APPEARANCE
Striking, courageous, powerful. Attractive head with confident expression; brown or hazel eyes; dropped ears, broad in width, set quite high; medium-length, strong muzzle. Body higher at withers than hips; well-sprung ribs; tucked-up flank; moderately wide, deep chest; straight front legs. Powerful hindquarters; long, muscular thighs, short and strong from hock to pad. Tail quite long, carried high with gentle, crescent moon curve

COLOR
Any shade of brindle, buckskin, solid black. Coat glossy, smooth, short to medium in length

APTITUDE
Hunting bear, boar, raccoon

WITH ITS CHARACTERISTIC and highly attractive brindle coat and sleek, athletic frame, the Plott Hound is among the most striking of the American Coonhound breeds. It exhibits grace and elegance, qualities that belie its hunting abilities, as well as tremendous courage and tenacity. It has been bred to hunt since the mid-eighteenth century, and hunting is its forte, although it can also make a companion animal as long as its exercise requirements are met.

The Plott Hound was developed and refined in North Carolina and owes its origination to a young German boy called Johannes Plott, who left Germany in 1750 with his brother, Enoch, to emigrate to the United States. The two boys took with them five hounds of unknown heritage, reportedly three brindle- and two buckskin-colored dogs. Enoch died during the long voyage but Johannes settled in North Carolina. His strain of hounds had been bred for centuries in Germany for hunting ferocious wild boar, and the dogs were noted for their stamina, courage, and gameness. These traits were indispensable for Johannes in his rural location where bear and large predators were common. He used his dogs for hunting bear and bred them to increase the size of his pack. It is stated that he never crossbred his dogs to other breeds or types.

In 1800 one of Johannes's sons, Henry, moved to Haywood County, North Carolina. He continued the tradition of breeding hounds, and developed a superior bear-hunting hound; his sons in turn continued to breed the hounds. Many local families acquired the dogs, some of which also had an influence on the breed. Although the hounds remained essentially pure, there was also some crossbreeding to other types to increase the gene pool.

In the late 1880s a hunter from Rayburn, Georgia, crossed one of the males with his Leopard Spotted Bear Dogs. Some of the puppies came back into the Plott family and were bred back to their hounds but with no apparent loss of bear-hunting skills. Other outcrosses occurred, and documents from the early twentieth century describe crosses to Blevins Hounds, which had black saddle markings and tan heads and were noted for their bear-hunting skills. Part of the modern foundation of the Plott Hound is attributed to Gola Ferguson, who bred a female brindle Plott to a Blevins Hound in 1928. This resulted in two male dogs, Boss and Tige. Almost every registered Plott Hound today can be traced back to these two dogs.

The Plott Hound was not officially named as such until 1946. The name "Plott" was eventually selected in order to reflect the long history of the Plott family with these hounds, despite the contributions of many others to the breed development. One of the most prolific breeders outside the Plott family was Dale Brandenburg, who established his Pioneer Kennels in the late 1940s and produced a great number of champion dogs.

The breed standard was drawn up in 1946, and the Plott Hound was recognized by the United Kennel Club. In 1953 the National Plott Hound Association was established, and in 1989 the breed became the official state dog of North Carolina. The Plott Hound is also recognized by the American Kennel Club. Plott Hounds are fearless when hunting bear and display enormous tenacity, but they are also a very popular hound for use in raccoon hunting and display an inherent instinct for "treeing"—chasing prey up a tree and continuing to bay at it. No terrain is too difficult or rough for a Plott Hound.

DETERMINED AND BRAVE

DACHSHUND

ANCIENT — GERMANY — COMMON

SIZE

Males/females, standard 16–32 lbs/miniature under 11 lbs

APPEARANCE

Long, low, lively. Head tapers to end of nose; fine, slightly arched muzzle. Strong jaws; almond-shaped, dark eyes; ears set high, broad, well rounded, moderate length. Long, muscular neck, powerful front end, prominent breast bone. Short front legs incline slightly inward. Body long in proportion to height. Level back with well-sprung ribs, muscular hindquarters with upper thigh set at right angle to pelvis, lower leg short, set at right angles to upper thigh. Tail is continuation of topline, not carried too high

COLOR

Black/tan, chocolate/tan, wild boar/tan, gray/tan, fawn/tan, solid red, sable, or cream, dapple or brindle. Coat either smooth haired being dense, smooth, short; or long haired being straight or slightly wavy; or wire haired, with rough, harsh, dense undercoat

APTITUDE

Hunting badgers or burrowing game, tracking, show, companion

THE DACHSHUND IS A GERMAN BREED whose name originates from *dachs*, meaning "badger," and *hund*, meaning "hound/dog," and it was as a badger-hunting dog that the breed was developed. There are now two recognized sizes of Dachshund, standard and miniature; they may be low in height, but they are tremendously efficient hunting dogs and largely fearless. The dogs developed into two types specifically to fulfill different hunting needs: the larger type was used for badgers or fox and the miniature for rabbits, hare, and smaller rodents. The Dachshund is unusual in that it hunts above and below ground. It will track prey above ground but will also dig into a set or hole and retrieve and kill prey that has gone underground. For this reason, in Germany, the dog is measured by the circumference of its chest, which determines into what size hole it can follow its prey. In Germany the dog is referred to as "Teckel" and sometimes as "Dackel," both of which are the same as the Dachshund, although the Teckel is considered a "working" dog.

Dogs that were long-bodied and low to the ground were known in the Middle Ages, or even earlier. Accounts dating to the sixteenth century indicate that a short-legged and powerful dog was used for hunting badgers in the German forests. In 1685 the author Christian Paullini refers to the Dachshund in his book on dogs, prescribing the qualities of a dog able to hunt underground.

The foundations for these charismatic and bold dogs are not clear, although it is thought that the German Pinscher, French hounds, the Bassett, and further Terrier blood might all have played a role. Certainly the Dachshund developed to be highly specialized at hunting down holes. The dog's sense of smell, like all scent hounds, is highly tuned; the anatomy of its front legs, which incline slightly outward, enables it to dig freely; and its slender yet powerful frame is well equipped for going down holes. Today there are three coat varieties in the Dachshund: smooth haired, long haired, and wire haired. The smooth haired is the oldest of the three and gave rise to the other two, and the wire haired did not develop until the nineteenth century.

During the nineteenth century Dachshunds became popular in Britain, mostly brought about by Queen Victoria's (1819–1901) enthusiasm for the breed. She was sent her first Dachshund from Germany in 1840. The first club for the breed, the Dachshund Club in Britain, was established in 1881. The first Dachshunds were registered with the American Kennel Club (AKC) in 1885, and the breed rapidly became popular; the Dachshund Club of America was formed in 1895. However, World War I had a devastating effect on the popularity of Dachshunds in the United States and United Kingdom because of their link with Germany. After the war, the breed picked up again in popularity, and by 1938 they were the fourth most popular dog breed in the United States.

Dachshunds have often been the dog of choice for celebrities, actors, politicians, presidents, and particularly artists. Pablo Picasso adored his Dachshund named Lump; Andy Warhol had a pair, Archie and Amos, who he often painted; and David Hockney has two, Stanley and Boodgie, who he has also painted and immortalized in a book.

RHODESIAN RIDGEBACK
ANCIENT – SOUTH AFRICA – COMMON

SIZE
Males 25–27 in./females 24–26 in.

APPEARANCE
Athletic, powerful, sleek. Head of fair length, flat, rather broad between ears. Long, deep, strong muzzle. Round, lively eyes that harmonize with coat color; high-set, medium-sized ears, wide at base, tapering to rounded point. Strong, fairly long neck; muscular front end with straight front legs. Deep chest, not too wide; powerful back and hindquarters. Tail tapers to tip, carried with slight curve

COLOR
Light wheaten to red wheaten. Coat short, dense, sleek. Distinctive ridge of hair on back that follows spine from behind shoulders to haunches

APTITUDE
Large game hunting, lure coursing, guardian, show, companion

THE RHODESIAN RIDGEBACK is one of only three known dog breeds in the world to exhibit a distinctive ridge of hair that grows in the opposite direction to normal hair growth, along the center of its back. The ridge starts just behind the shoulder blades and has two "crowns" or whorls of hair at the top before extending along the spine to end at a point between the prominence of the hips. The ridge is a hallmark of this breed. The other dogs to exhibit this unusual feature are of Asian origin: the ancient Thai Ridgeback, which developed in eastern Thailand, and the ridgeback dogs of Phu Quoc Island, Vietnam's largest island. The uniqueness of this feature suggests a common ancestry at some point, although there is no specific evidence to reveal whether the Asian ridgeback dogs were taken to South Africa, home of the Rhodesian Ridgeback, and were influential in its development, or the other way around. The most popular theorized movement of cultures in prehistory would, however, imply that the Asian dogs were taken to South Africa over the course of early history.

The foundations of the Rhodesian Ridgeback lie with the native South African dogs of the Khoekhoen (Hottentot) people, which developed specific adaptations to their environment over the centuries. These half-wild dogs, which exhibit the hair ridge on their backs, were able to withstand and flourish in the extreme temperatures of their South African homeland. The dogs were extremely tough, durable, and self-sufficient. In the late fifteenth century the Portuguese explored the coast of South Africa but showed little interest in settling. The first European settlers arrived in 1652, when the Dutch established a colony near the Cape of Good Hope, followed by Germans and French Huguenots. These European settlers brought their dogs with them, including breeds such as Mastiffs, Great Danes, Greyhounds, and Bloodhounds, which were widely interbred with the native ridgeback dogs. The colonists wanted to develop hunting dogs that were able to cope with the difficult climate, and crossbreeding their European stock with native dogs was the solution. How the early crosses were made is not recorded, but a type of dog began to emerge that combined the stamina and endurance of the native breed with the hunting and guarding skills of the European dogs. These included both sight hounds and scent hounds, and the Rhodesian Ridgeback of today exhibits considerable ability in both these types of hunting. In addition to their very great hunting qualities, these early crossbred dogs were also extremely loyal to and protective of their family, which made them valuable as guard dogs and much appreciated as companions. It is interesting to note that the ridge of hair seen in the native South African dogs was perpetuated through the crossbreeding.

The breed in its modern form traces to 1875 when the missionary Reverend Charles Helm (1844–1915) moved from Swellendam in the Cape Province of South Africa to Rhodesia (present-day Zimbabwe), taking with him two of the crossbred ridgeback dogs, Lorna and Powder. Helm established his Hope Fountain mission on a crossroads near what is now the city of Bulawayo. Many travelers and big game hunters would stop at the mission as they passed by and became familiar with his two dogs. This included a well-known big game hunter called Cornelius von Rooyen, who borrowed the two dogs for a hunting trip. Von Rooyen was thoroughly impressed with the dogs and immediately began a specific breeding program to produce dogs that

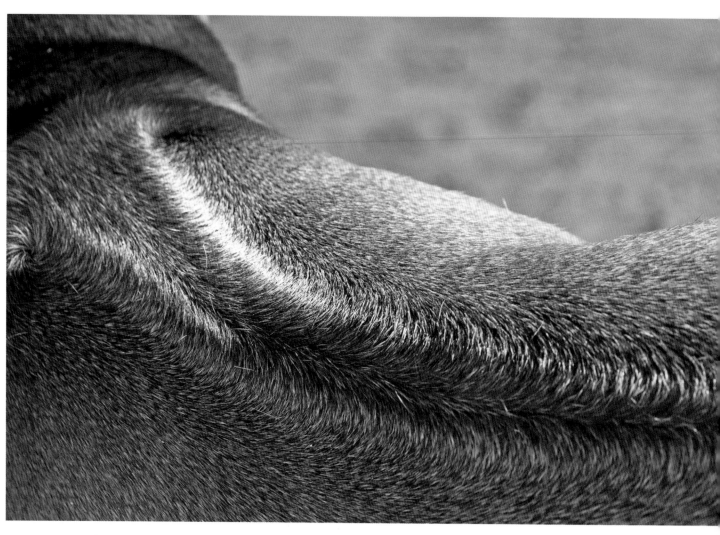

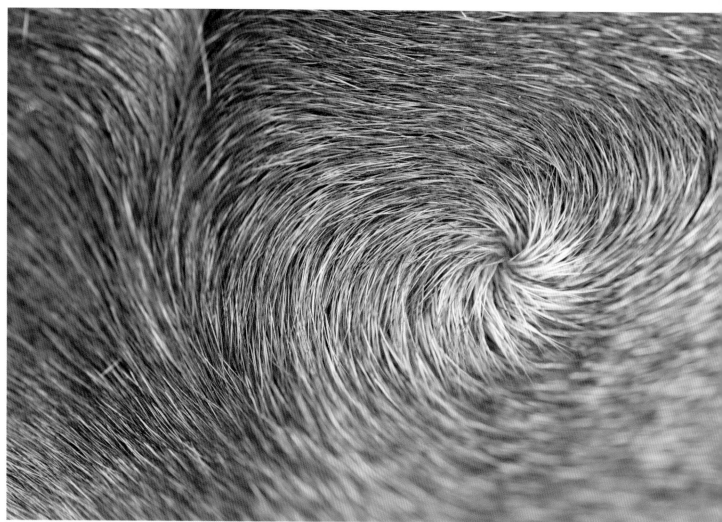

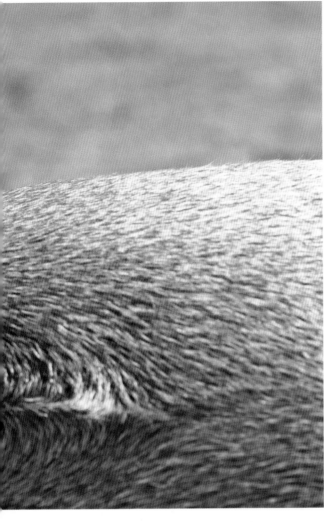

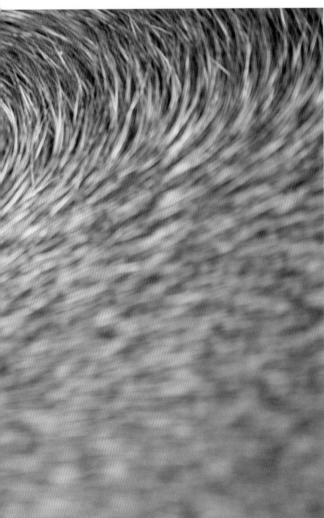

were capable of big game hunting; "big game" included lions. Von Rooyen wanted to produce dogs that could track prey silently and exhibit unequaled bravery: prerequisites for lion hunting. The dogs also had to have intelligence, tremendous stamina, the ability to go all day without food and sometimes water, and highly honed hunting skills.

The exact crosses Von Rooyen used are not known, although accounts by his daughter indicate that he experimented with a number of breeds, including the native South African dogs with Airedale and some kind of Terrier, Collie, Greyhound, Bulldog, and Pointer. According to Von Rooyen's son, one of the best hunting dogs he had was from a Collie female. Von Rooyen's hunting dogs, often referred to as lion dogs, became well known for their abilities, and he sold them in large numbers, spreading their fame and popularity across Rhodesia (Zimbabwe).

Another important figure in the breed's development was Francis Barnes, who was heavily involved with the Bulawayo Kennel Club. He acquired one of Von Rooyen's ridgeback lion dogs, quickly followed by several more. It was Barnes and dog breeder B. W. Durham who were instrumental in drawing up a breed standard for the newly named Rhodesian Ridgeback (Lion Dog) in 1922. A club was formed for the breed, and in 1926 the breed was recognized by the South African Kennel Union. Today the Rhodesian Ridgeback is one of the most popular dog breeds in South Africa.

It is not known when the first Rhodesian Ridgebacks were imported to Britain or the United States, although it is thought to have been early in the twentieth century. After World War II, however, the dogs began arriving in both Britain and the United States in quite significant numbers. The Rhodesian Ridgeback Club of Great Britain was established in 1952, and although initial numbers were low, the breed quickly became popular, with breed numbers estimated at around 11,000 by 2011. In the United States the American Kennel Club (AKC) recognized the Rhodesian Ridgeback in 1955, and today it ranks within the top fifty most popular dog breeds. Although these dogs were developed as hunting dogs and are capable of taking on the most aggressive of prey, they also make wonderful family dogs and are generally good with children. They are notably loyal, protective, and affectionate and will guard their territory with vigor.

CHAPTER 6
AGILE AND WISE

There are many gun dog breeds today, some of ancient origin and some of modern development. All of them were originally developed as working breeds and the dogs are known, virtually without exception, for their wonderful temperaments. Gun dog breeds are noted for their intelligence, obedience, trainability, loyalty, and affectionate nature. It is therefore no coincidence that a number of these breeds now rank among the most popular dog breeds across the world.

Significantly, throughout their development, the working gun dog breeds—often called sporting dogs—have been used either in pairs or individually with a single hunter, rather than in packs like many of the scent hound breeds. Although historically some of these breeds, such as the Hungarian Vizsla, Weimaraner, and German Shorthaired Pointer for example, were used for hunting small and even large game (Weimaraner), gun dog breeds today are mostly used for bird hunting.

Although the gun dog breeds originated as working dogs, from the late nineteenth century dog shows began to emerge, and many breeders specialized in producing dogs specifically for the show ring. This has led to clear differences in type in many, although not all, of the gun dog breeds. Working lines have been bred consistently for working ability over appearance, whereas show lines are bred to most closely resemble the breed standards. Dogs from working lines and from show lines make excellent companions, but those from working lines can have a greater exercise requirement.

The gun dog breeds of today fall into three main groups: flushers, pointers or setters, and retrievers. Flushing breeds are typified by the spaniel and work relatively close to the hunter or shooter. They work the ground busily to flush birds out of the undergrowth and into flight. Once the dog has done this, it watches the trajectory of the bird so that it knows where to find it if it is hit. Pointers and setters work farther away from the hunter or shooter and often in pairs. Once they have located a bird, they freeze and mark where the bird is in order to allow the hunter or shooter time to position themselves. On a command, they are allowed to scare the bird into flight. Again they watch where the bird falls so that they can retrieve it. Retrieving breeds are used for retrieving birds and waterfowl. They remain by the hunter or shooter and watch where the birds fall so that they can retrieve them. They will also "blind retrieve," which is when they are directed by the hunter or shooter using whistles or hand signals to where the bird has fallen. Gun dogs are required to be steady and obedient; they often work alongside other dogs and must respect the other dogs while working: for example, one dog should never retrieve another dog's bird.

Bird hunting with guns did not become widespread until the eighteenth century and from this time onward, and particularly during the nineteenth century, a number of gun dog breeds, such as the Labrador Retriever, Chesapeake Bay Retriever, Golden Retriever, and German Shorthaired Pointer, were developed. This was a period in which dog breeding in general became formalized and kennel clubs were established internationally, including the Kennel Club in 1873 and the American Kennel Club in 1884. Pedigrees and records were kept, stud books were started, and breed standards were established. However, many specialized

types of hunting dog existed for centuries prior to this. In addition to the sight hounds and scent hounds, specialized types included the old pointing types and the spaniel group, which gave rise to the setters. These dogs were used for hunting birds and small game, and worked in a highly specialized manner, typically by "air scent" rather than "ground scent" like the scent hound breeds.

Accounts from 17 B.C.E. mention "water" spaniels, and later accounts record water and land spaniels. The nineteenth-century writer John Walsh describes the Romans hunting with spaniels in 43 B.C.E. One of the earliest and most detailed accounts of different types of hunting dogs is the fourteenth-century *Livre de Chasse*, by Gaston Phoebus (1331–91), who describes spaniels coming from Spain and being useful for flushing birds and retrieving from water.

The "setting" family of dogs, now represented by the English, Irish, Gordon, and Irish Red and White, arose from the spaniel group and is thought to trace to around the fourteenth century. When a setter finds a bird it crouches down to indicate its location to the hunter, thus earning its name. Little is known regarding the origins of pointing dogs, although it is speculated that they developed alongside the spaniels and setters. Pointers are believed to have developed in Spain and spread through Continental Europe. The pointers indicate the location of birds and game through their "pointing": standing motionless, typically with one paw raised and tail held horizontally. The old Spanish Pointer, French pointers, and hounds are widely held to have contributed to the "modern" development of breeds such as the German Shorthaired Pointer and Weimaraner. Along with the distinctive Hungarian Vizsla, Spinone Italiano, and many more, these dogs are commonly referred to as hunt, point, and retrieve breeds. Many of these have developed within the last 200 years or so and are regarded as supremely versatile gun dogs, fulfilling all necessary roles of the hunt and shoot and doing so on land or in water.

During the nineteenth century field trials or tests were established by the various different gun dog breed societies and were designed to test the working abilities of the dogs in a competitive arena. They were structured to resemble a day's shooting in the field. The competitive nature of these trials meant that they also served to encourage the continual improvement of the breed's skills. One of the greatest and relatively rare achievements in the competitive forum is when a dog wins a dual championship: taking both show and working titles.

ENGLISH SPRINGER SPANIEL

ANCIENT – BRITAIN – COMMON

SIZE
Males ideal 20 in./females ideal 19 in.

APPEARANCE
Balanced, compact, proud, energetic. Medium-length, fairly broad skull, flat on top, slightly rounded to back and sides; muzzle approximately same length as skull. Medium-size, oval eyes, set well apart, with kind, trusting, intelligent expression. Long, fairly wide ears, hang close to cheeks; neck moderately long, muscular and slightly arched; strong, compact body.

Deep chest; well-sprung ribs; muscular loins with slight arch. Docked tail carried level with back or slightly elevated

COLOR
Liver and white or black and white or either of these with tan markings, or blue or liver roan. Double coat, outer coat medium length, flat or wavy, undercoat dense, short. Some feathering on ears, chest, legs, belly

APTITUDE
Hunting/shooting, bird flushing and retrieving, agility, drug and bomb detection, show, companion

THE ENGLISH SPRINGER SPANIEL is a delightful, busy, and intelligent breed, and a highly skilled working gun dog. It will work tirelessly all day over any terrain, including water, and do so with a characteristic enthusiasm for life. The English Springer Spaniel matches its gameness with a truly wonderful temperament and makes an excellent family dog for an active household. The Springer derives its name from its working method when flushing out birds; it will busily "work" dense undergrowth and startle birds so that they "spring" up into the air for the hunter. The English Springer Spaniel also makes an excellent retrieving dog and is worked in both capacities.

Although it was only accorded official breed status and its present name in the United Kingdom in 1902, this is a breed or type of extreme antiquity. Its history, however, is somewhat complicated because of the lack of documentation and the confusion over the use of the term "spaniel." This word is most commonly believed to trace back to the Roman name for Spain, Hispania, and as such the "spaniel" as a type is thought to have developed in Spain. With regard to the origins of domesticated dogs, the spaniel can be traced back further to Central Asia and China, from where it migrated west before eventually

reaching Spain, where it developed into a sporting-type dog. It is again speculated that this plucky dog accompanied the Romans across Continental Europe and into Britain. Specific reference is made to "water" spaniels in 17 C.E., which indicates that by this time there were two types of spaniel: land spaniels and water spaniels. The nineteenth-century British author John Walsh wrote about the Romans using "land" spaniels for pointing and flushing hawks in 43 C.E. Of specific interest with regard to the English Springer Spaniel, however, are the alleged tenth-century Welsh Laws of Howel Dha, which describe the attributes of the spaniel and outline the daily alcohol limitations placed on the chief officer trusted with the care of the "Springers."

Written references to spaniels are relatively frequent from the fourteenth century onward: the dog is mentioned, for example, by British poet Geoffrey Chaucer (c. 1343–1400) and most interestingly by Gaston Phoebus (1331–91) in *Livre de Chasse* (c. 1387), one of the best-known medieval hunting manuscripts. In this he describes the spaniel as coming from Spain and being used for hawking or falconry. He notes that the dogs were useful for hunting with nets and would retrieve fowl from water. Prior to the use of firearms in hunting and shooting, the spaniel (and other sporting dogs) were used to flush out birds, such as partridge, quail, and pheasant, and small game, such as hare and fox, from cover into nets. The manuscript refers to dogs of spaniel-like character, and they continue to appear in the arts particularly from the sixteenth century onward; although these depictions of dogs are not documented as "Springers," many of the images bear striking resemblance to the modern breed.

By the sixteenth century, although all hunting dogs from Spain were often referred to as spaniels, they were also further divided, in accounts, into land and water spaniels. Within these two subdivisions, different types of dog were referenced according to their game. Dr. Caius's publication

Of Englishe Dogges (1570) describes the spaniel that "spryngeth the birde" and another that located the bird by pointing (the old Spanish Pointer). This account, along with other written documents and physical descriptions of the dogs as brown and white or black and white with "floppy ears," indicates that these spaniels—most used for hawking and for "springing" the birds—were plausibly the ancestors of the modern Springer Spaniel. In the seventeenth century, reference is made specifically to "springing" spaniels, which were further divided into two sizes; the smaller was known as the "cocking" spaniel.

During the same period spaniels were often named according to the estate or kennels where they were bred. This is particularly relevant to Springers who were bred by the Duke of Norfolk (among others) and were typically also called Norfolk Spaniels. Spaniels, like other hunting breeds, were widely bred by the aristocracy or royal kennels. They were often part of the royal household, and James II (1633–1701) was particularly devoted to his Springer Spaniel, Mumper, whom he acquired from the Duke of Norfolk. Such was his love for this dog that when his ship, *Gloucester*, sank in 1682, he was accused of abandoning "all but his dog and the priests."

By the start of the nineteenth century, spaniels were regarded in three clear groups based primarily on size. The largest of the three was the English or Field Spaniel, and included the Springer or Norfolk, Welsh, Clumber, and Sussex. Next was the Cocking or Cocker Spaniel, which was slightly smaller and was used chiefly for woodcock, and the smallest was the nonsporting variety, then called Comforter or Toy. However, littermates could be called either Springer, Welsh, or Cocker depending on their size and coloring, which caused some confusion. During the nineteenth century there was little drive to maintain a pure strain of working dog, other than by breeding the best workers together. Author John Walsh wrote in his book *The Dogs of the British Isles* (1867): "The Norfolk spaniel resembles a thick made English Setter in shape and general proportions, but is a smaller size. This is a very useful breed, and is now generally spread throughout England, where, however, it is not kept very pure." An exception to this, however, and perhaps the true foundation of the modern English Springer Spaniel, is attributed to the efforts of the Boughey family of Aqualate in Shropshire,

who began to breed a pure strain of the type in 1812 and continued its interest in the breed until the 1930s.

The Sporting Spaniel Society was formed in 1899 by William Arkwright, and the first field trials were held at his Derbyshire estate. Although some breeders, such as the Bougheys, were already concentrating on keeping lines pure, it is believed that the formation of this club inspired other breeders to do the same. In 1902 the English Springer Spaniel, as a breed, was officially recognized by the Kennel Club, and the following year Ch Beechgrove Will, who belonged to F. Winton Smith, became the first English Springer Spaniel to be awarded a Challenge Certificate. The dog went on to win his championship in 1906. The English Springer Spaniel Club was formed in 1921, and during this same period a number of breeding kennels, such as the Beechgrove, Rivington, Avendale, and Tissington, were established. Breed registrations fluctuated during World War II but have since continued to rise exponentially, and the English Springer Spaniel is now one of the most popular breeds of dog. Significantly this breed, which was born to work, is a prominent competitor in field trials but also excels in the show ring and as a companion animal. There is often some difference in type between field trial and show dogs.

Dogs of spaniel type were taken to the United States by colonists—two were listed on the *Mayflower* (1620)— although there is no way to discern what type of spaniels these were. Spaniels of various types became so popular in the United States, however, that the American Spaniel Club was established in 1881; this is now the American Kennel Club (AKC) parent club for the Cocker Spaniel. Among the earliest true Springer Spaniels in the United States were those imported in 1907 by Ernest Wells for Robert Dumont Foote of New Jersey; in 1910 the first Springer Spaniel, Denne Lucy, was registered by the AKC. The English Springer Spaniel Field Trial Association was established in 1924, and the breed standard (modeled on the British one) was written in 1932. Until the 1940s breeders were able to produce "dual champion" dogs, which won in field trials and the show ring; however, in the years after the war the variance in type became greater, and, like in the United Kingdom, there is now some considerable difference between working and show Springer Spaniels.

AGILE AND WISE

ENGLISH COCKER SPANIEL

ANCIENT – BRITAIN – COMMON

SIZE
Males 16–17 in./females 15–16 in.

APPEARANCE
Cheerful, active, compact. Notable kind and intelligent expression; slightly flattened skull; strong squarish muzzle equal in length to skull; medium-sized slightly oval eyes with "soft" expression; low-set, lobular ears well covered in silky hair. Moderate length, arched and muscular neck; strong, compact body with deep chest and very slightly sloping top line down toward tail. Tail docked in the US

and carried horizontally

COLOR
Solid black, liver, or shades of red, few white chest hairs permissible. Parti-colors either clearly marked, ticked, or roan with white in combination with black, liver, or shades of red. Clearly defined tan markings can appear with black, livers, and parti-color combinations of these. Coat smooth, flat, and silky

APTITUDE
Hunting/shooting, bird flushing and retrieving, show, companion

THE ENGLISH COCKER SPANIEL is noted for its cheerful attitude, which is marked by the speed at which its tail wags. It is an industrious, busy, and energetic dog that will work tirelessly all day, much like its relative the Springer Spaniel. With its affectionate and obedient nature, it makes an excellent companion animal for an active household.

The history of the spaniel is complex, and much of it is speculated. It is only within the last century or so that the generic "spaniel" group has been divided into separate breeds; prior to this the dogs were regarded in two groups: water spaniels and land spaniels. Within the land spaniel group, the dogs were referred to by their hunting aptitudes or by the area in which they were bred. These dogs were then further divided by size and color, with the larger known as the English or Field Spaniel, and the smaller known as the Cocking or Cocker. These smaller spaniel dogs were ideal for flushing out small birds such as woodcock, from which they take their name.

It was not until the late eighteenth century that specific references to Cocker Spaniels began to emerge. An early written recognition of the terms "Springer" and "Cocker" appeared in 1790 in Thomas Bewick's *A General History of Quadrupeds*, although he appears to be referring to the same type of dog. A definitive difference is recognized in

1801 by Sydenham Edwards, who divided the land spaniel into two types in his *Cynographia Britannica*: the Springing, Hawking Spaniel and the Cocking Spaniel. In *The Dawn of the XIXth Century in England* (1886), John Ashton describes how "cock hunting with spaniels" was undertaken in 1804 using pairs of dogs. Although Cockers are now used for flushing and retrieving, they were traditionally used only for flushing. As the range on guns increased and birds fell farther afield, the flushing dogs were then trained to retrieve, too.

The Spaniel Club was formed in Britain in 1885 to promote the breeding of different types of spaniel for sporting events and to develop their breed standards, and in 1892 the Cocker Spaniel was recognized by the Kennel Club. The breed rapidly became popular both as a working dog and a companion dog, which led to the formation of the American Spaniel Club in 1881. One of the club's first objectives was to differentiate between the Cocker and the Field Spaniels and to separate the different breeds through the establishment of breed standards and the prevention of crossbreeding. This was achieved in 1905 when the Cocker achieved its own stud book and standard in the United States.

Despite its popularity as a pet, the Cocker Spaniel is a skilled hunting dog and great competitor in field trials. Its popularity as a field trial dog has fluctuated, but in the show ring the Cocker Spaniel has gone from strength to strength and is the most successful breed at winning Best in Show at Crufts. There are considerable differences between working Cockers and show Cockers, not only physically but also in their level of energy and activity. Working Cockers have been bred to have tremendous stamina and to be able to work over rough ground and in inclement weather. They also make excellent family dogs but require substantial exercise. The show Cocker has been bred as closely to the breed standard as possible and can be slightly less energetic than the working Cocker. Both types, however, are typified by a truly lovely temperament.

IRISH WATER SPANIEL
MODERN – IRELAND – RARE

SIZE
Males 22–24 in./females 21–23 in.

APPEARANCE
Smart, upstanding, strongly built, intelligent. High-domed skull; long muzzle, slightly square in appearance. Smooth, short facial hair; can have longer "beard and sideburns"; smallish, almond-shaped eyes, dark amber or medium to dark brown. Long, low-set ears hang close to cheeks. Powerful, arched neck; medium-length, compact body; muscular back; hindquarters level with or marginally higher than shoulder. Straight front legs with good bone, well-angulated back legs with low-set hocks. Tail, called "rat tail," thick at root where covered with curls, tapers to point where it is bare; or hair is smooth and short, reaches to just above hock, carried level with back

COLOR
Rich to dark liver with purplish tinge, can be referred to as "puce-liver." Double coated, waterproof, dense. Body covered in tight ringlets, head has topknot of loose curls

APTITUDE
Hunting/shooting retriever, agility, showing, companion

THE IRISH WATER SPANIEL IS A distinctive breed with its tightly curled, waterproof coat; long, loosely curled topknot of hair; and unique "rat tail"; it was traditionally referred to as a "whip tail" or "rat tail" dog. It is the largest of the spaniel breeds and the only surviving water spaniel breed, although its numbers have become low, which is a reflection of the fluctuating fashions in the dog world. The Irish Water Spaniel has been bred for many years, specifically as a working gun dog, and excels over any terrain, particularly in marshy, watery territory. It is noted for its tenacious character and great stamina, which, combined with its enthusiasm and intelligence, make it a great worker. It is an equally good companion dog but requires exercise and obedience training. The Irish Water Spaniel is a breed that displays an innate sense of humor.

Little is known of the origins of this energetic breed, which developed in its modern form in the nineteenth century but has ancient foundations. Dogs that resembled the Irish Water Spaniel are said to have been found in Shannon, southern Ireland, during the 1100s. One of the earliest descriptions of a "water spagnel" appeared in *Historie of the Foure-Footed Beastes* (1607) by Edward Topsell (1572–1625). By his own admission, Topsell based much of his work on the better-known *Historiae Animalium* by the Swiss naturalist Conrad Gessner (1513–65), written between 1551 and 1558.

Contributors to the development of the Irish Water Spaniel are thought to include the Poodle and various retriever or spaniel types. Prior to the nineteenth century there were two, perhaps three, strains of water spaniel seen in Ireland: the Southern and Northern, with possibly the Tweedy Water Spaniel as well. The three, all now extinct, exhibited differences: the Tweedy was pale colored; the Northern had short ears, a curled coat, and a liver color, sometimes with white; and the Southern was liver colored with long ears, curled coat, and feathering on its legs. The modern Irish Water Spaniel is believed to most closely resemble the Southern strain, although it is likely that these strains were interbred. The modern Irish Water Spaniel is attributed to Justin McCarthy who established a true type in the mid-1800s through his dog, Boatswain. Boatswain (1834–52) is said to have descended from the Southern strain of water spaniels and is acknowledged as the foundation of the modern breed. Descendants of McCarthy's dogs achieved notable success in the show ring during the nineteenth century, and in 1890 the Irish Water Spaniel Club was formed in Ireland.

The breed was first registered by the American Kennel Club in 1884, although in 1877 four of the dogs were exhibited at the Westminster Kennel Club. The Irish Water Spaniel Club of America was founded in 1937 by Mr. Marshall of Connecticut and Mrs. Hall of Massachusetts and in the same year held its first show and field trial. In Britain, the Sporting Irish Water Spaniel Club was formed in 1908 but it disbanded during the war years and was not reestablished until 1989. This club promotes the Irish Water Spaniel chiefly as a working gun dog. The second club, the UK Irish Water Spaniel Association, was formed in 1926 and works to preserve and promote the breed.

ENGLISH SETTER
ANCIENT – BRITAIN – RARE

SIZE
Males 25 in./females 24 in.
APPEARANCE
Elegant, graceful, athletic. Long, lean head; long, moderately square muzzle; dark nose, large nostrils, wide apart. Large, expressive, nearly round eyes; low-set, hanging ears, moderate length, rounded at ends, carried close to head. Long, muscular neck, arched at crest; deep chest, not too wide; back level or slightly sloped to rear; strong loins slightly arched. Tail set in line with back, medium length, tapers to end, feathering on underside. Carried horizontally, can have slight curve

COLOR
White base flecked with following colors (flecking referred to as "belton": black (blue belton), liver, orange, or yellow. Also tricolor, blue belton with tan markings. Coat flat, silky, medium length

APTITUDE
Hunting, bird setting, flushing, retrieving, showing, companion

THE ENGLISH SETTER IS AN ancient breed of hunting dog and is one of Britain's most elegant gun dogs; sadly, it is also currently registered on the Kennel Club's "vulnerable native breeds" list, although its numbers are more buoyant in the United States. This is indicative of fluctuating fashions in the dog world, although there are still not enough puppies being bred to fill demand. The English Setter combines a gentle, kind, and extremely affectionate temperament with excellent working qualities, making it a wonderful companion dog or working gun dog.

The breed is thought to trace to the fourteenth century and developed from the spaniel family. Originally, the English Setter was referred to as a "setting spaniel" or "sitter"; it was used on open moorlands to locate game birds using its sense of smell. Once it found a bird, it would "sett" or crouch down, facing the bird, and remain totally still, often with a paw raised to further emphasize the bird's location. This alerted the hunter, who would approach with his net, at which point the dog would jump up and scare the bird into the net. By the eighteenth century, the "setting spaniel" was called a "setter." Four setter breeds are now recognized: English, Irish, Irish Red and White, and Gordon.

Hunting was largely the province of the aristocracy who kept large kennels, and the development of setters is associated with these kennels. One important line was established by James Hay, Earl of Carlisle, in the seventeenth century, and his dogs were described as "marble blewe" in color, and white with flecks of black hair throughout their coat. The term "belton" is now used to describe this configuration of a white base coat with flecked color in the breed. By the nineteenth century, setters began to be differentiated into separate breeds, and the foundation of the modern English Setter is largely attributed to the breeding program of Mr. Edward Laverack (1800–77). He based his breeding on two dogs: a female named Old Moll and a male named Ponto. When Laverack purchased Old Moll he described her as being the most perfect specimen of a setter he had seen. Laverack bred and line-bred his dogs in order to establish a definitive type. His dogs became known as Laverack Setters and combined hunting skills with a show ring appearance. The first show for setters was held in 1859 in Newcastle-upon-Tyne.

With the development of dog shows and field trials, the English Setter began to develop into two specific types—a working type and a show type—and both of these are still seen. The modern show ring English Setter is often also referred to as a "Laverack." The working English Setter was chiefly developed by Mr. Richard Llewellin (1840–1925), an avid hunting and shooting man, who based his breeding on Laverack lines but also used other strains to create an ideal working dog. This strain of working English Setter is often referred to as a "Llewellin," and in the United States the field dog stud book of Chicago actually registers the Llewellin as a separate breed, although it is not recognized as such by the Kennel Club or the American Kennel Club (AKC). English Setters were first imported to the United States in the 1860s and were first recognized by the AKC in 1884. In Britain the English Setter Club for Field Trials was established in 1890 and the English Setter Association (for showing) was established in 1951.

GORDON SETTER
ANCIENT – BRITAIN – MODERATE

SIZE
Males 24–27 in./females 23–26 in.

APPEARANCE
Stylish, sturdy, muscular. Head deep not broad; fairly long muzzle; low-set, hanging ears, well folded, lie close to head; dark brown eyes with wise or intelligent expression. Long arched neck; deep chest, not too broad; strong back; short from shoulder to hip; broad loins. Topline slightly sloping from withers to loins. Straight front legs, plenty of bone; feathering, tail moderately long, tapers to end, feathering on underside, carried horizontally. Can have slight curve

COLOR
Black with tan markings. Coat soft, medium length, shiny

APTITUDE
Hunting, bird setting, flushing, retrieving, showing, companion

THE GORDON SETTER is one of the four setter breeds—the others are the English, Irish, and Irish Red and White—and it is the largest and heaviest in frame. The Gordon works at a slower pace than its relatives but will continue undeterred all day long; it is noted for its great stamina and tenacious hunting. It is a very intelligent dog and can be misunderstood, although it is loyal and affectionate to its loved ones. The Gordon is a working gun-dog breed and was developed over a number of centuries in this capacity; it is frequently described as a "personal gun dog" and works best as an individual, sharing its working and home life with its owner.

The origins of the Gordon Setter trace back to the fourteenth century to the "spaniel" group of hunting dogs. Over time these dogs developed specific characteristics. The "setter" or "sitter" dogs were those that would crouch down on finding a game bird and remain motionless to alert the hunter to the bird's whereabouts. Once the hunter had been shown the bird's location, he was able to lay his nets before allowing the dog to jump up and scare the bird into the net. The modern development of the Gordon Setter began in the early nineteenth century and is attributed to the 4th Duke of Gordon (1743–1827), who bred dogs at Gordon Castle in the Scottish Highlands. Although the duke contributed to the breed, there had been black and tan hunting and shooting dogs of setter type around for many years prior to his involvement. A reference to such dogs appeared in c. 1621 in *Hunger's Prevention: Or, The Whole Art of Fowling by Water and Land* by Gervase Markham, in which he describes "black and fallow setting dogs."

There were many kennels breeding black and tan working dogs in the north of England, including those of Thomas William Coke (1754–1842), who became the Earl of Leicester; it is thought that the Duke of Gordon obtained dogs from Leicester as part of his breeding program. Several books written in the nineteenth century suggested that the black and tan setters were crossed with Bloodhound to establish the Gordon Setter.

In 1873, after the formation of the Kennel Club, the dogs were first registered as Black and Tan Setters, and the name was not changed to Gordon Setter until 1923. Two influential early breeders were Robert Chapman at the end of the nineteenth century and Isaac Sharpe in the first half of the twentieth century. Chapman used the prefix "Heather" for his dogs, which were consistent winners in the show ring. Sharpe used some of the Heather lines at his kennels that were close to Gordon Castle and became a breeder of world repute. The first British club for the breed was established in 1891 but was disbanded during World War I. The British Gordon Setter Club was established in 1927 and still serves to preserve and promote the breed. Breed numbers declined as a result of both world wars and because many large shooting estates closed down, but after World War II the numbers began to pick up.

Some of the earliest Gordon Setters in the United States were imported in 1842 from the Gordon Castle kennels. Setters in their three varieties were becoming popular in the United States but were also often interbred at this time. The breed was recognized by the American Kennel Club in 1884, and in 1924 the Gordon Setter Club of America was formed. There is less difference between the working and show varieties of the Gordon Setter than is seen in the other setter breeds, and it is a notably versatile dog, an all-around working gun dog, and an excellent companion.

GERMAN SHORTHAIRED POINTER

MODERN – GERMANY – COMMON

SIZE
Males 23–25 in./females 21–23 in.

APPEARANCE
Intelligent, balanced, athletic. Clean cut and noble head; almond-shaped brown eyes with intelligent, good-humored expression. Length of muzzle equals length of skull; large brown nose with broad nostrils. Ears are broad, set high, and hang close to head. Muscular neck; powerful front end; short back; chest deep; defined tuck up; loin strong and

slightly arched; hips broad with hip sockets wide apart. Powerful hindquarters with well-muscled thighs. Tail docked in US to 40% its length, carried down when at rest or horizontal when active

COLOR
Solid liver or liver with white (ticking, roan, or patches of liver). Coat short, thick, smooth

APTITUDE
Trailing, retrieving, pointing, agility, obedience, showing, companion

THE GERMAN SHORTHAIRED POINTER (GSP) is an extraordinarily versatile hunting breed and is often heralded as a "wonder" breed in shooting circles. In its native Germany it is called Kurzhaar (Shorthair) and in Continental Europe the Deutsch Kurzhaar. The GSP is one of a number of breeds referred to as an "HPR," meaning hunt, point, and retrieve. The breed has become more popular in recent years not only for shooting but also for field trials and pointing tests. It is able to fulfill all the requirements of hunting a great range of quarry, from various birds to small game, and is adept on land and in water. The GSP is an elegant, energetic, and intelligent breed, and is also obedient and affectionate.

Its origins trace back to Germany in the 1800s. For the first time people other than the aristocracy had the right to hunt and shoot and were able to purchase or lease large tracts of land for this purpose. The German huntsmen set about developing a dog that was able to track, point, flush out, and retrieve this varied quarry. It had to be able to retrieve game from water and from land, and be bold enough to hunt game such as fox, wild cat, and deer. In addition, the dog had to be a companion and a family pet.

Prior to the development of the GSP there was a small number of pointing dogs in Germany of primarily Spanish pointer descent. Three pointers are recorded as being at a

well-known early kennel in Sondershausen in 1714. It is thought that Spanish pointing dogs, German pointers, and pointers from France were influential in the development of the GSP, along with various German scenting hounds, French Gascon, English pointers, and English Foxhound. The initial gene pool was very varied and a number of early dogs registered have "unknown" parentage. In 1872 a pedigree register was established, and the first dog, Hecktor I, was entered into the German Kennel Club stud book. Hecktor was a liver and white dog described as quite heavy and houndlike in appearance and still greatly removed from the sleek GSP of today. Two early dogs in the breed were Nero and Treff. Both of these are foundation dogs of the breed through their progeny.

An early breeder of pointers was Prince Albrecht zu Solms-Braunfels, who owned a large breeding kennel called Wolfsmuhle in Braunfels, Germany, where he bred pointers and setters, and crossbred various breeds. A breed club was established in 1880, and in 1891 the name was changed to the Klub Kurzhaar; it is now known as the Deutsch Kurzhaar Verband (DKV). Through years of rigorous breeding, the GSP has become a champion in both form and function; in order to be registered by the DKV it is required to pass conformation assessment and field tests. A testament to the modern qualities of the GSP is the number of these dogs that achieve dual championship status, winning in both the show ring and at field trials.

Dr. Charles Thornton of Montana is credited with being the "father" of the breed in the United States. He was instrumental in introducing and popularizing GSPs in 1925, and others began importing GSPs in the 1930s. The American Kennel Club (AKC) recognized GSPs in 1930. The first AKC licensed specialty show was held in 1941, and in 1944 field trials began with the German Shorthaired Pointer Club of America being established in 1962. GSPs rank among the most popular hunting dogs today and match their abilities with wonderful temperaments.

AGILE AND WISE

AGILE AND WISE

VIZSLA

MODERN — HUNGARY — MODERATE

SIZE
Males 22–24 in./females 21–23 in.

APPEARANCE
Distinctive golden rust color; athletic, noble, robust but rather lightly built. Skull moderately wide between ears; muzzle of equal length or slightly shorter than length of skull. Square, deep muzzle, tapers slightly to nose, which is brown. Medium-sized eyes blend with coat color; thin, silky ears, proportionately long, set fairly low, rounded, leather ends. Strong, moderately long, arched neck; strong body, slightly longer than height at shoulder; chest moderately broad; deep, underline has slight tuck up at loins. Tail set just below level of croup, carried horizontally when moving. Docked tail with one-third removed is preferred

COLOR
Varying shades of golden rust, minimal white markings on chest, toes allowed but discouraged, white markings elsewhere not allowed. Short, dense, smooth coat

APTITUDE
Hunting, pointing, retrieving, tracking, agility, showing, companion

THERE IS SOMETHING MAGICAL about the Vizsla. This intelligent and characterful dog has endured the tumultuous history of its homeland, Hungary, and nearly faced extinction in the twentieth century and the loss of many of its original pedigree records. Today the Vizsla has been reestablished in Hungary, where it has become the national dog.

The story of the Vizsla begins with the ancestors of the nomadic Magyar people, who heralded from northern, western, and central Asia. These dogs were probably of Mastiff and hound dog crosses that were found in the Himalayas and mountains of Tibet. By 895 C.E., the Magyar people had arrived in the Carpathian Basin, the vast Hungarian plains of east-central Europe, where they established themselves as herdsmen, hunters, and farmers. Their dogs needed to track, point, and retrieve, and to find food. The Magyars developed a skilled and intelligent dog with a keen sense of smell. It was able to locate game and drive birds toward the hunter. Specific breeding continued and accounts describe the dogs as "golden" in color. The earliest known reference to "Vizsla" dates to around 1350 and was the name of a village on the Danube, indicating that this was the area where the dogs were developed.

From the sixteenth century onward, hunting was popular as a sport among the nobility, who selectively bred hunting dogs. It is significant that the Vizsla was and continues to be considered a companion dog—even when bred and used for hunting. Historically it lived with the family, and it appears to achieve the height of its skills when it is treated with great affection and sensitivity.

By the nineteenth century Vizslas had been taken by the Germans, Austrians, and British back to their respective countries to breed to their own hunting stock, and gradually the foundation nucleus of Vizslas in Hungary diminished. In 1917 an organization called Hubertus was formed to preserve the foundations of the breed. It chose twelve Vizslas, and today all modern registered Vizslas in Hungary trace to these three males and nine females. In 1920 a group of breeders established the Magyar Breeding Association and drew up a breed standard.

World War II had a devastating effect on the Vizsla and nearly led to the breed's extinction. Thousands of Hungarians fled in the face of Soviet occupation, leaving their dogs behind. Some were able to take their dogs with them, and it is to these people that the breed owes its continuance. During the 1950s early Vizslas arrived in the United States, and the Magyar Vizsla Club of America was established in 1953. In 1960 the breed was accepted into the American Kennel Club, at the same time dropping "Magyar" from its name.

In the United Kingdom the Kennel Club recorded two Vizsla registrations in 1953. Other dogs were imported from the United States, and in 1963 a Vizsla called Joram de la Creste was imported from France and used as stud seven times; his offspring are found in many of the current pedigrees in the United Kingdom. The Hungarian Vizsla Club was founded in 1968, initially with just twenty-five members. The breed was taken off the Rare Breeds register at the Kennel Club in 1971, and today the Vizsla is a popular breed supported by truly dedicated enthusiasts.

WEIMARANER

MODERN – GERMANY – MODERATE

SIZE
Males 25–27 in./females 23–25 in.
APPEARANCE
Graceful, athletic, aristocratic. Moderately long head; noble, intelligent expression. Eyes set well apart, in shades of amber, gray, blue-gray. Long, lobular ears, slightly folded, set high. Moderate-length, powerful body slopes slightly from withers to loin; deep chest; well-sprung ribs; flank tucked up. Muscular hindquarters; well-angulated stifles; hocks well let down. Tail docked to 6 in., carried confidently
COLOR
Solid color of mouse-gray to silver-gray, small white mark on chest allowed. Coat smooth, short, sleek, looks like metallic sheen
APTITUDE
Originally big-game hunting, hunting, pointing, retrieving, tracking, agility, showing, companion

THE MODERN WEIMARANER is a beautiful and distinctive German breed of hunting dog that also makes an excellent companion animal. It is a perfect combination of working ability, temperament, and appearance and is the result of judicious and selective breeding in Germany that saw it develop as a type around 200 years ago. A defining feature of the breed is its unusual and attractive coat coloring, which ranges from silver-gray to mouse-gray and has the appearance of a metallic sheen. It is not known from where the coat coloring derives and it led to the dog often being referred to as a "gray ghost." Interestingly, although the Weimaraner is predominantly a short-coated breed, there are instances of long-haired Weimaraners. The long-haired variety is strictly not recognized by the American Kennel Club (AKC) but is recognized by the Kennel Club in the United Kingdom and in Continental Europe; the German Weimaraner Club has both long-haired and short-haired varieties as part of its club logo. The first known long-haired puppy was seen in 1973 and within the same time frame a second one was imported from Austria. Long-haired Weimaraners have since won both show and working classes in Britain but remain rare.

The origins of the Weimaraner are unclear. Some sources claim that the dog dates back to the seventeenth century, based on dogs of similar appearance in artworks. These early hunting dogs could have given rise to the Weimaraner when selective breeding was undertaken later. One of the propagating breeds in its origin is held to have been the St. Hubert Hound of Belgium, which in turn gave rise to the Bloodhound. Others claim that the Weimaraner and German Shorthaired Pointer share origins that include old German hounds, pointers, and the French Gascon.

The "modern" development of the Weimaraner is popularly traced to the German court of Weimar. Karl August, Grand Duke of Saxe-Weimar-Eisenach (1757–1828) was a keen sportsman and rider and maintained large kennels of hunting dogs. These are attributed as being at the foundation of the Weimaraner breed. At first the dogs were used for hunting big game, such as bear, wolf, wildcat, and deer; they became renowned for their skills and were referred to as the "gray hunting dogs." By the second half of the nineteenth century the emphasis of hunting had changed to birds and smaller game. The dogs were then bred for their hunting, pointing, and retrieving qualities. Breeding and ownership of the dogs were rigidly controlled by the German nobles, which greatly contributed to the rapid development of the breed type.

A breed standard was drawn up in 1896, and in 1897 the Club for the Pure Breeding of the Silver-gray Weimaraner Vorstehhund was established, now called the Weimaraner Klub; the stud book was opened in the same year. Membership of the club was restricted, and only members were allowed to own and breed the dogs. In 1928 Howard Knight, a hunter from New England, USA, applied for membership so that he could procure dogs and import them to the United States, but it was not until 1938 that he acquired any breeding stock. In 1943 the AKC recognized the breed in its Sporting Group category. A number of dogs from Germany were imported to the United States during the 1940s, and by the 1950s the breed had become popular, leading to indiscriminate breeding and a resulting loss in quality. The situation was rectified during the 1960s, driven by concerned and knowledgeable breeders.

SPINONE ITALIANO
MODERN – ITALY – MODERATE

SIZE
Males 23–27 in./females 22–25 in.

APPEARANCE
Robust, powerful, energetic. Unique shaped head with divergent head planes and gentle and intelligent expression. Oval-shaped, long skull; slightly Roman nose preferred, square in profile; kind, alert expression. Large, round eyes ocher colored, lighter in light coat colors, darker in darker coat colors. Ears carried low and almost triangular in shape with rounded tip and thick hair cover. Strong, muscular neck; deep chest; minimal tuck up at flank. Top line slopes gently downward from withers before rising slightly to muscular, well-arched loins. Tail thick at base, carried down or horizontally, docked to 5.5–8 in.

COLOR
Solid white, white/orange, orange/roan, white with brown markings, brown roan. Coat dense, coarse, flat or slightly crimped, between 1½ to 2½ in. in length

APTITUDE
Hunting, pointing, retrieving, showing, companion

THE SPINONE ITALIANO is an all-purpose gun dog and part of the hunt, point, and retrieve group of hunting dogs. Like many of these associated breeds, it is noted for its excellent temperament. The versatile Spinone will hunt game or birds and retrieve in water and on land. It is often described as being "slow footed" in relation to its speed and the purposeful way in which it hunts, although this can be a misleading description. It actually has a very active trot and typically hunts at this pace, although in general terms it is considered one of the slower-paced hunting dogs. The breed is renowned for its thick, protective skin and dense, coarse coat, which provides it with great protection from undergrowth and unforgiving hunting grounds.

It is thought to derive its name, which was not used until the nineteenth century, from the thorny blackthorn (sloe) bush—the *prunus spinosa*—that provided cover for small game, and it is one of very few dog breeds that is able to navigate it. The Spinone Italiano is also noted for its exceptional sense of smell, which was utilized to good effect by the Italians during World War II for tracking German troops; allegedly the dogs were able to differentiate between the shoe polish used by the Germans and that used by the Italians.

The origins of the breed are greatly contested and largely unsubstantiated. The Spinone is frequently dated back to prehistory and the time of the Roman Empire, although this is undocumented. Some theorists claim that the breed's ancestors came from eastern Europe; others maintain that it has Setter in its heritage or that it is derived from the ancient wire-haired Segugio Italiano, an Italian scent hound with similar characteristics. None of these claims are proven, but it is clear that the Spinone has "pointing" blood in its heritage and that it developed its characteristics in relation to its geographic home.

The lovely and charismatic breed almost died out during the first half of the twentieth century, partly as a result of Italian hunters turning their attention to different, faster breeds, such as spaniels and setters, and also because of the mass devastation caused by World War II. In 1949 a breed expert, Dr. Adriano Ceresoli, made a study of the Spinone in order to determine breed numbers and found that some breeders were resorting to crosses to Wirehaired Pointing Griffons, Boulet Griffons, and German Wirehaired Pointers to preserve the breed. He later wrote a leading book on the breed, *Lo Spinone Italiano* (1951).

During the 1950s the first Spinoni arrived in Britain, imported by the British-born pianist Alberto Semprini, who was of Italian descent. The breed did not, however, become popular until the 1980s. In 1981 four Spinoni were imported by Mary Moore and Ruth Tattersall, which were bred with other imports to establish the foundations of the breed in the United Kingdom. The Italian Spinone Club of Great Britain was founded in 1983 and held its first Open Show in 1989. The Kennel Club awarded the breed championship status in 1994; the first full champion was Ch Sentling Zenzero. The breed was recognized by the American Kennel Club in 2000 and remains in low numbers in the United States, although it is supported by an enthusiastic group. The Spinone Italiano is a kind and skilled dog and makes a loyal companion.

CHESAPEAKE BAY RETRIEVER

MODERN – UNITED STATES – MODERATE

SIZE
Males 23–26 in./females 21–24 in.

APPEARANCE
Strong, well-balanced, powerful, cheerful. Broad, round skull with intelligent expression; tapered muzzle of equal length to skull. Medium large, clear eyes, yellowish amber in color; small ears set well up on head. Medium length, muscular neck; short, powerful back, slightly higher at hindquarters than withers. Deep, wide chest; well-tucked-up flanks; powerful shoulders and hindquarters; well-webbed hare feet. Medium-length tail, either straight or slightly curved, carried level or slightly above top line in movement, but never curled over back

COLOR
Any shade of brown, dead grass, or sedge. Small, white spot allowed on chest, belly, toes, or back of feet. Double-coated, short, thick, waterproof coat. Outer coat oily, harsh, often wavy over the shoulders, neck, back, and loins. Undercoat oily, dense, woolly

APTITUDE
Loyal hunting companion, retrieving, especially waterfowl from water, showing.

THERE ARE FEW IF ANY BREEDS of dog that come close to exhibiting the extraordinary water-retrieving abilities of the Chesapeake Bay Retriever. These dogs have a natural affinity and enthusiasm for water and the breed has become specially adapted to working in extremely cold water. The Chesapeake Bay Retriever has been bred for the last 200 years as a working gun dog, and today, in addition to this role, it can excel at working trials, obedience, agility, and as a companion animal, providing its exercise requirements are met. The dogs are noted for their affectionate and loyal temperament and can also be protective of their loved ones and territory; they are intelligent dogs, often with an independent streak, and require early training.

The Chesapeake Bay Retriever is one of the few dog breeds whose origins are documented, at least partly, and these are based on a letter written by George Law in 1845, first published in 1852. The letter provides an account of a shipwreck of an English brig in 1807. Law was on board a US boat, the *Canton*, when he came across a floundering English brig, which was heading from Newfoundland back to Poole Harbor in the south of England. Law spotted her and instigated the rescue mission, during which he discovered two puppies. They were described as Newfoundlands, but were possibly the smaller and now extinct St. John's Water Dogs. Law purchased the male and female from the British captain, who said they were of "the most approved Newfoundland breed." Law docked at Norfolk, Virginia, to drop off the British crew and while there gave the male puppy, Sailor, to John Mercer of West River, and the female, Canton, to Dr. James Stewart of Sparrow's Point, before he continued on his journey.

A later account of Sailor describes him as of "fine size," strong, powerful, with a relatively long muzzle, dingy red in color with some white on his face and chest, and having very light eyes. This pale amber eye color is one of the distinguishing features of the breed today. The same account also refers to the thickness of the dog's coat, which is an almost waterproof, double-coated oily coat that is well suited to its water-based activities. Sailor was bred to a variety of dogs, which were thought to have included curly-coated retrievers, Irish Water Spaniels, setters, pointers, and various retrievers. Canton remained on the western side of Maryland, where she was also well known for her skills and was bred to various retrieving and hunting dogs. The progeny of Sailor and Canton in both east and west Maryland were used for the popular sport of duck hunting. In 1877, when both strains were exhibited at the Poultry & Fanciers Association Show in Baltimore, they showed sufficient similarity to be recognized as one breed—the Chesapeake Bay Ducking Dog—although three types were recognized within the breed.

The American Kennel Club recognized the Chesapeake Bay Retriever in 1878, and placed it in its Sporting Group category. In 1918 the American Chesapeake Club was established to preserve and promote the breed. It held its first licensed Retriever Trial in 1932, and the breed continues to excel in such events, field trials, and shows. The Chesapeake Bay Retriever was declared the official state dog of Maryland in 1964.

LABRADOR RETRIEVER
MODERN – CANADA/BRITAIN – COMMON

SIZE
Males 22½–24½ in./females 21½–23½ in.

APPEARANCE
Strong, athletic, handsome. Broad head; medium-length muzzle; expressive, intelligent, kind eyes, brown or hazel, set well apart. Wide nose, well-developed nostrils. Ears set quite far back on head and hanging quite close. Overall impression of short, coupled, balanced dog. Chest deep and reasonably wide; back level from withers to croup, underline

almost straight. Distinctive "otter" tail, thick at base, gradually tapers to tip with thick coat covering, rounded appearance

COLOR
Black, various shades of yellow from light cream to dark fox red, or chocolate. Double-coated, waterproof coat with short, straight, dense hairs

APTITUDE
Hunting/shooting, retrieving on land or water, assistance dogs, police, agility, obedience, showing, companion

THE LABRADOR RETRIEVER, commonly referred to as Labrador or Lab, is an astonishing success story of modern dog breeding and currently ranks as the most popular dog breed in the world. It is a superbly versatile dog and can switch from a working role to that of a domestic pet in an instant. This, combined with its great intelligence and kind temperament, lies at the foundation of its success.

The breed can be traced to the St. Johns Dog found on the Canadian island of Newfoundland. This dog developed over a long period from the sixteenth century, when fishermen and early settlers arrived from Britain, Ireland, and Portugal, and brought their working dogs with them. The dogs were used to pull in fishing nets, tow small boats, and to carry ropes between boats. They were natural water animals and developed a water-resistant coat, which are both features of the modern Labrador. The St. Johns Dog was medium sized with an amenable temperament, great retrieving instincts, and considerable intelligence.

There had been a healthy trade route based on the fishing industry between Poole Harbor in England and Newfoundland since the late 1600s, and from the early 1800s fishermen also began to trade their St. Johns Dogs in the English town. The high cost of the dogs meant that it was only the wealthy English aristocrats who could afford

them. The 5th Duke of Buccleuch, his brother Lord John Scott, the 2nd Earl of Malmesbury, and a Mr. Radclyffe all bought imported dogs in Poole in the early years of the nineteenth century. These men, and subsequent dukes of Buccleuch and earls of Malmesbury, were instrumental in developing the breed. It was from the Buccleuch and Malmesbury kennels that the foundation dogs of the breed originated. They are widely considered to be the male dogs Buccleuch Avon, Buccleuch Ned, and Malmesbury Tramp, and the female Malmesbury Juno, all dating to the 1880s. The early British breeding of these dogs coincided with the breed's demise in Newfoundland as a result of heavy taxes and an eventual ban on ownership, and during the twentieth century the St. Johns Dog all but disappeared. The name "Labrador" was coined by the British, who inaccurately grouped together the territories of Labrador and Newfoundland and termed them both "Labrador." One of the first written references to the name was by the 3rd Earl of Malmesbury, who referred to the dogs as such in a letter dated 1887.

The early Labradors were nearly always black in color but the occasional dog exhibited a small patch of white chest hair, known as a medallion, which reflected the influence of the St. Johns Dog. Accounts confirm that a few of the original St. Johns Dogs of Newfoundland exhibited yellow or chocolate coat colors, which indicated a recessive coat color gene. It is probable that early breeders tried to breed out this coat coloring and it was not until the end of the nineteenth century in England that the first yellow Labrador was registered with the Kennel Club (KC). The chocolate coloring did not become popular until the 1960s, when Cookridge Tango took the first championship for the color in the United Kingdom. The KC recognized the Labrador Retriever breed in 1903, and the national Labrador Retriever Club was formed in 1916.

Labradors started to become popular in the United States in the early twentieth century, when interest in the

breed matched a great enthusiasm for bird hunting. The talents of the Labrador quickly became apparent: in particular the Labrador's short, waterproof coat made it a great water dog because it was less susceptible to icing up than those of longer-haired breeds. Among the first Labradors to be registered in the United States were Brocklehurst Floss and Brocklehurst Nell in 1917, when the American Kennel Club (AKC) first recognized the breed, but registration remained fairly slow and only twenty-three dogs were registered by 1927. The fortunes of the Labrador in the United States were given a huge boost in 1928 when an article titled "Meet the Labrador Retriever" appeared in the *American Kennel Club Magazine*. The Labrador Retriever Club was formed in 1931, and in December of that year it held its first field trials event at Glenmere Court Estate in Chester, New York. The US diplomat and politician W. Averell Harriman, who was also a Labrador breeder and owner of the Arden Kennels, won the American Bred Stakes. The Arden Kennels became one of the leading breeding kennels of Labradors, and in 1938 the dog Blind of Arden became the first dog to appear on the cover of *Life* magazine. He became the first American Field Champion, and his sister, Decoy of Arden, won the first female American Field Champion title; another Arden Labrador, Shed of Arden, won the National Champion competition three times.

The first yellow Labrador, Kinclaven Lowesby, an imported son of a British dog, was registered in 1929 in the United States; the first chocolate (described as "liver") was Diver of Chiltonfoliat, who was registered in 1932 and was also British bred. The first US-bred chocolate was registered in 1940 and called Kennoway's Fudge. After World War II, the popularity of the Labrador in the United States grew rapidly and in 1991 it became the nation's most popular dog—a rank that the Labrador has now held for the last twenty years.

Today there are two different body types seen in the Labrador, although the AKC and KC incorporate both types within the single Labrador Retriever group. The field dog, bred specifically for retrieving and gun dog work, is generally longer in the leg, lighter in body frame, and more athletically built than the show-bred Labrador. Both types exhibit the characteristic Labrador qualities of excellent temperament, intelligence, and personality.

GOLDEN RETRIEVER
MODERN – BRITAIN – COMMON

SIZE
Males 23–24 in./females 21½–22½ in.

APPEARANCE
Golden-colored, powerful, confident, athletic with a kindly expression. Broad skull: muzzle has straight profile, slightly deeper at stop than tip. Friendly, medium-large, dark brown eyes, set well apart; rather short ears carried close to cheek. Medium-long muscular neck; body short, coupled; strong back, level from withers to croup, croup slightly sloping; deep chest; well-sprung ribs; very little tuck up at flanks. Tail well set on, following line of croup, thick at base with feathering

COLOR
Any shade of golden, feathering may be lighter. Few white hairs on chest permissible. Double-coated, top coat straight or wavy, flat to body, undercoat thick, dense, and waterproof

APTITUDE
Hunting/shooting, retrieving, assistance, agility, obedience, showing, companion

THE GOLDEN RETRIEVER is one of the most popular and versatile dog breeds in the world and is noted for its extremely good temperament. The dog was originally bred as a working gun dog, a role at which it continues to excel, but its extraordinary temperament means that it is also used for a wide range of other jobs. These include search and rescue, tracking, drug and bomb detection, and assistance for the blind and deaf; it also makes a superlative pet. The Golden Retriever is a talented agility dog and is particularly obedient and easy to train. It is little wonder that it has become such a popular breed.

The origins of the breed trace to Scotland in the nineteenth century and specifically to Sir Dudley Coutts Marjoribanks (1820–94), later Baron Tweedmouth, who kept large kennels and bred hunting and shooting dogs. In 1854 Tweedmouth purchased the vast Guisachan Estate, not far from Loch Ness. He expanded his kennels and dog breeding activities, and it was there that the Golden Retriever, or Yellow Retriever as it was then known, developed. An early dog in the breed was a yellow dog called Nous, who had been purchased in 1864. At this time Tweedmouth had several "retrievers" in his kennels as well as Tweed Water Spaniels, light-colored tenacious gun dogs with good water retrieving skills. In 1867 Tweedmouth was given a Tweed Water Spaniel female called Belle whom he bred with Nous the following year, which resulted in four yellow puppies. These dogs were crossbred with Tweed Water Spaniels, Red Setters, Wavy Coated Retrievers, and Bloodhounds to establish the modern Golden Retriever.

The first Golden Retrievers to be exhibited were seen at Crufts in 1908 and belonged to Viscount Harcourt, although at this time they were still not considered a separate breed and were affiliated with Flat Coat Retrievers. The Golden Retriever Club (GRC) was established in 1911 and was recognized in 1913 by the Kennel Club, at which time the breed status was also recognized as being separate from other retrievers. The breed standard was drawn up in 1911; it originally excluded cream colors because the darker golden color was preferred. This was later changed, and the standard now rejects "red or mahogany" colors. In 1931 the GRC held its first field trial event, in which the dogs proved their abilities, thus increasing the popularity of the breed.

By the 1930s, Golden Retrievers were being exported to countries including Canada, North and South America, Kenya, India, France, Holland, and Belgium. The first dog recognized by the American Kennel Club (AKC) and registered in the United States was Lomberdale Blondin in 1925, but it was registered as a "retriever." The breed was not officially recognized as separate until 1936, and in 1938 the Golden Retriever Club of America Inc. was established. One of the driving forces behind the club and the early establishment of the breed in the United States was Colonel S. Magoffin. He had been introduced to the breed by Christopher Burton of Vancouver, Canada, who used Golden Retrievers for shooting. Burton supplied Magoffin with a dog called Speedwell Pluto, who went on to become US and Canadian champion and was prolific as a sire. Magoffin established the Gilnockie champion breeding kennels in Colorado, which account for many of the pedigree lines of the breed in the United States today.

CHAPTER 7
TENACIOUS AND SPIRITED

The majority of terrier breeds developed in Scotland, England, Ireland, and Wales, and although a select few terriers made it into the royal household, terriers in general were the working man's dog and were used for vermin control and for hunting fox and badger above and below ground. It is the terrier's practice of digging out prey from holes, or of "going to ground," that gives rise to its name: "terrier" derives from the Latin *terra*, meaning earth.

The earliest evidence of terrier dogs is an engraving taken from a fourteenth-century illustrated manuscript that was reproduced in *Sports and Pastimes* (1801). The image shows a dog of unknown heritage digging a fox from a hole, assisted by three men with spades. The first written account of these dogs appeared in Dr. Caius's *Of Englishe Dogges* (1570), in which he described "the terrar" that hunts the fox and badger. Although there is much speculation regarding the foundations that gave rise to the original terrier type, there is simply no evidence. The very distinct terrier breeds of modern times only developed within the last 200 years or so, and prior to this there appears to have been only a generic terrier type of varied characteristics, largely governed by its geography. Terriers were not in fact described with any kind of informative detail pertaining to their specific appearance until the eighteenth century.

They were and still are used chiefly for hunting, either with huntsmen on foot or on horseback. Richard Blome's work *Gentleman's Recreation*, published in 1686, described terriers being used to hunt in pairs to dig out the fox. As foxhunting became more popular, terriers were used in addition to Fox Hounds. The hounds gave chase, but frequently the fox bolted down a hole, at which point the terriers were brought in to dig out the fox so that the hunt could continue. In order to confront a fox (or badger) within the confined space of its hole, terriers have to be tremendously brave; they must be great diggers and they must bark. The barking is essential to alert the huntsmen to where they are, both when above and below ground.

Terriers used for this type of hunting developed these characteristics over time. They also developed narrow,

flexible chests to allow maneuvering in tight spaces and a decent length of stride to enable them to keep up with hounds when necessary (although mostly they were transported to the fox holes). They were bred to be of sufficient size to get the job done, but not too big for the hole. Their hides are tough, their coats are thick, dense, and in some varieties wiry, and their jaws are powerful. Terriers are a whole lot of dog in a small package, and some varieties are extremely efficient at rodent control; unlike terriers used for foxhunting, these rodent-killing terriers have a high kill instinct and are also often silent when killing their prey. So good were their abilities in this respect that in the nineteenth century rat baiting became a popular sport, and the Manchester Terrier was one of the best at this endeavor. Great numbers of rats would be let loose in an enclosure and the dog was released to see how many of the rats it could kill in a given time frame. Typically, terriers of various types have been kept on farms and small holdings, and, in the nineteenth century, in industrial areas, docks, mines, and even public houses.

One of the earliest accounts that documents specific physical characteristics of different terriers was Peter Beckford's *Thoughts on Hunting* (1781), in which he mentions black, white, and red terriers. Some years later, in *Rural Sports* (c. 1802), terrier owner Reverend William Daniel described two types: a rough, short-legged, long-backed dog of black or yellowish color and a smooth-haired, beautifully formed dog of either reddish brown or black with tan legs. This latter type, known as the Black and Tan and thought to have existed in rough and smooth coats, is believed to be at the root of many of the modern terrier breeds, including most clearly the Manchester Terrier, but also the Airedale and Fox Terriers. During the same period, in *Cynographia Britannica*, Sydenham Edwards describes similar black and tan terriers with smooth and rough wire coats and in long- and short-legged varieties. Some fifty years later John H. Walsh outlines different specific types in his book *British Rural Sports* (1850s); these included the Dandie Dinmont (the only breed to be named after a fictional character), Black and Tan, Skye Terrier, Bull Terrier, a toy terrier, and a rough-coated terrier. The first organized dog show took place in Newcastle-upon-Tyne in 1859, and from this date onward the specialized breeding of dogs, record keeping, pedigrees, breed clubs, and breed standards really took off. As such, although the terrier in general terms originates far back in history and has been the huntsman's and farmer's friend through the ages, the modern terrier breeds of today date to the nineteenth century.

In the United States terriers were initially most prized as ratters and vermin control. They were seldom used in conjunction with Fox Hounds for ridden hunting, but were occasionally used for hunting on foot. An early reference to a specific terrier dates to 1777 and records an extraordinary moment in history. On June 6 during the battle of Germantown between the Americans led by George Washington (1732–99) and the British under General Howe (1729–1814), a little terrier, described as a "fox terrier," was seen wandering around in the area between the US and British lines. A colonial soldier rescued the dog, and on gathering it up saw a plate on its collar that identified its owner as General Howe. The soldier took the dog to Washington and suggested that it be kept as a mascot to raise the morale of the troops. Washington, however, who was missing his own dog, Sweet Lips, appreciated the nature of the relationship between a man and his dog. Accounts indicate that the little terrier was cleaned up and fed, a cease-fire was ordered, and the dog was returned to General Howe, accompanied by a note that read: "General Washington's compliments to General Howe . . . ."

Terriers were greatly appreciated in the United States during the mid-nineteenth century for their ratting abilities, and frequently competed in ratting competitions much like those in Britain.

Accounts indicate that during the California Gold Rush (1848–55) and the exponential growth of San Francisco, rats were rife and terriers bought and sold for high prices for their ratting skills. They were let loose to run riot up and down the streets after rats, drawing crowds of onlookers, and were also pitted against them in enclosures. Sadly, accounts indicate that many terriers were used solely for this purpose and were rather neglected otherwise. From the 1870s onward "pure bred" terrier breeds began to be imported to the United States from Britain and were established through the formation of breed clubs and the American Kennel Club in 1884.

The role of the terrier has moved away from that of a tenacious hunting dog and they are now primarily companion animals. Terrier breeds also excel at agility and any events that test their intelligence and athleticism. However, many societies strive to preserve the fundamental qualities of the terrier and still encourage the working qualities of these multitalented dogs.

MANCHESTER TERRIER

ANCIENT/MODERN – ENGLAND – RARE

SIZE
*Males/females Standard
15–16 in.; 12–22 lbs/
Toy 10–12 in.; up to 12 lbs*

APPEARANCE
*Sleek, elegant, agile. Wedge-
shaped, long, narrow head with
lively, keen expression. Almond-
shaped, small, dark eyes set
relatively closely together. Ears
can be naturally erect, button, or
cropped on the Standard, or
naturally erect on the Toy. Slim,
slightly arched neck; smooth
topline that arches slightly over
loins; narrow but deep chest;
tucked-up abdomen. Tail reaches
to hocks, thick at base, tapering to
point, carried in gentle curve*

COLOR
*Jet black, rich mahogany tan in
specific pattern marking that
includes black "thumbprints" on
each foreleg, black pencil
markings on toes. Coat firm,
short, smooth, glossy*

APTITUDE
*Ratting and hunting all
small vermin, agility,
showing, companion*

THE MANCHESTER TERRIER is a smart terrier breed that combines its elegant looks with the great intelligence and tenacity that is at the heart of the terrier breeds. In the United States the Manchester Terrier is divided into two types: the larger Standard and the Toy. In Britain these two types are recognized as separate breeds; the Standard is called the Manchester Terrier and the smaller version is the English Toy Terrier (Black and Tan). These dogs evolved from the original British Black and Tan Terrier that traces back to at least the sixteenth century. Early accounts indicate a stouter and less refined terrier than the modern Manchester, but the similarities are apparent. In this period the dogs were referred to as ratters, and although the Manchester today is primarily a companion animal, it retains its effective vermin-killing skills.

During the nineteenth century this distinctive terrier became widespread. The rat-catching abilities of the Manchester, or Black and Tan as it was then known, meant that the dogs were popular in the ports and wharves of central and northern England and also in the mining communities and farming areas, where they were put to good use. These terriers became most associated with Lancashire and eventually Manchester, which led to the breed's name in the 1890s.

By the nineteenth century Britain was overrun with rats, which led to the employment of professional rat catchers. One of the best known was Jack Black, a royal rat catcher who was in the service of Queen Victoria (1819–1901). One of Black's top rat-catching dogs was Billy, a Black and Tan Terrier who Black bred prolifically and who accounted for a large number of the Black and Tans in London.

The development of the Black and Tan into the modern Manchester is typically credited to the introduction of some Whippet blood in the mid-nineteenth century. The gently arched back of the Manchester, which is not typical of terrier breeds, could be attributed to Whippet influence. Some speculate that Italian Greyhound and Dachshund might also have been introduced. Thanks to its sophisticated appearance, the breed became popular with the gentry as well as the working classes and it was often referred to as the "gentleman's terrier." Equally, the smaller Manchester Terrier gained a following among women. This resulted in two distinct sizes of the terriers. The smaller variety was initially overexaggerated by eager breeders to the detriment of the dogs, but this was later rectified.

The Manchester Terrier typically had its ears cropped, which is still practiced in the United States for the Standard size. In Britain, ear cropping was banned in 1897 by the Kennel Club. In the United States the Black and Tan was first registered with the American Kennel Club (AKC) in 1886. The Manchester Terrier Club of America was formed in 1923 and recognized as the parent club for the Standard type; the American Toy Manchester Terrier Club was established in 1938. World War II had a devastating effect on the breed and many of the larger breeding kennels disbanded; by 1952 the situation was dire. The AKC authorized that the two separate breed clubs (Standard and Toy) be amalgamated into one organization that recognized two varieties. As such, the American Manchester Terrier Club was formed in 1958 and now preserves and promotes the interests of both types.

DANDIE DINMONT

MODERN – SCOTLAND/ENGLAND BORDERS – RARE

SIZE

Males/females 8–11 in.; weight 18–24 lbs

APPEARANCE

Long, low-bodied, distinctive head with silken topknot of hair. Broad between the ears with domed forehead; deep, strong muzzle. Large, round, bright, dark eyes, set well apart with intelligent expression. Ears set well back and low on skull, hang close to the cheek and 3–4 in. long. Topline is low at shoulder; slight downward curve and a corresponding arch over the loins, with a very slight gradual drop from top of loins to root of the tail.

Body is long, strong, and flexible; chest deep and sits well down between forelegs. Forelegs are short with good muscular development and set wide apart; hind legs are slightly longer. Tail 8–10 in. long, carried in a scimitarlike curve

COLOR

Pepper: any shade of gray or silver, topknot and ears silvery white, legs and feet tan; mustard: any shade of brown or fawn, topknot and ears creamy white with legs and feet a darker shade. Coat is a mixture of 2/3 hard hair to 1/3 soft hair

APTITUDE

Hunting, showing, companion

THERE IS GREAT DEBATE over the origins of the charming Dandie Dinmont Terrier, which has lived in the border areas between Scotland and England for many centuries. The long and low-bodied dog is said to date back to at least the seventeenth century. It has been attributed to crosses between Otterhounds and some type of native terrier, through terrier and Dachshund crosses, though it seems unlikely. What is known is that this small but feisty dog was used for otter hunting but also for going to ground after rabbits and rats, and for hunting badgers and all kinds of vermin. Its use on the latter underlines the bravery of the dog, which is considerably smaller in size than a fully grown badger. Farmers, poachers, and roaming gypsies all kept these plucky and useful dogs, and many colorful though unsubstantiated stories revolve around them.

One story tells of a seminomadic musician called Old Will "Piper" Allen (1704–79) who kept a pack of terriers for hunting otters in Northumberland. One of his dogs allegedly became famous for his otter-hunting skills, and Old Will was offered a vast sum of money for his dogs by the Duke of Northumberland, but he refused to part with them. At this time these terriers were not known by a specific breed name and it was not until the early nineteenth century the name Dandie Dinmont came into use, thanks to the Scottish author Sir Walter Scott (1771–1832). Before this time they were sometimes referred to as Mustard and Pepper Terriers, based on the two varieties of coat coloring they exhibited.

In 1815 Scott published his novel *Guy Mannering*, which featured a character called Dandie Dinmont, a farmer who kept six distinctive terriers. Scott's character Dandie Dinmont bore a striking similarity to a farmer called James Davidson, who lived near Scott and who kept the same type of terriers. As the book became popular, the terriers became known as Dandie Dinmonts.

The best known of the early Dandies was a dog called Old Pepper, who is alleged to have been caught in a trap in 1839 on the 5th Duke of Buccleuch's estate. Old Pepper had no pedigree, but he gave rise to Old Ginger, and this dog's name can be found at the foundation of all registered Dandies today. The Dandie Dinmont Terrier Club was formed in 1875 and is the second oldest dog breed club in the world. In 1876 a breed standard was accepted.

The first Dandies registered in the United States were imported from Scotland in 1886 and were registered with the American Kennel Club. The first champion was Ch King O The Heather in 1893, and the first US-bred champion was Auld Pepper O The Ark in 1931. The following year, the Dandie Dinmont Terrier Club of America was formed. Breed numbers were severely reduced as a result of World War II, but after the war, enthusiasts reestablished breeding and one kennel, the Bellmead in Old Windsor, England, became particularly well known. Dandies continued to be bred here until the 1990s, and Bellmead now forms part of the Battersea Dogs Home for strays and rescued dogs. Sadly, the Dandie Dinmont remains low in numbers today in both the United Kingdom and the United States but is supported by the dedicated efforts of breeders and enthusiasts.

BEDLINGTON TERRIER
MODERN – ENGLAND – RARE

SIZE
Male ideal 16½ in./female ideal 15½ in.; weight 17–23 lbs

APPEARANCE
Graceful, gentle, woolly coated. Narrow, deep, rounded head with full topknot of hair. Small, almond-shaped eyes, dark to hazel depending on body color; ears set low, hanging flat to cheek, triangular with rounded tips, velvety, covered in fine hair, forming a small, silky tassel at tip. Head carried high on long, tapering neck; muscular, athletic body; deep chest; flat rib cage,

definite tuck up in underline. Back has natural arch over loins and hind legs, which look slightly longer than front legs. Tail set low, scimitar-shaped, thick at base, tapers to point, reaches hocks

COLOR
Blue, sandy, or liver, or any of these colors with tan markings. Thick coat, a mixture of hard and soft hair that stands well out from skin, has tendency to curl round head and face. Profuse topknot of hair on head is lighter than body

APTITUDE
Hunting vermin, show, companion

THE BEDLINGTON TERRIER HAS a quite unique appearance that is remarkably lamblike, particularly in the woolly nature of its coat and the shape of its skull. It is also one of the "racier" of the many terrier breeds and is noted for its great turn of speed. Relatively light in frame, the Bedlington has a graceful arch to its back that has caused some to speculate on the influence of Whippet blood early in its development. It is also strongly associated with the Dandie Dinmont, which shares some characteristics and developed in a broadly overlapping area. The Bedlington is a sensitive and intelligent dog; originally bred for hunting vermin, it now makes an excellent companion animal. It is typically quiet, gentle, and comedic but also terrifically energetic and enthusiastic, and noted for its great stamina.

The breed developed in Northumberland in the northeast of England and is first mentioned in the eighteenth century. Terriers are popularly said to have been bred by gypsies and poachers for their great hunting skills. Given their turn of speed, terriers were able to catch any small game and vermin and were excellent at "going to ground" after rabbits and other prey. Many of the large estates employed gamekeepers to come in with their terriers and rid their grounds of rats, rabbits, badgers,

and even otters. The author Robert Leighton, writing at the beginning of the twentieth century in *Dogs and All About Them*, suggested that the Bedlington was a cross between the Otterhound and Dandie Dinmont; however, there is no evidence of this. Commonly, the Bedlington is thought to have developed from the Rough Coated Scotch Terrier. From these, a strain of terrier—with the characteristic woolly coat and outline of the modern Bedlington—developed in the Rothbury area. The small dogs took their name from the mining town of Bedlington near Rothbury and became popular in Northumberland.

The earliest recorded Bedlington was Old Flint who was born in 1782 and belonged to Squire Trevelyan. It was not until the 1820s that the breed was given its current name, by Joseph Aynsley, who bred his female, Phoebe, to a male dog called Piper. Both dogs traced their pedigree back to Old Flint. Another noted breeder was Thomas J. Pickett, whose dogs Tynedale and Tyneside were important in the breed foundation. The Cowney family was also instrumental, and brought Rough Coated Scotch Terriers from Scotland to Northumberland where they crossbred with local dogs.

When the first issue of the Kennel Club stud book was published in 1874 it listed thirty Bedlingtons. The first club in Britain was established in 1875 but later disbanded and reformed in 1882, when the breed standard and rules were published. This too disbanded, and a third club formed in 1887, lasting until 1892. The current club, the National Bedlington Terrier Club, is recognized worldwide, and was formed in 1893 and registered by the Kennel Club in 1898.

The first Bedlington was registered with the American Kennel Club in 1886. The Bedlington Terrier Club of America was formed in 1936; this later become the parent club of the breed. The breed was at its most popular in the United States during the 1960s when the dogs were fashionable, but registration numbers have now decreased, and the breed remains in relatively low numbers in the United States and the United Kingdom.

BORDER TERRIER
MODERN – ENGLAND/SCOTLAND BORDERS – COMMON

SIZE
Males 13–15½ lbs/females 11½–14 lbs

APPEARANCE
Alert, fearless, athletic. Head has "otterlike" appearance, broad between eyes and ears; muzzle short, dark, with a few whiskers; large, strong teeth. Dark hazel eyes with intensely intelligent expression; small, V-shaped ears set to sides of head, dropping forward. Strong, supple body, relatively narrow in frame; deep but not over-sprung ribs; relatively straight underline. Moderately short tail, thick at base, tapers to end, carried gaily when alert

COLOR
Red, grizzle, and tan, blue and tan, or wheaten. Short, dense undercoat covered by wiry, broken topcoat. Thick, loose-fitting hide

APTITUDE
Hunting fox and all vermin, agility, showing, companion

IN ITS SHORT HISTORY the Border Terrier has become the most popular truly working terrier breed. It is a small, workmanlike, rugged dog, utterly unpretentious in every way, and has a characteristic and unique "otterlike" head; it is game for any adventure and matches its enthusiasm with a loyal and affectionate temperament. The Border Terrier is characteristically obedient, highly trainable, easygoing, and thrives when integral to family life. The Border Terrier is also extremely tough, often described as "hard as nails," with tremendous endurance and an excellent length of stride for a small dog; all of these qualities can be traced to its working foundations.

The breed developed along the border areas of Northumberland and Scotland specifically to hunt foxes, although it was also used on other vermin. These wild and rugged areas are home to widespread sheep farming and equally to predators, particularly during lambing time. Foxhunting with hounds was one method of curtailing losses to foxes. However, foxes typically "go to ground," so the hound packs were augmented with terriers, who would follow the fox into its hole. In order to do this, the terrier needed to be able to keep up with the hounds and the riders on horseback and be fearless enough to confront a fox underground and persuade it to leave the hole so the hunt could continue. On a practical note, it also had to be small enough to fit down the hole but large enough to enforce its objective. The Border Terrier fulfills all these criteria and more. From a physical aspect this dog is relatively narrow in its frame, which allows it to access tight spaces, but has an excellent ground covering stride, enabling it to keep up with the hunters. It also has a hard, wiry double coat and a particularly tough and loose-fitting skin that helps to protect it when hunting. Unlike some terrier breeds that are worked alone, because of the hunting method in the Border Terrier's background, it is used to working in packs with other dogs.

Many will claim that the Border Terrier's history is ancient, which is not strictly true. The Border Terrier as a specific breed or type did not emerge until the nineteenth century. Prior to this there were terriers throughout northern England and Scotland, typically described as rough coated or smooth coated and exhibiting a vast array of physical differences. Breeding was by and large conducted purely for working ability, and types and breeds developed gradually in different areas and exhibited different characteristics. The exact heritage of the Border Terrier is not known, but it is associated with the Bedlington Terrier and the Dandie Dinmont, which developed within a broadly similar area. On a rare occasion, a Border Terrier will exhibit a soft topknot of hair, which is characteristic of the Bedlington and Dandie Dinmont breeds. The Border Terrier was often initially referred to as either the Coquetdale or Reedwater Terrier, based on the areas where they were bred. The actual name "Border" is thought not to have been in use until the 1880s.

The Border Terrier's development is largely attributed to the Robson family and to John Robson, who founded the Border Hunt in Northumberland in 1857. Robson, along with John Dodd of Catcleugh, hunted their hounds along Carter Fell, which is part of the Cheviot Hills and forms the boundary between Northumberland and Scotland, and they used small terriers in conjunction with hounds. The family bred these terriers for generations, and it was the

TENACIOUS AND SPIRITED

grandsons of these two men, Jacob Robson and John Dodd, who tried to get the Border Hunt's terriers recognized by the Kennel Club (KC). The first Border Terrier to be registered was The Moss Trooper, whose father was Jacob Robson's dog, Chip. However, The Moss Trooper was only accepted into the Any Other Variety listing with the Kennel Club, which formally rejected the Border Terrier breed in 1914. Finally, in 1920, the KC admitted the Border Terrier, and the first standard for the breed was drawn up by Jacob Robson and John Dodd. The Border Terrier Club was established, and Jasper Dodd became its first president. The breed rapidly gained in popularity and is a regular fixture in the show ring today as well as in a number of other events based on its working heritage. The Border Terrier Club (UK) has issued working certificates to dogs that have proved themselves "underground" since 1920, and breed clubs worldwide strive to maintain the working qualities of the breed.

Although there were a few Border Terriers in the United States in the first decades of the twentieth century, the American Kennel Club (AKC) first registered them in 1930. A breed standard was presented to the AKC in 1948, and the Border Terrier Club of America was formed as the parent club in 1949. It held its first specialty show in 1959 in conjunction with the Ladies Kennel Association. It also issues working and hunting certificates for the breed.

Although not as popular in the United States as in the United Kingdom, the Border Terrier is still widespread and enthusiastically supported. The first US champion was Pyxie O'Bladnoch of Diehard, who had been bred in the United Kingdom by Dr. Lilico and imported to the United States in 1937. The Diehard line became the foundation for the Border Terrier in the United States, and the first US-bred champion was CH Diehard Dandy who won his title in 1942. Dr. Merritt Pope's Ch Philabeg Red Miss became the first US-bred female champion in 1948; Dr. Pope was one of the founding members of the Border Terrier Club of America, the club's first president, and an influential figure early in the breed's US history through his Philabeg Kennels. Another of the important early kennels was the Dalquest Kennel owned by Marjorie van der Veer and Margery Harvey. Marjorie van der Veer became the first secretary of the club, a position that she held for thirty-four years.

AIREDALE TERRIER
MODERN – ENGLAND – MODERATE

SIZE
Males approx. 23 in./females smaller; weight approx. 55lbs

APPEARANCE
Muscular, lively, bold. Long, narrow, flat skull, little difference between length of skull and foreface. Small, dark eyes with intelligent expression; V-shaped, folded ears with fold above level of skull. Short, strong body; level back; deep chest; well-sprung ribs; muscular hindquarters. Tail set on high, carried gaily, of fair length and substance

COLOR
Black or grizzle saddle, topside of neck, topside of tail, all the rest tan. White hairs on chest allowed. Coat hard, dense, wiry, softer undercoat

APTITUDE
Hunting variety of game and birds, flushing, retrieving, tracking, police, military, showing, companion

THE AIREDALE TERRIER is the tallest of the many terrier breeds and is often referred to as the "king of terriers"; certainly the charismatic breed is among the most versatile of its type and has been used in a wide variety of ways since its development in the nineteenth century. There are few jobs that the Airedale is not willing to do, and over the course of time it has been used for vermin control, all types of farm work, hunting and retrieving, tracking, extensive police and military work, agility and obedience, and as a watchdog and devoted companion. It is noted for its fearless attitude and general enthusiasm for all that life has to offer; it also has a tremendous amount of character.

The breed traces to the county of Yorkshire in northern England and to the areas around the Rivers Wharfe, Calder, and Aire. It was developed by the working classes primarily as a hunting dog for vermin and small game. Surprisingly for a terrier breed, the Airedale can make an excellent retrieving dog, which further adds to its value as a hunting dog, and no doubt makes it popular among poachers. There is no record of the exact crosses that brought about the Airedale, although it is popularly attributed to the old Black and Tan Rough Terrier, which also gave rise to the modern Welsh Terrier, and the Otterhound, with further crosses to Bull Terrier and Irish Terrier. These resulted in a long-legged terrier with excellent scenting abilities, an affinity for water, and the tenacity that is typical of terrier

types. At first this dog was often referred to as either a Working, Bingley, or Waterside Terrier. It earned the latter name through the popular Yorkshire rat-hunting competitions that were held along the riverbanks. These events involved the dogs looking for "live" rat holes, often swimming from bank to bank in their search. Once they found a hole that had a rat in it—a live hole—a ferret was set loose to drive out the rat. When the rat fled into the water, the dogs would pursue it until it was caught. Points were awarded for finding the "live" hole and for the kill. These events remained popular into the 1950s.

When the dogs were introduced to the United States in the late 1800s, they were used for hunting coyotes, bobcats, and raccoons, often in conjunction with other hunting dogs. The versatility of the breed saw its popularity soar on both sides of the Atlantic. In 1879 a group of breed enthusiasts in Britain first coined the name "Airedale" for the dogs, and the British Kennel Club recognized the breed in 1886; the National Airedale Association was established in Britain in 1928. The breed first appeared in the show ring in the United States in 1881 when a dog called Bruce, imported by C. H. Mason of Bradford, Yorkshire, came to the public's attention. The Airedale Terrier Club of America was established in 1888, and it was recognized by the American Kennel Club in the same year. At this time the dogs were popular as show animals and pets but also in a sporting/hunting capacity. Some breeding lines for hunting were bred to be larger than the breed standard, particularly the Oorang line founded by Walter Lingo in Ohio. These dogs became noted as hunting dogs, but there was eventually a loss of breed type and character through breeding for size.

Airedales have particularly distinguished themselves in the service of man during wartime and owe much of their success in this capacity to Lieutenant Colonel E. H. Richardson, who established the first British war dog training center in the last years of the nineteenth century.

TENACIOUS AND SPIRITED

Richardson trained many different breeds and mongrels for military service and to fulfill a diverse range of roles. In 1904 the Russian Embassy in London approached Richardson to supply the Russian army with suitable war dogs for use during the Russo-Japanese War (1904–05). Richardson dispatched a number of Airedales to St. Petersburg, which were the first Airedales to arrive in Russia. Airedales were reintroduced in the 1920s and special Red Army service dog units were established. Today the Airedale is a popular breed in Russia and throughout Continental Europe and much of the world. The breed was also used in Germany by the military during both world wars, and extensively by the British army. Numerous accounts detail the bravery of Airedales during times of combat, in which they were used for bomb detection, message relay, search and rescue, patrolling, packing supplies, as ambulance dogs, sentries, and guards, and for rodent control. Airedales were drafted into the British police force in the early years of the twentieth century and the North Eastern Railway Police was the first force to employ dog patrols. They patrolled at night to catch "thieves, tramps, and other persons who may be sleeping out." Nearly all the other police forces followed suit, and a record from 1915 reveals that the Baltimore police force imported Airedales to the United States for patrolling.

Several US presidents, including Theodore Roosevelt (1858–1919), Woodrow Wilson (1856–1924), Warren Harding (1865–1923), and Calvin Coolidge (1872–1933), owned Airedales or Airedale crosses, which greatly popularized the breed. Of these, Harding's dog, Laddie Boy, was the best known because he frequently accompanied the president to cabinet meetings where he had his own special chair. Laddie Boy's birthday parties featured in the national press, and guests included dogs belonging to congressmen and senators. When Harding's administration was struggling, he published a fictional collection of letters between Laddie Boy and a dog named Tiger in an attempt to win public favor. Coolidge acquired one of Laddie Boy's half brothers, which later became a White House dog in 1923 when Coolidge was elected president. The Airedale Terrier is still supported worldwide and has recently started to compete in agility competitions and even in various hunt tests in the United States.

SCOTTISH TERRIER
MODERN – SCOTLAND – COMMON

SIZE
Males/females about 10 in.; weight 18–22 lbs

APPEARANCE
Short-legged, compact, powerful, bold. Long head, muzzle tapers slightly to nose; square, powerful jaw with large teeth. Small prick ears; small, dark, bright, almond-shaped eyes with piercing expression. Moderately short, muscular neck; strong, thick body; level topline. Broad, very deep chest with forechest extending in front of forelegs. Short legs with substantial bone; muscular hindquarters. Tail set high,

carried erect, can have slight curve forward, should be approximately 7 in. thick at base, tapers to point. Appearance should be of symmetry, balance without exaggeration

COLOR
Black, wheaten, or brindle of any shade such as grizzle, steel gray, sandy. May have few white/silver hairs in black or brindle coat, slight amount of white allowed on chest or chin. Outer coat hard, wiry; undercoat soft, dense

APTITUDE
Hunting vermin, showing, companion

THE SCOTTISH TERRIER, affectionately known as the Scottie, is one of the most distinctive of the many terrier breeds and has a distinguished profile. The modern Scottie, a rather different and more glamorous dog than its ancestor, has a wiry, weather-resistant coat that is allowed to grow longer around the legs and lower body, beard, and eyebrows while the rest of the body is kept trimmed. This grooming adds to the breed's unique appearance and clean-cut outline and serves as protection when hunting. Interestingly, when the US breed standard was revised in 1993, grooming was mentioned as a positive attribute for the breed because the modern Scottie grows a longer coat. This was in contrast to many Scottie breeders' views at the turn of the twentieth century, when the concept of enhancing a dog's appearance through grooming and trimming was largely rejected.

The Scottie is a small, powerful, and surprisingly agile dog given its heavy body and short legs. It was bred originally as a hunting dog and the gamekeeper's friend in the Scottish Highlands and used to rid estates of foxes, badgers, weasels, stoats, otters, rats, and any other vermin it came across. Although it has changed greatly in appearance since its early days, it has not lost its tenacious

spirit, love of digging, and excellent rodent-control abilities. The Scottie, like most terrier breeds, is an extremely "game" dog and will tackle any adventure with enthusiasm; today it is most commonly kept as a pet and makes an intelligent, charismatic companion but needs training and exercise. Throughout the centuries small, feisty terriers have been bred in large numbers by gamekeepers and farmers across Scotland for specific vermin control, with many keeping large packs of terriers with which they hunt. These dogs developed specific traits, such as pricked ears or drooping ears, longer or shorter backs, and different tail carriage and colors, and their relative geographic isolation and the difficulty of early travel meant that they maintained and evolved these unique identities. Despite this, they all share the same basic terrier characteristics of tenacity and great endurance, hunting instinct, and gameness, and all developed with working abilities at their foundation. An early reference to the terrier in Scotland was made by John Lesley, Bishop of Ross (1527–96), who wrote a history of Scotland between 1436 and 1561, referring to short dogs used for killing vermin.

Although the modern Scottie developed toward the end of the nineteenth century, its ancestors are of ancient and little documented origin, possibly first brought to Scotland by the ancient Celts or the Norsemen who had settled the Hebrides, Isle of Skye, and other Scottish islands during the eighth and ninth centuries. The vast rugged landscape of Scotland that includes highlands, lowlands, and extensive coastal areas has given rise to a variety of terrier breeds including the Scottie, Cairn, Skye, and West Highland White, all of which share similar ancestry and have been shaped by their particular environment. Many will claim the Scotch Terrier or Scottie is the oldest of these, but there is no proof.

The Scottie's ancestors are commonly thought to trace to the Black Mount range of mountains in the central Scottish Highlands and the surrounding areas, including the moorland area west of Loch Rannoch, and drawings of early terriers from this region show some similarities to the Scottie of today. By the nineteenth century, however, there was a concentrated population of terriers in the Aberdeen area, and as such they were often referred to as Aberdeen Terriers. Several figures stand out in the "modern" history of the Scottie; one of the earliest to write about the breed was Captain W. Mackie, who toured Scotland in the late 1870s and recorded the different types of terrier. He noted in his diaries that every gamekeeper in every locality considered his own terriers to be the Scotch terrier and the best in type. Mackie brought a large number of the "Scotch" terriers back to England with him and began to breed them to a type. This coincided with the rise of dog shows and the formation of the Kennel Club in 1873. At the same time, there was considerable difference of opinion over what constituted the Scottish Terrier; the debate was eventually resolved with the drawing up of a standard in 1880 by J. B. Morrison. Mackie showed his Scotch terriers with great success and by 1885 had produced Ch Dundee, one of the Scottie's foundation sires, and the champion female Ch Glengogo. Another hugely influential figure was Mr. J. H. Ludlow, who was instrumental in founding the Scottish Terrier Club of England in 1883 with a group of fellow supporters. Ludlow bred many champion Scotties, including Ch Alister who was the first significant black-coated winner, and Ch Dundee who was a foundation sire for the breed. Ludlow also owned Bonaccord to whom all present Scotties trace; he was grandfather to Ch Alister and also grandfather to Ch Kildee, a well-known show dog. Ludlow's female, Splinter II, is often regarded as the "mother of the breed" because she features at the foundation of very many Scotties.

Among the earliest Scotties imported to the United States were the male Tam Glen and the female Bonnie Belle, who were brought over by John Naylor in 1883. He continued to import the breed from Britain, including the male dogs Glenlyon and Whinstone. In 1884 Glenlyon was the sire of Dake, the first Scottish Terrier registered in the United States. He was registered with the American Kennel Register because the American Kennel Club (AKC) was in the midst of being established at this time and it was not until the following year that it accepted Scottish Terriers into its registry. Whinstone went on to become one of the

most important sires and a foundation for the breed in the United States. Whinstone was by the British Ch Alister. In 1895 the American Scottish Terrier Club was formed, but after several years it was disbanded. The Scottish Terrier Club of America, which is the parent club for the breed today, was formed in 1900 chiefly by Dr. Ewing and Mr. Mackenzie. Francis G. Lloyd, president of Brooks Brothers in New York and president of the Scottish Terrier Club of America, kept many Scotties under the Walescott prefix and was a consistent winner from the turn of the century until his death in 1920.

By the 1930s, the breed was extremely popular in both the United Kingdom and the United States, and two important British kennels—Albourne owned by Mr. Cowley and Heather Kennel owned by Robert Chapman— provided many dogs for import to the United States. Chapman was a prolific dog breeder who was also important in the Gordon Setter's modern history in the United Kingdom. It was during this period that British breeders began to produce a showier-type Scottie, with longer hair on the face and legs and a shorter body, which was sold for large sums of money to US buyers.

One of the best-known US-bred Scotties of the mid-twentieth century was Fala, who was born in 1940 and was the dearly loved pet of President Franklin D. Roosevelt (1882–1945). Fala was given to Roosevelt by his cousin, Margaret Suckling, and he became his constant companion. The dog slept in the president's bedroom and had a bone brought upstairs on a tray every day for his breakfast. He quickly won the hearts of the American public and traveled frequently with Roosevelt; he received so much fan mail that he was assigned his own secretary. When Fala died in 1952, he was buried at the feet of Roosevelt in the Hyde Park Rose Garden, New York.

Throughout the twentieth century, there has been a series of revisions to the Scottie breed standard in both the United States and the United Kingdom, and these changes have led to the appearance and character of the breed as it is seen today, with its prick ears, jaunty tail, and abundant hair on the lower body, chin, and eyebrows. Although different from its working ancestors, the Scottie, or Diehard as it is occasionally called on account of its tenacity, is a wonderful, intelligent character and an entertaining companion.

TENACIOUS AND SPIRITED

TENACIOUS AND SPIRITED

WEST HIGHLAND WHITE TERRIER

MODERN – SCOTLAND – COMMON

SIZE

Males ideal 11 in./females ideal 10 in.; weight 15–21 lbs

APPEARANCE

Small, strong, active, cheerful. Slightly domed skull; head has rounded appearance; medium-sized, wide-set, dark eyes with lively, intelligent expression; heavy eyebrows; small, pointed, erect ears set wide apart. Short, blunt muzzle tapers to black nose. Muscular neck; compact body with level topline; deep but not broad chest; strong, broad loins; relatively short legs with good bone; round feet. Relatively short, high-set tail, carried erect but never curled over back

COLOR

White. Double coated, hair hard, straight, approximately 2 in. long

APTITUDE

Hunting fox, badger, vermin, showing, companion

THE WEST HIGHLAND WHITE TERRIER, or Westie as it is affectionately known, has a relatively short history that dates to the end of the nineteenth century. Yet in little more than one hundred years, it has become a popular companion animal, noted for its lively and affectionate nature; it is also outgoing and independent, sometimes accused of stubbornness, and an enthusiastic digger and barker. It is excellent at "raising an alarm" in the event of an intrusion. Above all, the Westie is a "game" dog; it will embrace adventure, keep going all day, and tackle all types of terrain, all with characteristic enthusiasm.

This energetic, bold, and thoroughly "terrier" attitude traces to the breed's origins. The Westie was first bred for hunting aggressive prey such as fox and badger in the Scottish Highlands and will tackle all kinds of vermin. By the seventeenth century, Scotland had become home to various types of terrier with differing physical characteristics but all were rugged, enduring dogs that made fearless and proficient hunters. Different strains of terrier developed in different regions and were bred by farmers or on estates specifically for hunting and vermin control. There is evidence that many families in the western Highlands, particularly on the Isle of Skye, had kept and bred white dogs for many years. This is interesting because during the nineteenth and twentieth centuries white dogs were often considered weaker or poorer than their litter mates.

The Westie's development is popularly attributed to Colonel Edward Donald Malcolm (1837–1930), the 16th Laird of Poltalloch, who owned Duntrune Castle and the vast Poltalloch Estate on the west coast of Scotland. Colonel Malcolm cannot be solely credited with the breed's emergence because many families bred these small white terriers. However, he wrote many articles about the dogs, and it is for this reason that he is most often credited with developing the breed. There are no records documenting Colonel Malcolm's breeding program, although it is believed that Skye and Cairn Terriers formed part of it.

The breeding of the Westie may also stem from an alleged hunting incident. One of the colonel's brown terriers was mistaken for a fox or hare and shot dead, which led to him breeding white dogs. However, the same tale is also related to the foundations of Sealyham Terriers in Wales and various other breeders of terriers in the Scottish Highlands. Colonel Malcolm's terriers were typically referred to as Poltalloch Terriers after his estate. His dogs and those of other terrier breeders were bred purely for hunting, and although the Westie today likes to dig, they were not required to do this. They hunted their game up, over, and between the rocky surfaces of the Highlands and had a narrow, deep rib cage that allowed them to fit between rocks and awkward places.

Similar white terriers were also bred by the dukes of Argyll, in particular George John Douglas Campbell (1823–1900), the 8th Duke of Argyll, whose terriers were referred to as Roseneath Terriers. They took their name from Rosneath Castle (different spelling), which belonged to the duke's family. Although it is not known if the Poltalloch and Roseneath Terriers were bred together, it is clear that the two families knew each other. Equally, the two names seem to have been used interchangeably to describe the short-legged, white terriers. A further strain of similar white terriers belonged to Dr. Flaxman from Fifeshire. His terriers became known as Pittenween Terriers.

In 1905 Colonel Malcolm established the White West
Highland Terrier Club in Glasgow with a group of
supporters. He was uncomfortable that the breed was
called Poltalloch, and maintained that he was not
responsible for the breed because there had been terriers of
this type on Skye and in Argyle and the surrounding area
for many years; the colonel moved to have them renamed
with the more general nomenclature of White West
Highland Terriers. In 1906 a second club, the West
Highland White Terrier Club of England, was formed, and
at the same time the Kennel Club moved to change the
name of the breed to West Highland White Terrier; the
Kennel Club allowed dogs with Cairn and Scottish Terrier
in their pedigree to be registered as Westies until 1924. In
1907 a Westie was shown for the first time at Crufts, and
in 1908 the Kennel Club awarded challenge certificates;
the winner was Ch Morven, owned by Colin Young, Justice
of the Peace and the first Provost of Fort William.

Young's breeding program and his dogs were very
influential on the development of the Westie, and possibly
more significant than any others. He bred the first male
and female champions in the breed, and between 1907 and
1917 he bred six champions and accumulated forty-three
challenge certificates. His dog Ch Morven won twelve
challenge certificates; the only one he did not win was a
class judged by Colonel Malcolm. In 1976 the Westie Ch
Dianthus Buttons won the Best in Show award at Crufts;
the current record holder for the breed (UK) is Ch Olac
Moonpilot, who won forty-eight challenge certificates and
was Best in Show at Crufts in 1990.

The first Westies in the United States were Ch Kiltie and
Ch Rumpus Glenmohr, who were imported between 1907
and 1908 by Robert Goelet. At first the small white terriers
were known as Roseneath Terriers in the United States,
and the first US club for the breed was the Roseneath
Terrier Club established in 1908; in the same year the
breed was recognized by the American Kennel Club. In
1909 the name was changed to the West Highland White
Terrier Club of America. The first Westie to win the Best
in Show title at the Westminster Kennel Club Dog Show
in New York was Ch Wolvey Pattern of Edgerstoune, who
belonged to Constance Winant, and who took the title in
1942. Twenty years later a Westie, Ch Elfinbrook Simon
belonging to Barbara Worcester, took the title again.

IRISH TERRIER
MODERN – IRELAND – RARE

SIZE
Males ideal 18 in. and 27 lbs/ females ideal 18 in. and 25 lbs

APPEARANCE
Agile, athletic, spirited. Flat skull; long, fairly narrow head; strong jaws; black nose. Small, dark brown eyes with lively, intelligent expression; small V-shaped ears, set well on head, neatly folding forward. Topline of fold is above level of skull, ears darker than body hair. Head and neck carried proudly, small frill of hair to each side of neck. Chest deep but not too wide;, body moderately long, strong, straight. Loin slightly arched, muscular. Powerful hindquarters with long thigh and hocks near the ground. Tail set, carried high, a quarter docked

COLOR
Whole colored, bright red, golden red, red wheaten, or wheaten, some white on chest allowed. Coat dense, wiry, broken appearance with soft, fine undercoat

APTITUDE
Hunting all kinds of vermin, agility, showing, companion

THE IRISH TERRIER HAS BEEN REFERRED TO in traditional Irish writings as "the poor man's sentinel, the farmer's friend, and the gentleman's favorite," and there is perhaps no better way of defining not only this breed's great appeal but also its tremendous versatility. As with all terrier breeds, the Irish Terrier was originally developed as a working dog, primarily to rid farms, estates, and homes of rats and other vermin. The Irish Terrier is noted for its great bravery and will take on any kind of prey. It is also an efficient watchdog and loyal to family and loved ones.

Despite its working foundation, the Irish Terrier has always been in close contact with humans and was typically kept in small numbers as part of the family and home environment. This has contributed to its lovely, people-oriented nature. The Irish Terrier was also widely used in the military during World Wars I and II. Lieutenant Colonel E. H. Richardson, who established the first British war dog training center, used Irish Terriers extensively and described them as "extraordinarily intelligent, faithful, and honest. . . . Many a soldier is alive today through the effort of one of these very terriers."

References to Irish Terriers date back several hundred years in Ireland, although the nomenclature appears to have covered a wide group of sporting terriers. Diversity within the breed remained strong until the end of the nineteenth century, when the creation of a breed standard helped to produce a more consistent type. The early diversity was a result of breeding for working qualities, and as such there was variety in color as well as form. Today the Irish Terrier is only ever in shades of red to wheaten.

The Irish Terrier Club in Dublin was founded in 1879, and in the following year the controversial issue of ear cropping was addressed. Eventually the Irish Terrier Club became instrumental in the movement to ban ear cropping in all breeds in the British Isles, and a ruling was passed that all Irish Terriers born after 1889 and shown under Kennel Club rules must have uncropped ears.

There were a number of people who were of great significance to the Irish Terrier's development, among whom were George Krehl, who was editor of the magazine *Stock Keeper*, and Dr. R. B. Carey, who was secretary of the Irish Terrier Club for more than twenty-seven years. Another leading breeder was William Graham of Belfast, who did so much for the breed that the William Graham Memorial Challenge Trophy was established in 1901 in his honor.

An early winner was the female Ch Spuds, who went on to be the first well-known Irish Terrier to arrive in the United States. The first Irish Terrier to be exhibited in the United States was Kathleen, who was imported by James Watson. He showed Kathleen in 1880, and in the following year the Westminster Kennel Club Show offered classes only for Irish Terriers. The American Kennel Club recognized the Irish Terrier in 1885, and the Irish Terrier Club of America was formed in 1896. By 1929 the Irish Terrier ranked as the thirteenth most popular dog breed in the United States, and enjoyed similar popularity in the United Kingdom. In Britain the Irish Terrier Association was established in 1911. Since its heyday, the Irish Terrier has decreased in numbers and is now relatively rare in the United States and United Kingdom, although it is supported by enthusiasts around the world.

SOFT-COATED WHEATEN TERRIER
MODERN – IRELAND – MODERATE

SIZE
*Male ideal 18½ in.; 35–40 lbs/
female ideal 17½ in.; 30–35 lbs*

APPEARANCE
*Strong, hardy, squarish in outline,
distinctive coat. Rectangular-
shaped, moderately long head;
powerful muzzle; large, black
nose. Slightly almond-shaped,
dark reddish-brown or brown
eyes, set well apart; small to
medium ears that fold forward*

*with topline level with skull.
Compact, strong body; level back;
deep chest; well-sprung ribs; tail
set on high, docked, carried at 90°
to back*

COLOR
*Any shade of wheaten. Abundant,
soft, silky, single coat, gently wavy*

APTITUDE
*Hunting all kinds of vermin,
herding, watchdog, agility,
companion*

THE SOFT-COATED WHEATEN TERRIER (SCWT) was only recognized as a distinct breed in the twentieth century, but the foundations of this charming and characterful breed stretch back many hundreds of years. From very early on it seems that there were two clear groups of dogs: those that belonged to the aristocracy and those that belonged to the farmers and peasants. Over the years a type of general purpose, working farm dog of unknown heritage developed, and it is from these that the SCWT came about.

This general purpose requirement at the dog's foundation has greatly contributed to the SCWT's special characteristics and temperament. Although this dog possesses all the tenacity, intelligence, and plucky nature of the terrier breed, the SCWT is also calmer in temperament and suited to working in and around livestock. In January 2012 an American SCWT, Molly, owned by Linda Hallas, became the first of her breed to earn an American Kennel Club (AKC) Herding Title at the Mid-Florida Australian Cattle Dog Fanciers Herding Trials. It is a truly versatile dog and able to fulfill all the necessary roles on a small farm, and has even been trained as a retrieving dog.

The SCWT is one of three long-legged terrier breeds native to Ireland—the others are the Kerry Blue and the Irish Terrier—and doubtlessly the three share common roots. The fourth Irish terrier breed is the Glen of Imaal, which is a shorter-legged breed.

The SCWT, Kerry Blue, and Irish Terrier were closely interrelated at their foundation, and in the nineteenth century, with the rise of dog shows, all three breeds were exhibited in the same class for "Irish Terriers." The SCWT was the last of the three Irish terrier breeds to gain official recognition, and was accepted by the Irish Kennel Club in 1937. The breed made its debut in the Irish Kennel Club Championship Show on St. Patrick's Day, March 17, 1938; in the same year its breed club was established in Ireland. For many years the breed was required to qualify in field trials over rat, rabbit, and badger before being able to attain championship standard.

From the 1950s the SCWT began to be bred away from the original Irish type. This is seen most clearly in the development of an increasingly heavy coat, which is particularly popular in the United States. Understandably, this upset Irish breeders of the original Irish type of SCWT, and currently some breeders are turning back to the original type. In England and Ireland emphasis is placed on a natural appearance of the coat, although trimming is allowed to produce a clean outline. Greater emphasis on trimming and styling is seen in the United States.

In 1946 seven SCWT puppies were imported to Boston. Two of these were owned by Lydia Vogel of Massachusetts, who went on to show and breed her dogs, although they did not become popular for another ten years. In the late 1950s the Arnold family from Connecticut imported Gad's Hill and Holmenocks Hallmark from Ireland as foundation dogs for their Sunset Hills Kennels, and at the same time the O'Connor family from New York purchased Holmenocks Gramachree from Maureen Holmes and founded their Gramachree Kennels. The Soft-Coated Wheaten Club of America was formed on St. Patrick's Day in 1962. The breed was accepted for registration by the AKC in 1973 and has continued to grow in popularity in the United States. The breed is also found in conservative numbers across the world.

WIRE FOX TERRIER
MODERN – ENGLAND – MODERATE

SIZE

Males 15½ in./females slightly less; maximum weight 18 lbs

APPEARANCE

Playful, agile, keen. Top of skull almost flat, head no wider than 3½ in., ideally 7–7¼ in. long in males, less in females. Dark, moderately small, rather deep-set eyes with alert, intelligent expression. Small, neat, V-shaped ears with flaps neatly folded over. Topline of folded ear well above level of skull. Neck of fair length with graceful curve when viewed from side. Short, level back; slightly arched loins. Chest deep, not broad. Straight front legs; round, compact feet. Strong, muscular hindquarters; long thighs with hock joints well bent, close to ground. Tail set, carried high, not over back, quarter of length docked

COLOR

White should predominate, brindle, red, liver, or slate blue are objectionable. Otherwise, color of little or no importance. Coat broken, dense, wiry

APTITUDE

Hunting all types of vermin

UNTIL THE LATE TWENTIETH CENTURY Wire Fox Terriers and Smooth Fox Terriers were considered two different types of a single breed, although they are now recognized as separate breeds. There is much debate over their origins; some people believe that the two developed from similar roots, while others maintain that their origins are different. There is in fact no definitive answer, and for many years both the Wire and the Smooth were bred together, although this is now discouraged. The Smooth became more popular more quickly in show classes, but the Wire has now become the more prolific show winner of the two in the United States, and has taken a record thirteen Best in Show awards at the Westminster Kennel Club Show. Both the Smooth and the Wire are very lively, intelligent, and charismatic dogs that excel in agility, obedience, and earth dog classes, and make loyal, loving companions. Both retain their inherent "terrier" aptitude for hunting small vermin and "going to ground."

The Wire developed during the nineteenth century specifically as a working breed and primarily to augment fox hunts through its ability to go to ground after foxes, although it was also used on badgers, otters, rabbits, and other vermin. This fearless dog will hunt any vermin underground yet also has a remarkable turn of speed above ground. It was useful in alerting huntsmen to occupied fox holes by pinpointing them and standing beside them barking. The breed is thought to have developed through a combination of smooth and rough-coated Black and Tan Terriers, Bull Terriers, Greyhounds, and Beagles, although there are no records of its earliest emergence. A particularly interesting account of the Wire Fox Terrier appeared in *A History and Description of the Modern Dogs of Great Britain and Ireland* (1897), by Rawden Briggs Lee. From Lee's account it appears that the early Wires were seen in several colors, including blue grizzle, red, fawn, and pepper and salt, as well as black and tan, and it was not until toward the end of the nineteenth century that the vogue for predominantly white dogs with either black, tan, or black and tan markings arose. Today any color other than these are unacceptable for show ring purposes. It is believed that the Wire was bred with the Smooth to improve the predominance of white in the former and also to refine the Wire's general appearance.

Early illustrations from the beginning of the nineteenth century that depict terriers in relation to fox hunts show wire-haired black and tan dogs that are very similar in appearance to the modern Wire Fox Terrier, which indicates the influence of the Old Black and Tan Terrier in the breed's formation. One of the earliest references that differentiates the Wire and the Smooth appeared in the *Encyclopedia of Rural Sports* (1840), by Delabere Blaine. He describes two varieties of terrier with the Wire, or rough-coated, predominantly bred in the north of England and Scottish borders. Early authors also reference the introduction of both Bulldog and Bull Terrier blood to the working terrier to increase its bravery; early illustrations reveal the influence of the Bull Terrier, particularly in the shape of the head and characteristic patch markings over the eyes. The most concentrated breeding of the Wire took place in the Midlands and north of England, Durham, and

Yorkshire, although they were also bred across the country including in Devon, where they were kept by Reverend John Russell, a major influence in developing the Jack Russell Terrier. A journalist known as Robin Hood and writing for *The Field* magazine described a wire-coated terrier that was part of the Quorn hunt pack when Sir Richard Sutton was Master. This dog, with its long head, rough coat, and "ferocity of a lion" twinned with the "gentleness of a lamb," is said to have greatly contributed to the development of the Wire Fox Terrier in the Midlands through his stud duties.

The first class specifically for Fox Terriers was held in 1862 at the Islington Agricultural Hall at the North of England Second Exhibition of Sporting and Other Dogs. There were twenty entries, and the class was won by a dog called Trimmer, who was described as "workmanlike." The same year there was a class for smooth-coated terriers at the Birmingham National Exhibition. After this the Smooth Fox Terrier become very popular as a show competitor, but the Wire was rarely seen in the show ring for a further twenty years. The Fox Terrier Club in Britain was formed in 1876 to "foster, encourage and develop" what was at that time the most popular of the terrier breeds. The club oversees both Wire and Smooth Fox Terriers and drew up the breed standard the same year; barring a slight change in weight the standard has hardly changed. The Wire and Smooth were not judged separately until 1883 when there was a tie for the Grand Challenge Cup between Wire Briggs and Smooth Spice. Spice eventually took the cup, and after this a separate Grand Challenge Cup was established for the Wire and the Smooth. The Wire Fox Terrier Association was incorporated in 1913 and the Smooth Fox Terrier Association in 1932.

The Smooth Fox Terrier arrived in the United States in 1879, followed several years later by the first imports of Wire Fox Terriers. The American Fox Terrier Club (AFTC) was formed in 1885, the same year that the Fox Terrier was recognized by the American Kennel Club. The two varieties were not divided into two separate breeds until 1985. The AFTC adopted the British breed standard and based its own on this. Although the Fox Terrier became popular during the mid-twentieth century, it is now much more conservative in numbers in both the United States and United Kingdom, and the Wire is more popular than the Smooth.

PARSON RUSSELL TERRIER/JACK RUSSELL

MODERN – BRITAIN – COMMON

SIZE
Males ideal 14 in./females ideal 13 in.; weight 13–17 lbs

APPEARANCE
Confident, alert, strong. Skull flat, broad between ears; strong, rectangular muzzle; powerful jaws; large teeth. Almond-shaped, dark eyes; small V-shaped ears drop forward neatly with fold level or just above topline of skull. Moderately arched neck of fair length; square, balanced body; topline level with slight arch over loins. Strong, flexible back.

Narrow chest, of moderate depth, compressible. Tail docked, set level with topline, carried gaily or on horizontal

COLOR
Predominantly white with black or tan markings, or combination, moderate body markings or grizzle allowed, brindle not allowed. Coat smooth or broken, hairs harsh, close, dense

APTITUDE
Fox bolting, agility, showing, companion

THE LIVELY AND FRIGHTENINGLY CLEVER Parson Russell Terrier was developed in Britain around 200 years ago specifically to prevent red foxes going to ground, or to drive them out of their holes once they had. It has developed a number of characteristics that are suited to this endeavor, which the breed has retained to the present day. These include its narrow and flexible chest, which allows the dog to maneuver in tight spaces underground, endless energy, an athletic frame with good stride, great strength and endurance for digging after the fox, and a persistent bark to alert the huntsmen to its whereabouts both above and below ground. Although the Parson Russell Terrier makes an excellent companion, it will also dig and bark and requires frequent exercise and diversions.

The origins of the Parson Russell Terrier trace to the nineteenth century to the parson (Reverend) John Russell, after whom the breed was named. John Russell was born in 1795, the son of a clergyman who was also a fanatical fox hunter. Russell grew up with a love of hunting and hunting dogs. This was during a period when foxhunting in Britain was reaching an ascendency thanks to the development of faster, more agile hounds by Hugo Meynell (1735—1808). These hounds increased the pace of the hunt, and the British people were enthralled. Terriers, collectively

referred to as fox terriers, were used with hounds to locate fox holes down which the fox had bolted, to alert the huntsmen, and to "persuade" the fox to leave the hole so the pursuit might continue. According to Russell's memoirs, in 1819 he bought a terrier called Trump, who became the matriarch of Russell's own line of fox terriers.

In 1826 Russell moved to Devon, southern England, where he continued to hunt and breed his dogs. By this time he had established his own pack of Fox Hounds and Fox Terriers, and Russell himself became known as the "sporting parson." His Fox Terriers were legendary and tenacious, and predominantly white. This coloring meant that the terriers were easily distinguished from the red fox and were not set upon by the hounds.

After the advent of dog shows in 1859, Russell became a noted judge of terriers and hounds; he also became a founding member of the Kennel Club, established in 1873. As dog shows became increasingly popular, there began to be a divergence in the Fox Terrier between the showier dogs that were bred for the ring and the working stock bred for hunting, characterized by Russell's own. The Fox Terrier Club was established in 1876; this club is still the parent club for Fox Terriers (Smooth and Wire) in Britain. Russell died in 1883, and his friend, Arthur Heinemann, took over as the true working breed's major supporter. In 1894 Heinemann set up the Devon and Somerset Badger Club, later changed to the Parson Jack Russell Terrier Club, to preserve the original type of terrier. He drew up a breed standard in which the ideal height of the dogs was 14 inches (13 inches for females); this height later became crucial in the ensuing controversies over the breed.

The Smooth Fox Terrier became popular both in the show ring and as a pet during the first two-thirds of the twentieth century, although tragically today they are listed as "rare" by the Kennel Club. The more rugged Russell Terrier was seen far less often in the public forum but was widespread among the farming community and with

huntsmen. Gradually, any small, white-colored terrier became referred to as a Jack Russell, and many of these began to be bred to be shorter in the leg. They became popular after World War II as companion dogs and were all generically called Jack Russells; the original longer-legged terrier type was in danger of disappearing. In the 1970s a number of clubs were formed to protect the Jack Russell and set height standards between 10 and 15 inches to take account of the great diversity in the dogs; the Jack Russell Terrier Club of Great Britain, formed in 1974, still looks after the interests of Jack Russell Terriers within this wide height range. This caused consternation among the proponents of the original Parson Jack Russell, whose height was approximately 14 inches. In 1983 the Parson Jack Russell Terrier Club was resurrected, and the members strove for Kennel Club acceptance for the original type of terrier. Finally, in 1990, the Parson Jack Russell Terrier standard was accepted by the Kennel Club; in 1999 the breed name was changed to the Parson Russell Terrier.

The Jack Russell Terrier Club of America (JRTCA) was formed in 1876 and adopted Heinemann's original breed standard, which advocated the longer-legged, original working variety. The JRTCA was opposed to American Kennel Club (AKC) recognition because it wished to keep the breed away from the show ring and true to its working roots. However, in 1985 a group of breeders established the Jack Russell Terrier Breeders Association (JRTBA) to promote the same type of terrier but through AKC affiliation. The AKC recognized the Jack Russell Terrier in 2000, and in 2003 the breed name was changed to the Parson Russell Terrier to reflect the established breed in Britain; at the same time the JRTBA name was changed to the Parson Russell Terrier Association of America (PRTAA). Today, there is still friction between this association and the JRTCA. Ironically, it is the short-legged variety of the Jack Russell that appears to have won the public's heart, certainly in the United States where they are affectionately referred to as "Shorties." These small dogs are below the height standards for the JRTCA and PRTAA, but they have their own group of supporters. In 1996 the English Rustler's Terrier Club was formed to preserve these dogs and was replaced by the English Jack Russell Terrier Club Alliance in 1999. The short-legged "Russell Terrier" is now in the AKC Miscellaneous breed grouping.

CHAPTER 8
DEVOTED AND LOYAL

Archaeological evidence and artistic representations indicate a number of different early types of dog: the versatile spitz types, sight hounds, mastiff types, mountain dogs, and various hound types were all used for a variety of important purposes. Since the earliest times, dogs have provided companionship in one form or another to humans as working dogs, hunting dogs, guard dogs, or draft dogs. Often these same dogs shared the homes and hearths of their owners around the world once the working day was over. History has revealed, however, that there was another type of dog of ancient origin that was totally different in form and function and who not only shared the hearth, but also crept into bed with their owners. These were small, and sometimes even tiny, dogs whose main role in life was to provide comfort, companionship, and entertainment. Evidence of these dogs traces back at least 2,500 years to Asia and the Mediterranean, although their history may extend further back. They were bred for their small size and amiable nature, and became the playthings of emperors and those who were wealthy enough to afford the luxury of an animal that did not earn its keep. This is, in fact, a little unfair because these small dogs of various types did perform a myriad of jobs from catching, or at least deterring, rats to providing a measure of personal protection to their owner.

Images from Ancient Greece and Rome that date to c. 500 B.C.E. show small dogs that are similar in appearance to the modern Maltese. These dogs were frequently referenced in ancient literature, and Aristotle used the name *Melitaei Catelli* and compared them to a small weasel in around 370 B.C.E. Early in the first century C.E. the Greek historian Strabo suggested that they originated from the Mediterranean island of Malta and wrote of the noble women of his time favoring the dogs; other sources have linked the Maltese to the Tibetan Terrier.

It was in ancient Tibet and China that the breeding of companion dogs reached an ascendency, which continued to the end of the nineteenth century. The Chinese philosopher Confucius (c. 551–479 B.C.E.) is said to have described short-legged, "short-mouthed dogs" with long tails and ears. They were also referred to as *ha pa* or "under the table" dogs. The tables were approximately 8 to 10 inches (20 to 25 cm) high to allow for people sitting on the ground, which indicates how small these dogs were. In Tibet the tiny dogs were associated with the Buddhist monasteries and bred by the monks. Their origins are bound to the myths and legends of the area and religion, particularly to the lion, which is an important Buddhist symbol. The little dogs were bred to resemble lions and became known collectively as lion dogs. They were sent as gifts by the dalai lamas to the Chinese emperors and were popular in the imperial Chinese palaces; with the spread of Buddhism from Tibet to China they continued their association with monasteries and as lion dogs.

These tiny dogs, which included the Shih Tzu, Lhasa Apso, Pekingese, and Pug, were small enough to fit inside the sleeves of imperial garments and became known as "sleeve dogs." They were secreted within the sleeve and were a formidable personal alarm should an unsuspecting person come too close to the emperor. The dogs lived in great luxury and were utterly pampered; in return they provided constant, loyal, and loving companionship, kept the imperial corridors free from rats, and were used in ceremonial processions. Often the emperor would be preceded by little dogs wearing bells and ribbons that were trained to bark to announce his presence. Other dogs are said to have held the train of the imperial garments in their mouths. Although these dogs were closely guarded by the imperial palace and were not for public sale, many of them were smuggled and sold to wealthy individuals; others given as gifts. The opening of trade routes and the establishment of the Silk Road that began in the Han Dynasty (206 B.C.E.–220 C.E.) saw the exchange of produce, and dogs of various type were distributed throughout Central Asia and into Europe.

Small, companion dogs were popular across the royal households of Europe, and Toy Spaniels were particularly prevalent. Pets of all kinds, and dogs in particular, were favored by the royal houses and traded between them as gifts. It has been suggested that these animals were provided for young royal children as companions (they had few others); almost without exception in Britain future monarchs were raised in the presence of pets, notably dogs. It could be argued that these loving and devoted creatures provided the most secure and trustworthy relationship for any royal; several unfortunate British royals were accompanied all the way to their execution by their pet dogs. Small, companion dogs were not the sole preserve of European royalty, but were, historically, most associated with the aristocracy and the wealthy. The little dogs would provide warmth at night and frequently slept in bed with their owners; they were often referred to as "comforters" and were used by ladies as hand or feet warmers. An old wives tale attributes them some degree of healing powers, and their body warmth was said to relieve joint aches and indigestion, as well as anxiety and neurosis. They were also said to be good at attracting fleas away from their owners and onto themselves.

Small dogs were favored by ladies, but were also popular with men: both King Charles I and II were great enthusiasts of little dogs, particularly Spaniels. Alongside their association with the aristocracy, small dogs of various type have also had a long history with courtesans and prostitutes. The French Bulldog was a great favorite within both these sectors of life and became a must-have accessory. The fickle hand of fashion has often played a role in the history of small companion breeds, most recently led by the film industry and advertising. Small dogs have been "de rigueur" among Hollywood's finest for many years. However, sudden surges in popularity are not always in a breed's best interests. Excessive demand can lead to unscrupulous breeding, over-producing, and the use of inferior stock to make a quick profit. Equally, trends for exaggerated features, such as greatly reduced size, over-flattened faces, and excessively

domed skulls have caused serious health issues in some breeds and continue to cause great controversy.

Although many breeds have been bred as companion dogs, others have developed gradually. The Standard Poodle was originally used primarily as a water retrieving bird dog, whereas the Miniature Poodle was prized as a truffle-hunting dog. Both types were employed in circuses, yet today they are chiefly companion dogs. The Dalmatian was prized as a carriage dog and used extensively by the fire service in the United States for clearing the way for horse-drawn fire trucks and for guarding fire houses. The elegant Yorkshire Terrier was once employed throughout much of northern England ridding mills and factories of rats.

Dogs as companions provide immeasurable comfort, humor, entertainment, solace, and dependability: qualities that greatly enrich our lives. Although any breed of dog can be a companion, some are more suited to the role.

SHIH TZU

ANCIENT – TIBET/CHINA – COMMON

SIZE	
Males/females 9–10½ in.; weight 9–16 lbs	than height at withers. Legs have good bone substance, jaunty gait. Tail heavily plumed, set high, carried curved over back
APPEARANCE	**COLOR**
Compact, solid, lively, proud. Broad, round head; wide-set, large, dark, round eyes with friendly, alert expression. Short, square-shaped muzzle; undershot jaw. Large, heavily coated ears, set just below level of crown. Head carried high; compact body with overall impression of balance. Topline level; body slightly longer	Any color. Outer coat long, dense, flowing, slight wave allowed. Moderate undercoat. Hair grows upward on bridge of nose contributing to characteristic "chrysanthemum" look, hair on top of head tied up
	APTITUDE
	Showing, companion

THE SHIH TZU IS A LIVELY, PLAYFUL, and intelligent breed that has a long and somewhat regal history; this little dog was one of the favored pets of Chinese emperors during the Qing Dynasty (1644–1912) and was often given as an imperial gift. Fittingly, the Shih Tzu has an imperial air about it and is typically a proud, confident breed with a cheerful countenance and a bold approach to life. Although the Shih Tzu is a small and beautiful lapdog, it is unafraid to sound the alarm, which it will do with vigor.

The history of this extroverted dog is long, controversial, and unsubstantiated in parts. It is most commonly traced to the wilds of Tibet, where it was kept as a domestic pet alongside the much larger Tibetan Mastiff, which was used as a guard dog. Accounts indicate that the small, long-haired pet aided the Mastiff types by vigorously sounding the alarm if intruders were present and was expected to know the difference between friends and family, and unwanted guests. The small dog was often called Tibetan Lion Dog, based on its appearance—the (Mandarin) name Shih Tzu loosely translates as "little lion"—and is popularly associated with the ancient Buddhist monasteries. It is thought that Buddhist monks bred small dogs to resemble lions, because the lion is an important Buddhist symbol and is believed to bring luck. A Buddhist legend recounts that the Buddha Manjusri, the God of Learning, always

traveled with a small lion dog who would turn into a full-sized lion and transport him on his back over vast distances. Lions were not in fact indigenous to Tibet and China, although some were imported at an early date. The little dog therefore came to be the closest representation of the much admired animal.

Despite the remoteness of Tibet, the little lion dogs made their way into China, sent as gifts from the Dalai Lama to the Chinese emperors, and it is in the imperial palaces that they began to develop. The dogs, the smallest of the Tibetan "holy dogs," were greatly admired by the Manchu emperors of the Qing Dynasty, who bred them in large numbers. Other small dogs, particularly the Pekingese and Chinese Pug, were also kept at the palaces, and it is likely that these were crossbred. However, the Shih Tzu also developed away from its ancestor in Tibet, the Tibetan Lion Dog, and these eventually developed into the Lhasa Apso. Although related, the Shih Tzu and the Lhasa Apso have very different characteristics. Within the Chinese imperial palaces, the Shih Tzu was often referred to as an "under the table" dog, because of its small size, and as a "sleeve dog," because it was small enough to be carried in the wide sleeves of garments worn by the elite. It was also associated with the "Foo" dog, which were lionlike images that were typically placed outside temples as guardians. Within the palaces it was the job of the eunuchs to breed and raise the small dogs and to create the most beautiful types to meet the emperor's approval. The flattened nose was much appreciated, and this was selectively bred for. In order to reproduce certain characteristics it is clear that some heavy inbreeding was practiced.

The "modern" Shih Tzu's history began in the nineteenth century and at the hands of the formidable dowager empress Cixi (T'zu Hsi), China's most powerful political figure of the time. She was a great dog lover and kept imperial breeding kennels where she raised Pugs, Pekingese, and Shih Tzu; she is credited with paying

DEVOTED AND LOYAL

special attention to family lines and color. It is not known whether palace staff crossbred any of these three breeds together, although it would seem likely that they did. Her dogs gained considerable fame during her lifetime but after her death in 1908 the kennels were dispersed and the dogs sold to individual breeders or given away as gifts. The Shih Tzu and Lhasa Apso were frequently grouped together as one breed and referred to as Lhasa Lion Dog, Lhasa Terrier, Lion Dog, or Shih Tzu Kou, and it seems that records were not kept. The situation worsened with the Chinese Revolution (1911–12), which saw the Qing Dynasty overthrown and the establishment of the Republic of China.

The Chinese Kennel Club was formed in 1923 and the Peking Kennel Club in 1934, but it was not until 1938 that a breed standard for the Shih Tzu Lion Dog was drawn up. By this time, however, a few of the dogs had made it outside their country. In 1928 Lady Brownrigg, who was instrumental in establishing the Shih Tzu in the West, brought two Shih Tzu back to England with her from a trip to China. These two were the male Hibou and the female Shu-ssa. In 1933 Mrs. Hutchins from Ireland procured another called Lung-fu-ssa. These three dogs and Lady Brownrigg's Taishan Kennels were of great importance in establishing the breed. At first the Kennel Club would not differentiate between the Shih Tzu and the Lhasa Apso but eventually supporters of both breeds were able to have them recognized separately, and in 1934 the Tibetan Lion Dog Club was formed and a breed standard drawn up; in 1935 the club name was changed to the Shih Tzu Club. By 1939 more than one hundred Shih Tzu had been registered. In that same year Gay Widdrington became involved with the breed. She later established the Lhakang Kennels, which were well known for their Shih Tzu. She operated strict selective breeding with the introduction of new Shih Tzu blood to her stock in order to keep the gene pool at a healthy level and to try to prevent hereditary illnesses.

As the breed became more established in Britain, it began to suffer in China, particularly during the civil war of 1948 to 1952 when dog breeding ground to a halt, and many dogs were killed. By the end of the war the Shih Tzu was extinct in its homeland. Luckily, eight dogs had been imported to Britain and a further three had gone to Norway, prior to their demise in China. However, this overlapped with the war years in Britain, and World War II saw the end of breeding programs for several years. By the end of the war the numbers of Shih Tzu in Britain and Europe were reduced, and breeders had to work hard to reestablish them. In 1952 Freda Evans, a Pekingese breeder, introduced Peke blood to the Shih Tzu to try to improve on some faults that had appeared as a result of the small gene pool. The progeny of this breeding was then bred back to pure Shih Tzu a number of times, thus diluting the Pekingese influence. This move was very controversial, and many people believed that it undermined their efforts to have the Shih Tzu recognized as a pure breed. The Kennel Club would only accept dogs that had Pekingese in their lines once they had passed four generations, and in the United States the American Kennel Club (AKC) maintained that seven generations had to pass before a Shih Tzu carrying Pekingese blood was accepted. Despite this, a large proportion of Shih Tzu today trace to this Pekingese both in Britain and the United States. By the 1960s a number of top kennels were breeding Shih Tzu in Britain.

A few Shih Tzu are thought to have been imported to the United States during the late 1930s, but it was not until the early 1950s that they began to be imported in any number. US servicemen were instrumental in bringing the breed to the United States, having come across them when stationed at US air bases in Britain. The first to establish breeding kennels were Maureen Murdock and her nephew Philip Price, who imported two Shih Tzu from Britain in 1954; the following year the AKC entered the breed in its Miscellaneous category. The Shih Tzu Club of America was formed in 1957, and by 1960 there were three clubs for the breed, which indicated how quickly it was becoming popular. By 1961 more than a hundred Shih Tzu were registered in the United States—a surprisingly large number given their short history—but by 1964 this figure had risen to more than 400. The Shih Tzu Club of America and the Texas Shih Tzu Society merged in 1963 to form the American Shih Tzu Club, responsible for all the records of the breed. In 1969 the Shih Tzu became the AKC's 116th recognized breed and was placed in the Toy Group. The breed immediately won championship titles across the United States, and its popularity soared; today it regularly ranks in the top ten most popular breeds in the United States and is similarly favored in the United Kingdom.

LHASA APSO

ANCIENT – TIBET – COMMON

SIZE
Males 10–11 in./females slightly smaller; weight 12–18 lbs

APPEARANCE
Small, long coated, confident, joyful. Narrow skull, not quite flat; head covered with profusion of heavy hair particularly whiskers and beard. Straight foreface; medium-sized dark eyes; black nose; heavily feathered ears. Body is longer than height at withers; well ribbed up with strong loins. Front and hind legs heavily furnished with hair; round, catlike feet. Well-feathered tail carried over back in a screw

COLOR
Any color, with or without dark tips to ears and beard. Hard coat of good length, heavy, straight, and very dense

APTITUDE
Showing, watchdog, companion

THE LHASA APSO WAS DEVELOPED in Tibet hundreds of years ago. Given the remoteness of this wild land, the Lhasa Apso developed relatively uninfluenced by other dog types. The dog's development is largely bound to the Buddhist monasteries of Tibet where it was bred and cared for; this association with the monasteries led to the dogs being revered among the local villages. In Tibet the dog is said to have evolved from wolves living in the Himalayas and made its way to the monasteries, encouraged by offerings of food. This small dog is certainly a product of its harsh environment. It is tough and sturdy and has a long, dense, and highly insulating coat with long facial hair that protects its eyes from cold, wind, and snow glare.

The Lhasa Apso was historically kept indoors where it was a useful watchdog and provided a backup alarm to the Tibetan Mastiff, which was generally kept outside. Tibetans believed dogs to be living representations of the mythical Tibetan Snow Lion or Kang Seng, who appears on the traditional Tibetan flag. There is an ancient saying, "When the snow lion is in the mountains, it is a snow lion; if it comes down to the plains, it becomes a dog."

The Lhasa Apso is friendly, loyal, and playful with those whom it knows and loves but has a highly protective streak and is able to distinguish rapidly between individuals it knows, those it does not know, and those whom it perceives as a threat. It is typically reserved with strangers and will bark vigorously if its territory is intruded upon by a potential threat. The breed is also highly intelligent and has acute hearing. Its Western name derives from the capital of Tibet, Lhasa, where the dogs were bred in the highest numbers. Apso is thought to derive from either its native name or from the Tibetan words *ara* meaning "mustache" and *sog-sog* meaning "hairy."

It is generally accepted that the Lhasa Apso was bred and raised primarily within the many Buddhist monasteries and in the homes of Tibet's most wealthy. The dogs were considered very lucky and were given as highly esteemed gifts but never (allegedly) sold. It was seen as a great honor to receive one of the special dogs, and they were occasionally given to foreign dignitaries by the Dalai Lama. It was through the Dalai Lama's gifts that the dogs were first seen outside their native Tibet. From the seventeenth century they were often given to Chinese emperors.

In the early years of the breed's emergence in the West there was great confusion between the small, exotic Eastern breeds, most particularly between the Lhasa Apso and the Tibetan Terrier. The first standard for the Lhasa Terrier (also known as the Lhasa Apso) appeared in 1897. The Tibetan Breed Association was formed in 1934 to distinguish between the different breeds, and in the same year a proper breed standard was drawn up for the newly named Lhasa Apso; distinction had been made between the Tibetan Terrier and Lhasa Apso in India in 1931.

Some of the first Lhasa Apso in the United States were gifts from the 13th Dalai Lama to the naturalist C. Suydam Cutting of New Jersey in 1934. In 1935 the American Kennel Club recognized the breed. World War II affected the development of the breed, but after the war breeders renewed their efforts, and numbers increased. Cutting's Hamilton Farm Kennels were sold to Mrs. Dorothy Cohen who was influential in the Lhasa Apso development in the United States. The American Lhasa Apso Club was established in 1959, and the dogs are now popular companion animals and also make good agility candidates.

PEKINGESE

ANCIENT – CHINA – COMMON

SIZE	slightly longer than height at
Males/females 6–9 in.; weight less than 14 lbs	withers. Straight topline; underline rises from deep chest to
APPEARANCE	lighter loin to form narrow waist.
Solid, regal, bold. Massive, broad, flat skull (in balance to body), appears broader than long from front. Wide-set, dark, large, round eyes; aloof or bold expression. Heart-shaped ears, heavily feathered, lying flat. Flat, broad muzzle, with wrinkle extending over bridge of nose in inverted V-shape. Broad, black nose; undershot lower jaw. Compact, pear-shaped body, appears heavier on front end than hindquarters; low to ground;	*Heavily feathered tail, set high, slightly arched, carried over back. Wide-set, short, sturdy forelegs, moderately bowed. Hind legs reasonably close together, of lighter bone than front*
	COLOR
	Any color. Double coated. Topcoat long, coarse, straight, stands out, undercoat softer. Coat forms cape around shoulders, feathering on ears, tail, legs, toes
	APTITUDE
	Showing, companion

EXOTIC MYTHS AND LEGENDS SURROUND the early history of the Pekingese, a breed with ancient, regal, and spiritual associations. Although the modern Pekingese is a very different dog in physical appearance from its ancestors, it has retained its aloof and dignified character. It is a loyal dog and devoted to its loved ones, but at the same time it can be independent in nature and occasionally stubborn.

The history of the Pekingese is believed to trace back to around 500 B.C.E., when there is evidence of short, muzzled dogs in China. By around 200 B.C.E. trade routes had opened between China and the West that saw produce traded between Rome, Egypt, the Middle East, Tibet, and China. It is speculated that the small, flat-faced dogs in China were influenced by Maltese dogs that had arrived from Rome. These small dogs were kept primarily as pets, although they were also capable of ferocity and were useful watchdogs. They were associated with the wealthiest strata of society, because pets were an unaffordable luxury for most.

The Chinese philosopher Confucius (c. 551–479 B.C.E.) is said to have described short-legged, "short-mouthed dogs" with long tails and ears. They were also described as *ha pa* or "under the table" dogs; tables at that time were often only

8 to 10 inches (20–25 cm) high to allow for people sitting on the ground, which indicates that the dogs were very small. Even smaller ones called "sleeve dogs" were bred. These were secreted within the wide sleeves of garments worn by the wealthy and were used as a form of personal protection. These tiny dogs were ferocious when provoked.

The dogs were specifically bred to have the appearance of miniature lions, a tradition that traces to Buddhism. Buddhism developed in India during the fifth century B.C.E., and much of its spiritual symbolism involves animals common to that country. The lion became one of the most important Buddhist symbols, and many legends surrounding the religion also involve this animal. One recounts how Buddha would ride his tame lion up into the sky and from his fingertips would produce hundreds of tiny lions that would gather as if they were one and protect him from his enemies. Buddhism gradually spread into Tibet and China from 1 to 400 C.E. and, with it, the symbol of the lion. Lions did not live in China or Tibet, so the people had to create a stylized form of the great beast. One legend suggests that the Chinese Emperor Ming Ti (28–75 C.E.) had a number of small *ha pa* dogs, which a member of court thought resembled lions; the dogs were trimmed to make them even more lionlike and suddenly the emperor was accompanied by one of the great Buddhist symbols, leading to the specialized breeding of the "lion dogs."

The little lion dogs were very much the preserve of the emperors and elite society, and their stylized image appears in many sacred works of art and sculptures. These were later known as "Fu" or "Foo" dogs and were placed in pairs at the entrance to Buddhist temples or crafted as small, lucky amulets. Folklore sprang up surrounding the lion dogs, including one that relates how Buddha's celestial lion approached him one day and told him of his love for a female marmoset. The marmoset was terrified by the lion's great size, and so he beseeched Buddha to make him smaller so that he might be with his beloved lady. Buddha

DEVOTED AND LOYAL

agreed and told the lion that he would make his body small but that his spirit and courage would remain as it was. The lion married the marmoset, and it is said that their offspring gave rise to the lion dogs.

It was during the Tang Dynasty (618–907 C.E.) that the lion dogs really gained ascendency. The Tang emperors were devoted to the dogs and lavished enormous luxury and money on their care, breeding, and upkeep. There were a number of different types of small dog in the imperial palaces by this time, and these were bred together. The objectives at this time were not to maintain pure breeding lines but to breed the most lionlike dog and that which would curry the greatest favor from the emperor. They were bred for specific color, too, and fawns and reds (lion colors) were the most popular. White was also popular, and a white mark on the forehead, said to be a mark of Buddha, was particularly sought after. The palace staff, who were mostly eunuchs, were in charge of the dogs, and competitions were held for the best dog in which the eunuch in charge received a prize. The best dogs had their portraits painted and were even awarded titles and honors. One of Emperor Ling Ti's (156–189 C.E.) dogs was given the most distinguished of the literary ranks in China. The dogs formed an integral part of ceremonial occasions and several would precede the emperor's arrival, uttering short, sharp barks. The lion dogs eventually became the sole preserve of the imperial palace, and anyone caught dealing in the dogs was punished with death. Even so, some dogs were smuggled out and sold to wealthy individuals.

The vast Forbidden City imperial palace was built in Beijing between 1406 and 1420 by the Ming Dynasty; the lion dogs were less popular during this period as a result of the decline in Buddhism, but with the establishment of the Qing Dynasty (1644–1912) breeding was renewed with vigor, and the dogs took up residence in this huge palace. The dogs began to be traded to Europeans who, it is said, liked those with black, spotted tongues. Despite this, numbers of Pekingese in Europe were insignificant until the mid-nineteenth century. During the Second Opium War in 1860, British and French troops ransacked the Summer Palace in Beijing. By the time the troops arrived, the emperor and his family had fled, but the emperor's aunt and her five dogs had been left behind. When the troops burst in she took her own life and the dogs were

taken by the British; these later formed the foundation for the breed in Britain. The smallest of the five was given by Captain John Hart Dunne to Queen Victoria (1819–1901). In 1861 he appeared in the *Illustrated London News* and earned much fame as the first Pekingese in Britain.

By this time, some of the palace lion dogs, including the Pekingese, had made their way out into the homes of individuals in China. A monthly dog sale lasting six days was inaugurated in 1865, and the dogs not deemed suitable for the palace were sold. Some of these were exported and formed the basis for the breed outside China. An exception was two palace dogs that were smuggled out of China in 1896 by Douglas Murray. These two are seen in many of the modern pedigrees. In 1902 the dowager empress Cixi (T'zu Hsi) returned to the Forbidden City and later made several gifts of the palace dogs to foreign dignitaries. This included sending a Pekingese to Alice Roosevelt, daughter of US president Theodore Roosevelt, and another to financier J. P. Morgan. These two dogs formed the foundation of the US bloodlines for the breed.

When Pekingese first arrived in Britain in the 1860s they were called Pekingese Spaniels and were grouped together with the Japanese Chin—then called the Japanese Spaniel (until 1977). The Japanese Spaniel Club oversaw both breeds, changing its name to the Japanese and Pekingese Spaniel Club, before the Pekingese Club was formed in 1904. The Pekingese Club of America was formed in 1909, and the breed rapidly became popular in both countries. In the United States, in particular, the ensuing dog shows were high society events patronized by the rich and famous. The American breed standard for the Pekingese was drawn up in 1909, based on the British one, although it has since been revised several times. At this time there was controversy over the size and weight of the breed, which at 18 pounds (6.5 kg) was considered too big by some. In retaliation another British club, the Pekin Palace Dog Association, formed in 1908 with a much smaller weight to keep the size of the dogs small and nearer the original type; it developed its own breed standard. Both these British clubs still promote the interests of the Pekingese, but there is now only one breed standard (a compromise) for the Pekingese in Britain, which lists the ideal weight as 11 pounds (4 kg). In the United States the top weight limit is 14 pounds (5 kg).

PUG

ANCIENT – CHINA – COMMON

SIZE

Males/females 10–11 in./ideal weight 14–18 lbs

APPEARANCE

Solid, muscular, "square" body type. Relatively large, rounded head with short, blunt, square muzzle. Defined wrinkles on forehead; large, round, dark, prominent eyes with lustrous expression, full of fire when excited. Small ears, either rose shaped or "button" ear, the latter preferred. Strong, slightly arched neck; short, cobby body; level back; broad chest. Strong, straight forelegs, powerful hindquarters; tail set high, tightly curled over back, double curl preferred

COLOR

Black or fawn with black "mask," ears, cheek moles, "trace" line down back. Smooth, short, glossy coat

APTITUDE

Showing, companion

PUGS HAVE OFTEN BEEN DESCRIBED AS *multum in parvo*, which in relation to these dogs equates to "a lot of dog, in a small package." There is perhaps no better description of the little Pug dog, whose enormous character makes up for any lack of size. The Pug is among the most charismatic and charming of dogs, whose lively and vivacious nature combined with a natural intelligence makes it an excellent companion animal.

The Pug is also one of the ancient dog types, dating to at least 400 B.C.E. and it is thought to have originated in the Orient. China is most commonly given as its native home, although there are no written documents that definitively give evidence for its earliest development. Dogs described as "short mouthed" are mentioned by the Chinese philosopher Confucius (551–479 B.C.E.), and it is thought that this referred to the early Pug, a small dog called the Lo-Chiang-Sze (or Lo-Sze). However, depictions on ancient illustrated scrolls also indicate that there were several different types of small companion dogs in the Orient that are now known as the Pekingese, Lhasa Apso, Shih Tzu, and Japanese Chin. Although this early history is rather vague, it is clear that small dogs were greatly favored by the ancient Chinese emperors and were specifically bred at the royal palaces as companions. They were treated extremely lavishly, and often provided with their own caregiver and fed a rich and exotic diet.

One of the many distinguishing features of the Pug is its wrinkled forehead. Through the way the skin folds, the wrinkles can produce the Chinese character for the word "prince" or "king." This consists of three parallel lines dissected with a single vertical line. Great importance was attached to this "symbol" on the early breeding of the dogs.

The popularity of these little dogs spread to Tibet, where they became favorites among the monks at the Buddhist monasteries, and to Japan where they warmed the laps of emperors. With the network of trade routes, known as the Silk Road, that began in the Han Dynasty (206 B.C.E.–220 C.E.), and the extensive exchange of produce, the dogs were spread throughout Central Asia and beyond. They began to arrive in Portugal and Spain during the sixteenth century, but it was the Netherlands that was most significant in the Pug's early European history. This came about through the Dutch East India Trading Company (DEITC) and its principal trading station at the Japanese city of Nagasaki, which was opened exclusively to Dutch trade in 1570. Many of the DEITC commodities, of which dogs were one, passed through Amsterdam where a specific dog market had been established by 1619, when it was described by the author James Howell. The Amsterdam dog market was later immortalized in paint by artist Abraham Hondius (1638–95). Pugs were an immediate success in the Netherlands, primarily based on the role model of William I, Prince of Orange (1533–84). William was an enthusiastic dog owner of a variety of breeds but it was Pugs that he favored, and a Pug that saved his life. He always took his Pugs with him when on military campaigns against the Spanish. One night, in 1572, the Spanish launched an attack on William I's camp at Hermingny, silencing his guards. His Pug, who was in bed with him, alerted the prince, which allowed him to make his escape. Thereafter he always kept Pugs, and they became the official dog of the House of Orange. There is even the image of a Pug carved into his tomb in Delft

Cathedral. Unsurprisingly, Pugs remained extremely popular in the Netherlands and were introduced to England in 1688 when William III (1650–1702) of the Netherlands landed in Torbay, England, before becoming the king of England in 1689. He took a number of his favored Pugs with him, and they rapidly became the fashionable pet accessory of the aristocracy. They remained incredibly popular in England, largely due to the patronage of the breed by the ruling monarchs until the end of the nineteenth century. Queen Victoria (1819–1901) owned thirty-six Pugs during the course of her long reign. Some years later they were again propelled into the public limelight by the Duke and Duchess of Windsor who owned nine Pugs and invested in numerous artworks depicting the exuberant dog.

Pugs had arrived in Russia by the eighteenth century when Peter the Great (1672–1725) is recorded as sending an embassy to the court of Emperor K'ang His (1662–1723). The emperor sent a Chinese envoy to welcome the Russian, and gifts of dogs were made by both parties. Although there is no documentary evidence, it is believed that Pugs were bred in Russia and sold to Europe. The breed had by this time become popular throughout Europe, particularly in Italy, France, Spain, and Germany, and many works of art depicted Pugs.

By the 1790s Pugs had become particularly fashionable in France, again very much within the realm of the rich and famous. Josephine de Beauharnais (1763–1814), the first wife of Napoleon Bonaparte (1769–1821), was devoted to her Pugs. Her favorite Pug, Fortune, had been indispensable to her when she was imprisoned during the French Revolution while still married to first husband, Alexander. Fortune was allowed to visit her daily, and she was able to place messages to officials on the inside of his collar in an effort to delay her proposed execution. Alexander was taken to the guillotine, but Josephine was eventually released and went on to marry Napoleon. Napoleon was not fond of dogs, particularly Fortune who was allowed to sleep in the marital bed and had by accounts bitten the French general during the course of his wedding night activities. After the injury, Fortune and Josephine's other dogs were barred from the bedroom but given their own adjacent room. They also had a private carriage and caregiver.

In Britain in the first part of the nineteenth century, the Pug suffered some physical decline through being crossed to bulldogs; it was also briefly subjected to ear cropping. In the 1850s, however, there was a reverse in its fortunes, which began with the parent stock of Lord Willoughby, a pair of Pugs called Mops and Nell who were referred to as "salt and pepper" in color. Another influential pair from the same period were the "golden fawn" colored Punch and Tetty who belonged to Mr. Chas Morrison, owner of the White Hart pub in Fulham, London. Toward the end of the century, two rough-coated Pugs were obtained by the Marquis of Wellesley direct from the emperor's palace in China. Wellesley later gifted them to a Mrs. St. John. These two produced Click, who was described as the ideal Pug. Click went on to be influential in Pug show lines in the United Kingdom and United States for many years.

Black pugs had undoubtedly turned up in litters over time but had probably been put down as "undesirable." This changed when a pair of black Pugs was introduced in the latter half of the century by aristocrat and breeder Lady Brassey; they promptly became very fashionable. Her efforts resulted in a class for black Pugs only in the Maidstone Dog Show in 1986. The Kennel Club was established in 1873, and around sixty pugs are listed in the first volume of the stud book. The Pug Club was established in the United Kingdom in 1883 and drew up the breed standard.

There is no documentation of the earliest Pugs in the United States, although it is thought that they first arrived in the mid-1860s, and twenty-four are listed as being shown at the Westminster Kennel Club Show in New York in 1879. Their popularity had a slow start in the United States, however, and the American Kennel Club (AKC) stud book shows that by 1920 there were still only a very few breeders registering their puppies. The Pug Dog Club of America was formed in 1931 by a group of enthusiasts and was recognized by the AKC the same year. Today, the Pug is a relatively popular companion dog and consistently ranks within the top twenty-five dog breeds in the United States and within the top twenty in the United Kingdom. It is a dog for the discerning dog owner, and it is said that once acquainted with a Pug no other breed will suffice. The Pug has a wonderful, affectionate, and lively character with a long and fluctuating history but one that always sees it eventually come out on top.

DEVOTED AND LOYAL

CHINESE CRESTED
ANCIENT – CHINA – COMMON

SIZE
Males/females ideally 11–13 in.; weight 5–12 lbs

APPEARANCE
Elegant, fine-boned, graceful. Wedge-shaped head; arches gently between ears, tapers to muzzle. Almond-shaped eyes, dark in dark-colored dogs, lighter in lighter-colored dogs; large, erect ears. Lean, elegant, slightly arched neck; body slightly longer than it is high. Level topline slopes slightly through croup. Underline has moderate tuck up at flanks. Long, slender legs; hare feet. Tail carried gaily in motion, tapers to curve, reaches hocks

COLOR
Any color or combination. Two varieties: hairless only has hair on head (crest), bottom two-thirds of tail (plume), and feet (socks). Body skin soft, warm, smooth. Powderpuff covered in double-soft, silky, long coat

APTITUDE
Rat catching, showing, companion

THE CHINESE CRESTED DOG comes in two distinct varieties: the essentially hairless and the fully coated Powderpuff. Both types can be found within a single litter of puppies. They are both also particularly unusual in their appearance: the hairless variety carries a charismatic crest of hair on its head and ears, a plume of hair on the bottom two-thirds of the tail, and hairy "socks," whereas the Powderpuff is covered in long, silky hair. These delightful dogs are extremely sensitive and intelligent; they thrive on human companionship and will form strong bonds with their family. Equally, they can become distressed if left on their own for periods of time. These are special dogs that require particularly empathetic owners.

The history of hairless dogs is one that stretches far back into prehistory. They are first thought to have evolved in Mexico or South America, where several varieties of hairless dogs are still commonly found. These dogs formed the basis for many superstitions and spiritual traditions; they were frequently included in ritual sacrifice and were widely eaten. The Spanish conquistadores documented the hairless dogs in the sixteenth century. Hairless dogs were also found in Africa, Turkey, Egypt, and Asia. It is not known from which stock the Chinese Crested originally developed, but it is speculated to be the hairless dogs of Mexico. It is known that these dogs were in China by the sixteenth century and were popular with Chinese seafarers. They were used for keeping rats at bay on board ship and were traded at ports as curiosities, which led to them being widely dispersed.

In the 1860s some Chinese Crested dogs were brought to Britain as part of a zoological show, but none were registered until 1881. The breed was established slowly in the United Kingdom, and the Chinese Crested Dog Club was not formed until 1969, and in 1971 there were still only twenty-six members. The Kennel Club did not recognize the breed until 1995, but it is well supported with more than 500 registrations a year. In the United States the breed was supported by New Yorker Ida Garrett, who came across them in 1880. Garrett began breeding the dogs and wrote about them extensively for sixty years. In the 1920s she met Debra Woods, and together these two women were a driving force in establishing the Chinese Crested in the United States. Woods established the Cresthaven Kennels and kept detailed records of her dogs from the 1930s. By the 1950s this stud book was comprehensive enough to found the American Hairless Dog Club and its registration for the breed; at its inception there were only two members! Within four years there were 160 Chinese Crested and 200 Mexican Hairless dogs registered.

Another leading figure early in the breed's US history was the dancer and performer Gypsy Rose Lee. Lee's sister had rescued a Chinese Crested dog from an animal shelter in Connecticut and given it to Rose to use in her act. The performer was instantly taken with the little dog and became a serious breeder, doing much to promote and publicize them. The American Chinese Crested Club was founded in 1978, and in 1986 the American Kennel Club (AKC) placed them in its Miscellaneous category; they were finally officially recognized by the AKC in 1991 and are now in the Toy group. Although best known for being lovely companions, this breed can also excel in agility, obedience, and as a pet therapy dog.

DEVOTED AND LOYAL

CHIHUAHUA

ANCIENT – MEXICO – COMMON

WEIGHT
Males/females maximum 6 lbs
APPEARANCE
Small, compact, cheeky. Apple dome skull with moderately short, slightly pointed muzzle. Ears set well apart, large, and erect when alert, flaring to the sides at 45° when resting. Round eyes with saucy, intelligent expression, dark in dark-colored dogs, may be lighter in paler coats. Graceful, slightly arched neck; body slightly longer than height at withers and slender. Level topline, well-developed chest and strong front

end; small, dainty feet. Tail is moderately long and carried in a curve or curled over back
COLOR
Any color, solid, marked, or splashed. Two coat varieties: long coat soft, flat, or slightly wavy with undercoat. Feathering on ears, feet, legs, "pants" on hind legs and large neck ruff. Tail has heavy plume. Smooth coat soft, close, and glossy
APTITUDE
Originally ceremonial, consumable, now showing, companion

THE CHIHUAHUA IS THE SMALLEST BREED of dog and one that is instantly recognizable. Although small in stature, this dog has enormous character and is highly intelligent. In the past few decades it has shot to public awareness through its use in advertising and in films such as *Legally Blonde* (2001) and *Beverly Hills Chihuahua* (2008). This is a very special breed of dog, and it requires a particularly sensitive and devoted home. It is not suited to being left alone and is not, generally speaking, ideal with very young children. The Chihuahua develops a strong attachment to its owners and is a loyal and charismatic dog. It is also a useful watchdog because it is naturally wary of strangers and will sound a vigorous alarm in the case of intruders.

The early history of the Chihuahua is one of great debate, but what is known is that this little dog is of ancient origin. It is typically said to have developed in Mexico, and it is the state of Chihuahua in northern Mexico from which it takes its name—although it did not derive this until the nineteenth century. However, it is to the ancient Techichi dogs of the Toltec civilization (c. 800–1000), which flourished in central-eastern Mexico, that the breed is most popularly said to trace. Many carvings and pottery figures dating to the ninth century show dogs of similar

characteristics to the modern Chihuahua. Dogs were an important part of early Central and South American life and existed in several varieties. Frequent mention is made of the Techichi dogs of the Toltecs, and of the Mexican Xoloitzcuintli (also known as Xolo or Mexican Hairless), the latter of which is believed to trace back 3,000 years.

The dogs were often eaten as a delicacy and played an important role in ritual sacrifice and spiritual ceremonies. It was believed that dogs acted as vessels to carry the spirit of the recently deceased across the river of the Underworld to the Underworld itself. Sometimes pottery figures of dogs that bear some similarity to the modern Chihuahua were placed in graves to watch over the deceased, and often actual dogs were ritually killed and placed in the grave alongside their master. The remains of these that have been discovered bear a resemblance to the Chihuahua. Dogs were also used as a sacrifice to the gods, and the Techichi were kept in large numbers in the various temples. After the Toltecs, the Aztecs continued these beliefs.

When the Spanish conquistadores arrived in the fifteenth century and plundered the native cultures, the little dogs are thought to have escaped into the wild. Some returned to Europe with the Spanish. There is no evidence documenting the fate of the little Mexican dogs in Mexico at this time, but it is possible that they survived and lived a feral existence until they were "rediscovered" 300 years later. Other theories suggest that the small dogs in Mexico originally heralded from Asia, and even from Europe; the latter theory is based on artistic representations that date to the fifteenth century. In truth it is not known, but it is Mexico with which the dogs are most associated.

The dogs were not "discovered" by the Western world until the 1850s in Chihuahua, hence their name, after which a few trickled into the United States and the United Kingdom. One was exhibited at a dog show in Regents Park, London, in 1897, and they were described in *A*

History and Description of the Modern Dogs of Great Britain and Ireland (1897) by Rawden Briggs Lee, but not very favorably. In the early years of the twentieth century the Chihuahua does not appear to have gained much of a following. One of the early British breeders was Mrs. Powell, who exhibited her Chihuahuas from 1930, and by 1937 had six imported dogs, some of which she showed in the United Kingdom, as well as in the United States at the Westminster Kennel Club Show. Tragically, when World War II broke out, Mrs. Powell's house received a direct bomb hit, and all of her dogs were killed. Other breeders in Britain continued to support the breed, and in 1949 the British Chihuahua Club was established; the first long-haired Chihuahua appeared in 1955.

The breed gained greater popularity in the United States, and the first to expand on the breed was the writer and dog judge James Watson. He acquired his first Chihuahua in 1888 in El Paso, Texas. In 1884, the first smooth-coated Chihuahua had been exhibited in Philadelphia. Both smooth and long-coated Chihuahuas formed part of the early imports from Mexico. Over the next few years Watson purchased several more of the dogs from north of the El Paso border and Tucson, Arizona; they were of quite diverse type, and at this time there was debate over whether they were a breed or not. Owen Wister and his friend, Charles Stewart, became significant early Chihuahua breeders. They purchased Caranza, a red long-coated dog, whose progeny went on to found the Merron, Perrito, and La Rex Doll lines; the Merron and Perrito lines also carried predominant long-coated genes. In the 1920s and 1930s the author and dog breeder Ida Garrett was involved in crossbreeding smooth-coated Chihuahuas with Pomeranians and Papillons to produce long-coated dogs, and in 1952 the American Kennel Club (AKC) divided the two coat varieties. The AKC first registered a Chihuahua in 1904, and the Chihuahua Club of America was formed in 1923, producing a breed standard at the same time. The breed steadily increased its following, aided by the Spanish American bandleader Xavier Cugat, known as the Rumba King. The little dogs became his trademark, and appeared with him in his weekly television shows. By the 1960s the Chihuahua had become the third most popular breed in the United States; they are still very popular in the United States and the United Kingdom today.

PAPILLON

ANCIENT – FRANCE – COMMON

SIZE

Males/females 8–11 in.; weight 4–11 lbs

APPEARANCE

Dainty, fine-boned, elegant, lively. Small head, slightly rounded between ears. Ears either large, erect, rounded tips, forming 45° angle to skull when erect, or of "drop" type, carried drooping. Eyes round, dark with intelligent expression; fine muzzle tapers to nose. Medium-length, elegant neck. Level topline, underline has definite tuck up at flanks. Chest of medium depth; well-sprung ribs. Slender, fine-boned legs, harelike feet. Long tail set high, carried arched over back, heavily feathered, curled

COLOR

White with patches of any other color. Facial markings of any color other than white should cover ears and eyes, ideally with white blaze and band over nose. Long, fine, silky coat, short on head, front of legs, longer frill on chest, fringes of hair on ears, back of forelegs feathered, hind legs have "culottes" of feathering, feet may have tufts of hair, tail heavily feathered

APTITUDE

Showing, agility, companion

THE PAPILLON IS A TOY BREED that combines its dainty appearance with a joyful approach to life. It is a superb companion, and is devoted, loyal, friendly, and intelligent; it also responds very well to obedience training. It can excel at performance classes, agility, and makes a good therapy pet; historically it was often referred to as a "comforter," and was never happier than when lying on a warm lap.

The name "Papillon" comes from the French for "butterfly," which, with their erect, feathered ears and dainty face, they resemble. There is a drop-eared variety of the Papillon called the Phalene, which is French for "moth," and this equally beautiful dog with its long, silky ears has a mothlike look. This breed has symmetrical facial markings that are much prized within the breed. The Phalene is uncommon in the United Kingdom and United States now, although it is still seen frequently in Europe. It was these drop-eared dogs that were dominant throughout their history until the late nineteenth century, when the prick-eared variety became fashionable.

Traditionally Papillons and Phalenes were associated with the royal households of Continental Europe, and although France is now listed as their country of origin, the breed actually developed across Europe, particularly in Spain, Belgium, and Italy. It traces to a dwarf spaniel type referred to as Continental Dwarf Spaniel, Toy Spaniel, and even Titian Spaniel. This dog was of a similar type and similar origin. As a result of its popularity among the rich, it was frequently given as a political gift between foreign dignitaries, and sea merchants also traded the dogs extensively, spreading them across Europe.

The history of this small dog can be traced to the sixteenth century when it begins to appear with some frequency in works of art. Among the earliest appearances was in the work of Titian (c. 1488–1576), who frequently painted these dogs. The dogs became a regular feature of the French court, forming part of Louis XIV's (1638–1715) household, and were a favorite pet of Madame Pompadour, mistress to Louis XV (1710–74). The tradition for these dogs continued in the French Court; Marie Antoinette, wife of Louis XVI (1754–93), is said to have been accompanied by her Papillon when led to the guillotine.

Some of the first Papillons arrived in the United States at the end of the nineteenth century; the author Edith Wharton (1862–1937) is known to have owned one at this time, although their history here really begins in 1908 when the Englishwoman Mrs. Storr Wells brought two from Paris to the United States and gave them to Mrs. de Forest Danielson of Massachusetts. In 1911 she bought two more females, and one of these bred with her male, Gigi, to produce Joujou. Joujou was the first Papillon to be registered with the American Kennel Club (AKC) in 1915 and was the first American-bred champion. In 1930 a group of enthusiasts established the Papillon Club of America. The AKC officially recognized the breed in 1935, and after this, classes for them began to be included at the various dog shows. World War II greatly affected the breed, and by the end of the war the club had disbanded but was reestablished in 1948. Since then the Papillon has continued to grow in popularity.

POMERANIAN
ANCIENT — GERMANY/BRITAIN — COMMON

SIZE
Males 3–7 lbs/females 4–6 lbs

APPEARANCE
Compact, active, self-confident. Wedge-shaped head, broad at back, tapers to nose; muzzle quite short; foxlike face; alert, intelligent expression. Dark, almond-shaped eyes; small, pointed, erect, ears, set high. Head carried high; proud, compact body; pronounced forechest; level topline with strong back. Tail set high with extensive plume, carried arched over back to lie flat

COLOR
Any color or pattern. Coat very thick. Topcoat long, harsh, stands away from body, undercoat soft, dense, short. Coat forms ruff round neck to frame face

APTITUDE
Showing, companion

THE LIVELY, INTELLIGENT POMERANIAN is a loyal and vivacious companion animal with a long, surprising history. The small lapdog of modern times is a very different dog from its ancestors, which developed in the frigid expanse of the Arctic alongside breeds such as the Siberian Husky, Samoyed, and Malamute. The Pomeranian is a Spitz and exhibits the classic characteristics of this group of dogs, seen, for example, in its thick, long coat, pointed ears and muzzle, and tail that curls over the back. The Pomeranian's ancestors would have been used for pulling sleds and herding reindeer by the Nordic people. Spitz types were popular in Germany by the sixteenth century; the word "spitz" is German for pointed and was probably coined in reference to the dog's pointed muzzle. They were commonly called Wolfspitz or Wolfspitzen and were used for a variety of jobs including sheepherding and draft work. With their thick, weatherproof coats, the dogs were able to withstand the worst weather, and this, combined with their amenable temperaments, made them valuable working stock. In Germany and through breeding, the Wolfspitzen developed into five different types, the smallest of which gave rise to the Pomeranian.

The Pomeranian is thought to have derived its name several hundred years ago from Pomerania, a historical region of Germany and Poland on the southern coast of the Baltic Sea. It was there that breeders selectively bred the smallest Wolfspitzen, and the dogs were named after the region accordingly. However, this area was subject to great political unrest and devastating wars throughout its history, which resulted in the loss of any breeding records in connection to the Pomeranian. The breed's modern history and the development of a standardized appearance traces to Britain and in particular to the patronage of the breed by two queens: Queen Charlotte (1744–1818) and the great dog lover Queen Victoria (1819–1901). Despite the activities of breeders in Pomerania, the Pomeranian was still exhibiting great differences in appearance and was considerably larger than the present-day breed, as evidenced in many paintings of the eighteenth century and photographs from the nineteenth and twentieth centuries.

One of the earliest tales of a Pomeranian in Britain dates to the late seventeenth century and pertains to the great physicist Isaac Newton (1642–1727). Newton is said to have had a Pomeranian called Diamond to whom he was devoted; descriptions of her indicate that she was a medium-sized dog of approximately 30 pounds (11 kg), which is far greater in size than the modern Pomeranian. According to a letter written by Newton, one evening when he had almost finished making revisions to his treatise on the law of gravity and was nearing a point when it might be ready for publication, he lit some candles in his study, and placed them on his desk next to the groundbreaking work; Diamond was sleeping nearby. When a visitor knocked on Newton's door he shut the dog in the room to allow in his visitor. Diamond woke up, heard the strange voice in the next room, and became very animated, wanting to protect her master. She rushed around the study, and knocked the table. The candles tipped over and set light to Newton's manuscript, which was completely destroyed. The event was so traumatic to Newton that he became seriously depressed and took to his bed, accompanied by Diamond, for some weeks. It took another whole year before he was able to resurrect his theory of gravity in full.

The breed did not reach the wider public until the eighteenth century. In 1767 the German-born Queen Charlotte, wife of George III, imported two white Pomeranians from the Pomerania area. The place of these dogs in the royal household brought the breed as a whole to the nation's attention. The well-known British artist Thomas Gainsborough (1727–88) painted the two dogs and several other pictures of Pomeranians, including *Pomeranian Bitch with Puppy* (c. 1777) and *Mrs. Robinson with Pomeranian* (1781–82). The former depicted the dogs of his friend, the cellist Carl Friedrich Abel, whereas the latter shows the actress "Perdita" who had had a scandalous affair with the Prince of Wales (George IV). In the painting she is seen holding a miniature painting of the prince in her hand, accompanied by the beautiful Pomeranian dog, which was a popular painterly symbol for love and devotion. A few years later the well-known artist George Stubbs (1724–1806) painted *Fino and Tiny* (1791), which depicted the Pomeranian Fino who is thought to have belonged to the artist. These images all show dogs of much greater size than the modern Pomeranian, and with quite varied characteristics; they were, however, referred to as "Pomeranians."

Queen Victoria, granddaughter of Queen Charlotte, greatly popularized the breed. After a visit to Italy in the late 1880s, she imported the male Pomeranian Marco, who became her devoted companion, and whose photograph was frequently taken. Marco was followed by a number of other Pomeranians and the queen established large breeding kennels for them. Marco was notably smaller than other Pomeranians in the country, and the queen developed a liking for this small size. The others she imported from Italy were similarly small, and she specifically bred the dogs to reduce their size. It is largely thanks to her efforts that the Pomeranian began to reach the size it is now required to be. There were fourteen Pomeranians exhibited at the first Crufts dog show in 1891, of which several belonged to the queen. The public were enamored with the charming little dogs, and they became almost instantly fashionable. The Pomeranian Breed Club was established in the same year, and a standard drawn up for the breed. One of the last dogs that Queen Victoria owned was a Pomeranian called Turi, who was with her when she died.

As the characterful breed was taking hold in Britain, it was also becoming popular in the United States, and the first Pomeranian was registered with the American Kennel Club (AKC) in 1888 in the Miscellaneous category. The dogs made their debut in the show ring in 1894 when Sheffield's Lad, owned by Mr. Toon and Mr. Thomas, came joint second in the Miscellaneous category. Sheffield's Lad does not appear to have had a further show record after this. Although he is listed as the first known Pomeranian to be shown in the United States, a dog called Chubb had been a prize winner at the Springfield Dog Show in 1876; he was listed as a Spitz, but it is likely he was a Pomeranian. In the early days the two names were occasionally interchanged.

Pomeranians appeared sporadically over the next few years at dog shows, but the first landmark for the breed was in 1899 when the American Pet Dog Thanksgiving Show (Philadelphia) was the first to hold classes only for their breed. At least eighteen Pomeranians were exhibited. In the following year the American Pomeranian Club (APC) was established by Mrs. Williamson and Mrs. Smythe, and in the same year the Pomeranian Nubian Rebel, who had been imported from Britain and was owned by Mrs. Smythe, won his class at the celebrated Westminster Kennel Club Dog Show, New York. Nubian Rebel went on to be a multi–prize winning dog. Important early breeding kennels were the Lakewood Kennels and Mrs. Smythe's Swiss Mountain Kennels, both of which produced champions. The AKC recognized the breed in 1900, and in 1909 the APC was made a member club; it held its first specialty show in 1911 and had 138 exhibits. The show was held in the Sun Parlor of the Waldorf Astoria, New York, and was a high society event. The judging, however, proved contentious, and the judge, Mrs. L. Dyer from Wales, deemed many of the classes of insufficient quality to merit a first placing. Mrs. Dyer commented that it was not the quality of the dogs that was lacking but their poor presentation and dire trimming. Interest in the Pomeranian continued to grow exponentially and dog shows attracted more entries; some entries came from breeders in Britain and Italy who shipped their dogs over to compete. Pomeranians have now been within the top twenty most popular dog breeds in the United States for a number of years.

DEVOTED AND LOYAL

POODLE

ANCIENT — GERMANY — COMMON

SIZE
Males/females Standard over 15 in./Miniature 10–15 in.; weight 12–18 lbs/Toy under 10 in.; weight 4–8 lbs

APPEARANCE
Squarely built, elegant, active, distinguished. Moderately rounded skull; long, straight, fine muzzle; very dark, oval eyes; long ears hanging close to head. Head carried high on strong, well-proportioned neck; level topline; deep, moderately wide chest; well-sprung ribs; short, broad, strong loins; straight tail set high, carried up, docked to sufficient length for balanced appearance

COLOR
Any solid. Coat curly, harsh, dense

APTITUDE
Originally water retrieving, tricks, circus performer, now agility, showing, service dogs, companion

THE ELEGANT AND DISTINGUISHED POODLE is widely recognized as being among the most intelligent of dog breeds; it has a tremendous personality and is frequently attributed to being almost humanlike in its nature. This is a dog that thrives on human companionship and excels in any event that draws upon its intelligence and closeness to its owners. The Poodle forms a strong and loyal attachment to its loved ones, and it is said that once an owner has had a Poodle, no other breed will suffice. There are three size varieties of Poodle: the Standard, the Miniature, and the Toy, and all three share similar characteristics.

The Poodle is most commonly associated with France, and became most popular there during the eighteenth century; it is the French national dog. However, the Poodle originated in Germany and has also been linked to Russia. Some theorists even place the Poodle's development as far back as Ancient Rome. Perhaps surprisingly, the Poodle was originally bred as a water-retrieving bird dog and was in wide use in this capacity in Germany by the sixteenth century. It is from Germany that it derives its name, *pudel*, meaning to "splash in water." It is thought that the early Poodle shared some similar heritage with other water-retrieving breeds, such as the Portuguese Water Dog, the Irish Water Spaniel, the Hungarian Water Hound, and the French Barbet, all of which exhibit some similar characteristics, notably in their coats.

The Poodle is, of course, well known for its coat and has been rather maligned in recent years because of the nature of this, particularly when trimmed. The Poodle's coat is extremely dense and waterproof with characteristic tight curls. It is generally trimmed into a manageable lamb or sporting trim unless being shown, in which case it is trimmed in a specific and unique way. This actually derived from the breed's working heritage. As a result of the time the dogs spent retrieving from water, the coat was trimmed to remove excess hair that became waterlogged, but sufficient coat was left in place to protect and keep key areas of the dog warm, such as its chest and joints. Its tail was docked to stop it getting caught in undergrowth and a ribbon tied around its topknot of hair to enable the hunter to identify easily where his dog was. This trimming also made the dog's appearance smart and appealing.

The breed became extremely popular in France, and France has become the breed's surrogate home; the Fédération Cynologique Internationale recognizes France as the country of origin. It was first popular for its working abilities and was known as *chien canard* or *caniche*, meaning "duck dog." However, thanks to its attractive looks and wonderful temperament, it also became popular as a companion. The Poodle has always been of different sizes, but it was not until showing began in earnest that the sizes were specified. In the eighteenth century the smaller Poodle became fashionable as a "sleeve dog," or "comforter," particularly with ladies at court throughout Europe. The smaller Poodle was also used for truffle hunting in France and later in England because its sense of smell and dexterous feet were perfect for finding and digging out the delicacies. In the eighteenth century the fashion arose for elaborate trimming, decoration, and even color dying of Poodles, particularly in France.

The Poodle also become a favorite among gypsies who taught it elaborate tricks for entertainment. By the end of the seventeenth century, troupes of French Poodles were performing extraordinary tricks, including playing cards and dominoes. In 1700 a troupe from Louvain, called The Ball of Little Dogs, was taken to England at the special request of Queen Anne for her amusement. The best-known circus Poodle was probably Munito, who was taught to walk a tightrope. A photograph in the British Royal Collection shows Sammy the Standard Poodle, who belonged to Princess Victoria of Wales (1868–1935), balancing on the back of two chairs with a baton in his mouth. Sammy was a much-loved companion for Victoria and is the subject of several images in the Royal Collection; tragically he died after eating rat poison.

One of the most fascinating accounts of a specific Poodle dates to the seventeenth century and to Prince Rupert of the Palatine, nephew to King Charles I of England. Rupert was given a white Standard Poodle called Boye while he was a prisoner of war in Austria. On his release, Rupert was accompanied back to England by Boye, to fight in the Civil War on the side of King Charles and the Cavaliers. King Charles became attached to Boye and, allegedly, allowed the dog to sit in a thronelike chair next to him

during meetings. Boye came to be seen as a good luck charm by the Cavalier soldiers and was viewed with deep resentment by the Roundheads. When Boye was killed during the battle of Marston Moor, Rupert went into a decline, which could be said to have been matched by the Cavalier forces who were eventually overthrown.

In the twentieth century Winston Churchill (1874–1965) was devoted to his Poodles; he had two, Rufus I and Rufus II. It was, however, the US writer John Steinbeck (1902–68) who brought the Poodle to life in the US public's imagination through his book, *Travels with Charley*, published in 1962. The Poodle continued to grow in popularity worldwide throughout the twentieth century and particularly after World War II. In North America, where it had first been registered with the American Kennel Club (AKC) in 1887, it became the most popular dog for twenty-two years between 1960 and 1982, which is an AKC record for any breed. Although the Poodle's popularity has waned slightly, it is still very highly rated and regularly features within the top ten breeds. It is also extremely popular in the United Kingdom.

FRENCH BULLDOG
MODERN – FRANCE – COMMON

SIZE
Males/females less than 28 lbs

APPEARANCE
Short-faced, compact, muscular with distinctive ears. Large, square head; skull flat between the ears; muzzle short, broad, and deep; lower jaw is undershot. Wide-set, round, dark eyes with intelligent and curious expression; ears are broad at base, elongated and rounded at tip—called "bat" ears—set high on head and carried erect. Thick, well-arched neck; compact, muscular body with heavy bone; broad at shoulders and narrowing over loins. Roach back; broad, deep chest and belly tucked up. Short, low set tail either straight or screwed. Forelegs are short, muscular, and wide set, and the hind legs are longer

COLOR
All brindle, fawn, white, brindle, and white. All colors are acceptable with the exception of solid black, mouse, liver, black and tan, black and white, and white with black, which are disqualifications. Black means black without a trace of brindle. Coat is moderately fine, smooth, short, and brilliant

APTITUDE
Showing, companion

THE SMALL, COMPACT FRENCH BULLDOG is a delightful companion breed that excels at being pampered. Although small in height it is a solid, muscular animal with a great personality. It is frequently described as the clown of the dog world. However, it is also an extremely bright dog, to such an extent that it has a great ability to train its owner, rather than the other way around; it can be stubborn on occasion but is entirely cheerful in nature and for the most part aims to please. The French Bulldog requires lots of interaction and stimulation, but little exercise, and for this reason makes an excellent town dog.

The roots of this breed trace back to Bullenbeissers and British Bulldogs. The Bullenbeisser was a descendent of the ancient Molossian dogs, which also gave rise to the Mastiff breeds. The Bullenbeisser dogs were used for dogfighting and bullbaiting. In Britain the Bulldog developed for the same purpose. These practices were outlawed in Britain in 1835, and these dogs had to find a new role. A fashion arose for small Bulldogs as companion animals, and some were specifically bred down in size.

During the nineteenth century, many artisans moved to France and took their small dogs with them. In France these small British Bulldogs were introduced to the existing Bullenbeissers. The resulting dogs were small Bulldogs of French character, and quickly became known as the Bouledogue Français. They became essential accessories among upper-class women and artisans.

In 1903 Mr. W. J. Stubbs published a booklet titled *The History of the French Bulldog*, in which he attributed the foundation of this breed to the miniature British Bulldog. This was disputed by both the French and the Germans, who claimed that the British dogs had only enhanced the already developing French Bulldog. Other authorities claimed that Spanish Bulldogs lay at the root of the breed.

It is possible that the French Bulldog's character was further cemented through terrier and pug crosses, although records in France were scant. In 1893 some French Bulldogs were taken to Britain, where they were largely shunned. To combat this, a group of enthusiasts formed the French Bulldog Club of England in 1902. In 1905 the Kennel Club recognized the breed as Bouledogue Français; in 1912 this changed to French Bulldog.

By this time the French Bulldog was firmly established in the United States, and was particularly popular among high society. Breeding kennels were established by 1885, and in 1896 nineteen of the breed made their debut at the Westminster Kennel Club Show. In the following year the "ear controversy" took hold. At this time not all French Bulldogs exhibited their now-characteristic erect bat ears; some still had the "rose" ear type where the ear is folded. At the show, however, all the winning dogs exhibited the rose ear type. A group of US breeders formed the French Bulldog Club of America (1897) and set the breed standard, specifying bat ears. This was accepted and is now one of the defining features of this breed. The American Kennel Club accepted the French Bulldog shortly after the club was formed, and by 1906 it was the fifth most popular breed in the country. Now it ranks within the top twenty breeds in the United States.

DEVOTED AND LOYAL

BOSTON TERRIER

MODERN – UNITED STATES – COMMON

SIZE
*Males/females 15–17 in.; weight
up to 25 lbs*

APPEARANCE
*Short-headed, strong, compact,
short-tailed. Square head, flat
between ears with short, square,
wide, deep muzzle. Large, round,
dark eyes, set well apart, with
intelligent, kind expression; small,
erect ears, natural or cropped.
Slightly arched neck; short,
compact body. Level topline with
rump curving slightly to set of tail.
Tail short, straight, or screw,
carried below horizontal. Chest
deep with good width; forelegs set*
*moderately wide apart; small,
round feet. Hindquarters have
strong, muscular thighs;
well-defined hock joints*

COLOR
*Brindle, seal (appears black but
has a red cast when viewed in
sunlight), or black with white
markings. White markings must
include: muzzle band, blaze
between eyes, forechest, and
should include: collar, blaze over
head, part or all of front legs, and
hind legs below hocks. Coat is
short, smooth, bright, fine*

APTITUDE
Show, agility, therapy, companion

THE CHARMING BOSTON TERRIER goes by the nickname of "the American Gentleman" and deservedly so. This small dog is big on personality and is noted for its extremely gentle nature, which, combined with its good looks, makes it highly appealing. The Boston is a devoted, loyal, and playful companion that thrives on a close and constant relationship with its family. It is an intelligent and energetic dog that can excel in agility and obedience classes and has frequently been used as a therapy pet.

The Boston is an "all American" breed that developed in Boston, Massachusetts, in the last decades of the nineteenth century but traces its ancestry back to the British Bulldog and the White English Terrier. One dog in particular is attributed as being at the very beginnings of the Boston Terrier, and this was Hooper's Judge, a Bulldog/English Terrier cross. Judge, as he was known, was imported to the United States from England and bought by Robert Hooper of Boston in the mid-1860s. Judge is described as being dark brindle with a white blaze, and having a "short, blocky" head. Judge was bred to Burnett's Gyp (Kate) owned by Edward Burnett of Massachusetts; she is described as being stocky, strong, low stationed, and again having a short, blocky head. Burnett kept several similar dogs, which he said were excellent ratters. The most important puppy they produced was Well's Eph, also a low-stationed, strongly built dog, dark brindle with white markings, and exhibiting an even mouth. Well's Eph was bred to a golden brindle female called Tobin's Kate, and she produced the puppy Barnard's Tom in 1877, owned by John Barnard. Tom is considered to be the first true Boston Terrier type. He had a red brindle coat with white markings and exhibited a screw tail. Tom was bred to a female called Kelley's Nell, and John Barnard was given the pick of the litter in lieu of the stud fee. He chose a male called Mike with full, round eyes, which are now distinctive of the breed; other dogs that were influential on the breed development were Hall's Max and Bixby's Tony Boy and the females Reynold's Famous, Saunder's Kate, and Nolan's Mollie, among others. French Bulldogs were also used in the early days to help establish type and size.

The first dog show in Boston was held in 1878 and had classes for Bull Terriers. In 1888 the dog show opened classes for "round-headed Bull Terriers," and the Boston came to be referred to as the Round Head, the Boston Round Head, or the Boston Bull. A group of breeders formed the Boston Terrier Club of America in 1891, at the same time naming the breed after the city of its origin. They drew up the first breed standard, and the American Kennel Club (AKC) officially recognized the breed in 1893; it was the first all-American breed to be registered.

As an all-American breed, the Boston was the source of national pride and became very popular; its image was used on many advertisements. Bostons remained among the top ten most popular breeds in the United States until 1935 when their popularity waned slightly; however, the Boston has worked its way back into the hearts of the American public and is regularly ranked within the top twenty-five breeds in the country. Bostons are also popular in the United Kingdom and are found in many other countries across the world.

DEVOTED AND LOYAL

CAVALIER KING CHARLES SPANIEL

ANCIENT/MODERN – BRITAIN – COMMON

SIZE
Males/females 12–13 in.; weight 13–18 lbs

APPEARANCE
Elegant, graceful, active. Head appears flat between ears; full muzzle, slightly tapered. Large, round, dark eyes, set well apart, with gentle, sweet expression. Long ears, set high on head, covered with plenty of feathering. Neck fairly long; slightly arched, short-coupled body; topline level; moderately deep chest. Feathered

tail, carried happily although not much above level of back. Can be docked but no more than one-third taken off

COLOR
Black/tan, ruby (rich red), Blenheim (rich chestnut/white), tricolor (black on white with tan markings). Coat silky, of moderate length, can have slight wave. Feathering present on ears, chest, legs, tail, feet

APTITUDE
Flushing small game, showing, companion

THE CAVALIER KING CHARLES SPANIEL is a delightful companion breed that matches its gentle, loving disposition with a beautiful appearance. This small dog is joyous in every sense with a superb temperament and a desire to please; it is intelligent, highly trainable, playful, loyal, and quiet. The Cavalier King Charles enjoys a romp outside and will display an inherent ability to flush small birds from undergrowth; historically it was occasionally used for such endeavors, although its chief role has always been as a companion animal. It traces its roots back many centuries and shares the same initial history as its smaller relative, the King Charles, or English Toy Spaniel as it is known in the United States; however, its breed status as the Cavalier was only recognized in the twentieth century.

Small, toy spaniels have appeared in European paintings certainly since the sixteenth century and possibly even the fifteenth century. A well-known painting by Antonio Pisanello (1395–1455), *The Vision of St. Eustace* (c. 1438–42), depicts two very small dogs of spaniel type that could be among the earliest images of toy spaniels, although there is no documentation to substantiate this. Certainly toy breeds used as "comforters" had been in existence for many centuries, primarily developed in ancient Asia. It can be speculated that breeds such as the Japanese Chin and Tibetan Spaniel were spread westward and into

Continental Europe where they influenced European spaniels, resulting in the small toy varieties. These little dogs, often described as "Spaniel Gentile" or "Comforters," became companions for Europe's elite and provided warmth and comfort. The dogs were said to relieve aches, pains, and illness, and to attract fleas away from their owners onto their own bodies. They were in great demand in the royal courts and stately homes across much of Europe, proved by their inclusion in paintings from Italy, Germany, Spain, Holland, and France from the sixteenth century onward. Under the Stuart monarchs (seventeenth to eighteenth centuries), the Cavalier King Charles/King Charles (English Toy) reached its ascendency.

The fate of the little spaniels, however, matched those of the royals in England with whom they became associated, and this had a considerable impact on the breed. Charles I (1600–49) was a great supporter of the spaniels, and legend recounts that every spaniel in England wept when he was executed. The artist Anthony van Dyck included a number of his spaniels in courtly paintings, including *The Five Children of Charles I* (1637), which depicts a tiny red and white spaniel alongside a vast Mastiff. One of Charles's favorite toy spaniels was a black and white one called Rogue, who is said to have accompanied the king to his execution; afterward Oliver Cromwell is said to have paraded the unfortunate dog as a trophy of his victory over the king. The breed is most linked to Charles II (1630–85), the Cavalier King who was always accompanied by several of the little dogs. Such was his devotion to the spaniels that he dictated they should be allowed entrance into any public building, including Parliament and public houses— although no actual record of this has been found. Undoubtedly they became closely identified with him and were accordingly named King Charles Spaniels. He was followed to the throne by James II who also kept the spaniels at court. Next came the Dutch William III (1650–1702) of the House of Orange, whose preferred dogs

DEVOTED AND LOYAL

were Pugs, and the King Charles Spaniel was quickly ousted from royal favor. Despite this, some aristocrats continued to breed them, including John Churchill, 1st Duke of Marlborough (1650–1722), whose family seat is Blenheim Palace. According to an often quoted story, when the duke was fighting in the Battle of Blenheim (August 13, 1704) one of his female red and white spaniels began to whelp. His wife soothed the dog by rubbing the spaniel's forehead. When news of the duke's victory was heard, the puppies were born, and all had a red mark on their forehead—now known as the Blenheim spot—and their mother's red and white coat colors; this color combination is now described as Blenheim.

Although Pugs became favorites at court, King Charles Spaniels were still very much in evidence in England's aristocratic homes. However, their physical appearance had begun to change, probably as a result of the fashion for short-faced dogs such as the Pug, led by the royal court. Gradually, through crossbreeding, the King Charles began to exhibit a much shorter face with a domed skull and low-set ears, which was the opposite of the traditional, historical dog with its fairly long muzzle, flat skull, and high-set ears; the historical type eventually became known as the Cavalier King Charles. Despite the general trend, one of Queen Victoria's (1819–1901) favorite dogs was a traditional (Cavalier) King Charles called Dash. Dash was a tricolor given to Princess Victoria in 1833 and was the first of her dogs to be painted by Sir Edwin Landseer. When Dash died in 1840, he was buried in the grounds of Windsor Castle with the following epitaph, "His attachment was without selfishness, his playfulness without malice, his fidelity without deceit. Reader, if you would live beloved and die regretted, profit by the example of DASH."

Toward the end of the nineteenth century, the fashion for short-faced, dome-headed King Charles Spaniels took hold; this coincided with the development of dog shows and the drawing up of breed standards. The King Charles standard required the short face and domed skull, and as a result the traditional, historical type all but disappeared. This quintessentially English breed was saved by an American called Roswell Eldridge. In the 1920s Eldridge came to England to try to find a "nosey" spaniel similar to ones he had seen in historic European paintings. He was appalled that no dogs of this type were to be seen in British

dog shows, so he took the extraordinary step of offering a prize of £25 at Crufts Dog Show to the male and female King Charles most like those seen in the days of King Charles II. British breeders, who were then solely concentrated on their dome-skulled, little spaniels with short noses, were outraged but nonetheless entered their "worst" dogs (with the longest noses). Sadly, Eldridge died before he found the traditional dogs he was looking for, but his enthusiasm had sparked the interest of some breeders, led by Mrs. Hewitt Pitt, who began to re-create the original historical type.

These dogs were called Cavalier King Charles after the Cavalier King. In 1928 a club was founded for them and a breed standard drawn up, which has altered little since. However, numbers were still low, and the Kennel Club (KC) refrained from recognizing the Cavalier. The dogs did, however, begin to be seen on the show circuit, which helped bring them to public notice. Eventually, the KC accepted the breed in 1945, and it became eligible for challenge certificates. The first champion of the breed was Ch Daywell Roger, who went on to be very influential in the Cavalier's development. Breed numbers were affected during World War II, but by 1960 registration numbers with the KC had reached four figures. The breed's fortunes changed in 1973 when Ch Alansmere Aquarius won the coveted Best in Show at Crufts, thrusting the Cavalier into the limelight both in the United Kingdom and overseas.

The little Cavalier had a slower road to success in the United States. Early Cavalier types are thought to have accompanied colonists, but there were no documented imports of the dogs until the early 1950s. In 1956 the Cavalier King Charles Spaniel Club (CKCSC) was established by a group of dedicated breeders and supporters; due to low numbers, the American Kennel Club (AKC) would only register the Cavaliers in the Miscellaneous group. The CKCSC organized its own championship shows and maintained records of all the pedigrees, and eventually the AKC recognized the breed in 1996. A new club was formed as the parent club for the breed, the American Cavalier King Charles Spaniel Club; the Cavalier King Charles became the 140th breed to be recognized by the AKC. These charming dogs have continued their rise in the public's affections and are loved throughout much of the world.

YORKSHIRE TERRIER
MODERN – ENGLAND – COMMON

SIZE

Males/females 8–9 in.; weight 4–7 lbs

APPEARANCE

Small with straight, neatly parted hair, lively, self-important. Small head, rather flat on top; medium-sized, dark eyes with intelligent, sparkling expression; small, erect, V-shaped ears. Compact body with short back, level topline; tail carried slightly higher than level of back, docked to medium length

COLOR

Dark steel blue/tan, puppies born black, develop their color. Blue from back of neck to root of tail, tail a darker shade of blue. Rich, golden tan hair on head, bright rich tan on chest, legs. Tan and blue hairs should not mingle. Coat quite long, straight, fine, silky, glossy. Hair on head long, tied in one central or two side bows, hair on muzzle very long.

APTITUDE

Ratting, showing, companion

THE YORKSHIRE TERRIER is one of the smallest of the terrier breeds, but its diminutive size has not extended to its sense of self-importance. Like a number of the small companion breeds, the Yorkie, as it is affectionately known, has an awful lot of personality rolled into a very small package. This is a self-confident, charismatic, and lively little dog that demands respect and attention. It also has one of the most luxurious coats known, which requires extensive maintenance to keep it in tip-top condition. The Yorkie in full show presentation is a beautiful spectacle; it is, however, a terrier at heart, and while it might be subjected to endless pampering by some owners, it also enjoys "being a dog," having a romp, and chasing rodents. Its compact size and endearing qualities have seen it become one of the most popular breeds in the United States.

The Yorkshire Terrier developed in Yorkshire and Lancashire in northern England from the middle of the nineteenth century. Mills and weavers kept small terriers to combat the extensive rat population and bred them for this specific purpose but kept no records. Many of these workers had originally come from Scotland, and brought their terriers with them. The Yorkie of today traces back to those terriers of the nineteenth century, and in particular to the Clydesdale, the Waterside (Otter Terrier), and the Old English Toy Terrier (rough and broken coated), all of which are now extinct. The Clydesdale, which was of most significance to the Yorkie, had developed from the Skye Terrier and is described as a "blue and tan" dog. Also developed from the Skye was the Paisley (extinct), which was described as all blue and thought to have had a minor influence on the Yorkie. The Old English Toy Terriers were black and tan or blue and tan and were also influential in the Yorkie's emergence; some early Yorkie breeders showed and registered their dogs as Toy Terriers, prior to the nomenclature of Yorkshire Terrier.

Three important dogs in the foundation of the Yorkie are Swift's Old Crab, born around 1850, and Kershaw's Kitty, and a female Old English Terrier owned by J. Whittam. Kitty is said to have produced around eighty puppies during her lifetime. The most influential dog, however, was Huddersfield Ben. He won many prizes for show classes and ratting, and it is said that every Yorkshire Terrier today traces back to him, through his ten sons and one daughter.

The Yorkshire Terrier's popularity spread across the Atlantic to North America with Mr. and Mrs. Ferdinand Senn of New York establishing the earliest American bloodline for the breed; they began exhibiting in 1878 and remained active in the breed until 1916. Yorkshire Terriers first appeared in the National American Kennel Club stud book in 1883. In the following year, the American Kennel Club was established, and the Yorkshire Terrier was officially recognized in 1885. Between 1900 and 1920 there were forty-five Yorkies awarded championship status. The first Yorkshire Terrier Club of America was founded around 1913 and continued until 1919. The Yorkshire Terrier Association of America was established in around 1915; it existed alongside the first club for several years, before being abandoned in 1924. A third club was organized in 1937 but folded with the onset of World War II. Breed numbers fell during the war, although afterward breeders rallied around. The Yorkshire Terrier Club of America was founded in 1951 and is still going strong.

DEVOTED AND LOYAL

DALMATIAN
ANCIENT – YUGOSLAVIA – COMMON

SIZE

Males/females 19–23 in.

APPEARANCE

Spotted, muscular, alert. Head flat between ears; top of skull as wide as it is long; powerful muzzle, same length as backskull. Medium-sized eyes, somewhat rounded, set moderately well apart, either brown or blue. Ears set high, carried close to head, wide at base, tapering to rounded tip. Fairly long, nicely arched neck; deep, moderately wide chest; level, strong back. Smooth topline with slightly arched loins,

underline has moderate tuck up. Legs have good bone; feet round; compact, well-arched toes. Tail is natural extension of topline, tapers to point, reaches hocks. Carried with slight upward curve

COLOR

Ground color white with black or liver spots. Clearly defined, round spots, evenly distributed. All born white with spots beginning to develop at two weeks. Coat short, dense, fine, glossy

APTITUDE

Coaching, firehouse, hunting, military, agility, show, companion

THE DALMATIAN'S STRIKING SPOTTED COAT pattern makes it one of the most distinctive of dog breeds. The dogs are born pure white, and their spots begin to develop at around two weeks of age. Until this point there is no way of knowing whether they will have black or liver spots. Given its attractive appearance and great character, the Dalmatian has also frequently appeared in movies and advertising, most famously in the Walt Disney classic *101 Dalmatians* (1961), based on the book by British author Dodie Smith, published in 1956. The dog's media appeal has perhaps been detrimental to the breed, and ill-equipped families have acquired them based on the "cute" factor. In reality, although the Dalmatian is a super dog, it is also a high-energy breed that requires lots of exercise. It is an intelligent dog that excels in challenging situations. Its trainability, intelligence, and athleticism have seen it perform in a range of roles, including hunting (tracking, flushing, and retrieving), ratting, military duties, farm duties, watchdog, circus performer, firehouse duties, and as a carriage dog.

It is in these latter two capacities that the breed is perhaps best known and most associated with the United States and Britain. The Dalmatian has an inherent affinity to horses and a natural instinct to run alongside a horse without interfering with the animal or causing it any alarm; it is accepted by horses readily, whereas other breeds are not. Coaches and carriages began to appear in Britain in the sixteenth century; they gradually became more frequent, which culminated in the "Golden Age of Coaching" in the nineteenth century. Dalmatian dogs were an integral part of this mode of transport. They ran alongside the coaches and private carriages to prevent stray dogs from attacking the horses, and when the carriages were stopped the dogs would sit beneath them to guard them. At night they slept with the horses to protect and guard them from animal or human predators. Wealthy private carriage drivers were not only great admirers of the dogs' skills but also their highly attractive looks added to the overall elegance of the turnout. In nineteenth-century Britain the dogs were often called the "English coach dog," "carriage dog," "plum pudding dog," or the "spotted dick."

In North America in the nineteenth century the Dalmatian became well known for its work in the fire department. The first horse-powered fire trucks began to be used in the mid-1800s, and Dalmatians were used to accompany them. As with the carriages in Britain, the dogs would run alongside the fire trucks, barking to clear the way, and guarded the trucks and the horses when they were not in use. The breed became known as the "firehouse dog" and is still kept at firehouses as a mascot or companion. In 1951 the National Fire Protection Association officially designated Sparky, a Dalmatian dog, as its mascot.

Although the modern history of these lovely dogs is well documented, their origins and development are far less evident. The breed is popularly said to have originated in Dalmatia, western Yugoslavia, although this is wholly unsubstantiated. In fact it appears that the dogs did not arrive in Dalmatia until 1930 when Vane Ivanovic, the Consul General of Monaco to Great Britain and a member of the British Dalmatian Club, took a pair of Dalmatians to

Dalmatia as a present for his stepfather, Bozo Banac, who had expressed a wish to introduce them there. Spotted dogs have appeared in the arts and literature since very early times; there are instances of spotted or "splodged" dogs appearing on Egyptian tombs and in frescoes from Ancient Greece (c. 1700 B.C.E.), including one taken from Tiryns to Athens, which is now on display in the National Archaeological Museum. The piece depicts black- and liver-spotted hounds hunting boar. Some theorists speculate that these dogs may have originated in the Balkans and spread throughout the Mediterranean through the extensive trade networks. Spotted dogs of Dalmatian type can also be seen in Italian frescoes of the fourteenth century in Santa Maria Novella, Florence. The Dominican order of friars associated with this church wears white gowns with black capes, and the church was often symbolically represented in the arts by a black and white dog, perhaps suggesting a deep-seated association between the church and the forerunners to the Dalmatian.

Another source of the breed's name and origin may have been the sixteenth-century Serbian poet, Jurij Dalmatin (c. 1547–89). Letters written by Dalmatin to a Bohemian duchess refer to two Turkish dogs that she gave him in 1573, which he is believed to have bred, and which gave rise to the Dalmatian. In truth it is not known where these dogs originated or whether they were descended from the spotted varieties seen in prehistory. The Fédération Cynologique Internationale lists Dalmatia as their origin, but their modern, traceable history is most associated with Britain and the United States.

The current British Dalmatian Club, originally called the Southern Dalmatian Club, was established in 1925. By 1930 the breed had become increasingly popular across the country, and the name was changed to reflect this. They held their first specialty show in the same year with 143 entries. The club gained championship status in 1933 and has held championship shows annually since then, apart from during the years of World War II. Ch Fanhill Faune became the first and, to date, only Dalmatian to take the title of Supreme Champion at Crufts in 1968. The Dalmatian Club of America was formed in 1905 by a small group of breed enthusiasts; Ch Spotted Diamond, born in 1901, was the first champion female recognized by the American Kennel Club.

INDEX

CREDITS

Endpapers *Savannah* (Saluki)
Al Zorbair Arabian Horse Stud, Sharjah
Owners: J. Wickham & S. Jones
jacidw@hotmail.com
sara@bespokegcc.com

2 *Maisie* (Vizsla)
Willowhunt Daisy
Owners: Mr. & Mrs. D. Hill
jsmith7@its.jnj.com

5 *Lady* (Pembroke Welsh Corgi)
Lady Foxway
Owner: Miss R. Crosby
Rcc2123@Sbcglobal.Net
Max (Pembroke Welsh Corgi)
Llandian's Max
Breeder: D Connolly
Owner: Mrs N Esdorn
Nickiesdorn@Mac.Com

6–7 *Jasper* (Labrador Retriever)
Adula Jade
Owners: Mr. O. & Mrs. F. Morley
ollycooper@btinternet.com

8–9 *Puppies* (Chinese Shar Pei)
Abbey Pontshannon Aint I Smart
Owner: Mr. C. & Mrs. L. Walker
ll.walker@live.co.uk
www.pontshannonshar-pei.com

10 *Molly* (English Cocker Spaniel)
Folderslane Gold Bangle
Owner: Ms. L. Bruce
lynn.bruce@cwgsy.net

14–15 *DayDay* (Borzoi)
GCH Go Lightly's Big Day
Breeders: Mr. & Mrs. P. Zobel, Go Lightly Borzois
Owners: M. Zobel & R. Stachon
golightlyborzoi@sbcglobal.net

16 *Minnie* (Saluki)
Plas Yr Wregin Minnie HaHa The Amazonian Queen
Owner: Miss T. Charles-Jones
tilericj@aol.com

19 & 20 *Seren* (Sloughi)
Moulay El-Mehdi Al Tisha of Falconite
Owner: Mrs. J. Harris
julia@falconite.co.uk
www.falconite.co.uk

23 *DayDay* (Borzoi)
GCH Go Lightly's Big Day
Breeder: Mr. & Mrs. P. Zobel, Go Lightly Borzois
Owners: M. Zobel & R. Stachon
golightlyborzoi@sbcglobal.net

24, 26 & 27 *Leo* (Afghan Hound)
GCH Kassan Windwalker of Skyview
In loving memory of June Boone
Owners: M. & D. Suess, J. Boone
doc@afghan-hound.com
www.afghan-hound.com

28 & 31 *Foxy & Wease* (Greyhound)
Marry Late & Flying Weasel

33 *Zipper* (Ibizan Hound)
BIS MBISS CH Harehill's Love On The Run
Breeders: W. & K. Anderson
Owners: K. & D. Gindler, W. & K. Anderson & L. Mattson
kikigin@me.com
www.harehillhounds.com

33 *Jackie* (Ibizan Hound)
GCH Harehill's Ace In The Hole
Breeders: W. & K. Anderson
Owners: K. & D. Gindler & W. & K. Anderson
kikigin@me.com
www.harehillhounds.com

34 & 37 *Glanton* (Irish Wolfhound)
Madiamoy Glanton Gilbert
Owner: Mrs. S. More-Molyneux
m1521562@googlemail.com
www.loseleypark.co.uk

39 *Whisper* (Scottish Deerhound)
Ehlaradawn Whispers
Owner: Master L. Rae
suzi@goldenoakeventing.com

40 *Poppy* (Whippet)
Derohan Attraction
Owner: Diana Webber
diana@whippets.plus.com

43 *Ditto* (Whippet)
Dittander Lilac Moon
Breeder: Miss P. Rose
Owner: Miss N. Cardale

44–45 *Stoney* (Siberian Husky)
Khovaki's Elfstone of Kascaram

Owners: C. & K. Doss
conker20630@mypacks.net

47 *Nik & Cain* (Alaskan Malamute)
Shomont Rasin Hell & Showmont Rasin Cain
Shomont Malamutes
Owners: S. P. Thompson & K. Givens
sue@shomont.fsnet.co.uk
www.shomontmalamutes.webeden.co.uk

48 *Wyatt* (Siberian Husky)
CH Sno-Magic's Gunslinger
Behind is *Seeley* (Sno-Magic's Devil in a Black Dress
CGC, RN), *Sarah* (CH Sno-Magic's Northern
Serenade, SD), & *Spicy* (Khovaki's Red, Hot 'n Spicy)
Sno-Magic Siberians
Owners: Mr. & Mrs. M. Lavin
susan@snomagic.com
www.snomagic.com

50 & 51 *Musher: Mike Lavin* (Siberian Husky)
Teton (Sno-Magic's Teton) (*right lead*), *Stormy*
(Sno-Magic's Dark N Stormy) (*left lead*). Behind is *Seeley*
(Sno-Magic's Devil in a Black Dress CGC, RN), *Wyatt*
(CH Sno-Magic's Gunslinger), & *Sarah* (CH Sno-Magic's
Northern Serenade, SD)
Sno-Magic Siberians
Owners: Mr. & Mrs. M. Lavin
susan@snomagic.com
www.snomagic.com

52 *Maggie* (Samoyed)
CH Sunfire's Amethyst Stardust, WSX, Th.D, CGC,
HCT-II, TDI
Sunfire Samoyeds
Breeders/owners: Mr. & Mrs. M. Emmett
sunfiresamoyeds@sbcglobal.net
www.sunfiresamoyeds.com

55 *Kasey & Misty* (Samoyed)
CH Lhotse's Sunfire On Kara Sea, WS, CGC, TDI
(*Kasey*)
CH Mystiwind's Sunfire 'N Ice, WS, CGC HCT-II,
TDI (*Misty*)
Sunfire Samoyeds
Breeders: Mr. & Mrs. L. Tusoni & J. & J. Ritter
Owners: Mr. & Mrs. M. Emmett
sunfiresamoyeds@sbcglobal.net
www.sunfiresamoyeds.com

56 *Blu* (Akita)
CH Snow Crests Rhythm N Blus
Snowcrested Akitas
Owner: Miss T. Liles
snowcrestedakitas@yahoo.com
www.snowcrestedakitas.com

59 *Glacier* (Akita)
GCH Snow Crest's Blu Ice
Snowcrested Akitas
Owner: Miss T. Liles
snowcrestedakitas@yahoo.com
www.snowcrestedakitas.com

60, 62 & 63 *Poh* (Chow Chow)
Jamarhys Chow Chow
Owner: Mrs. J. Powis
janepowis@btinternet.com

65 *Koru* (Norwegian Lundehund)
C'Ciqala Casey Lonewolf
Sakari Kennels
Owners: Mr. & Mrs. P. Rousseau
sakarikennel@yahoo.com
www.sakarikennels.com

66 *Leif* (Norwegian Elkhound)
Arctic Ridge's Leif Worfson
Owners: B. Oxley & Mr. & Mrs. Wagner
wagnerrl@earthlink.net

71 *Snoopy* (Keeshond)
Brykin Big Chief
Owner: Mrs. J. Waller
brykin.kees@btinternet.com

73 *Zeno* (American Eskimo Dog)
Snodreams Zeno of Peyton
Owner: Mrs. K. Conrad
ekconrad@msn.com

73 *Abel & Kiya* (Basenji)
Annandael's Land of Nod (*Abel*)
White Wind Anpu's Lil Secret (*Kiya*)
Breeder/owner: Miss D. J. Johnston
Haus Annandael Basenjis
annandael@gmail.com
www.annandael.com

76–77 *Lullah* (Great Dane)
Owner: Mr. D. Coughlan
dean@deancoughlan.com

79 *Boris* (Mastiff)
Sle-P-Holo's White Russian At Gavin
Breeders: T. Hyland & D. Golden
Owners: P. & J. Brown & T. Hyland

tonihyland@sbcglobal.net
dbpb@sbcglobal.net

80 *Wally* (Mastiff)
Owners: Mrs. A. Barroll Brown & family
absbarrollbrown@hotmail.com

83 & 84 *Bertie* (Bulldog)
Owner: Mr. D. Roderick
davidroderick1949@btinternet.com

87 *Sonny* (American Staffordshire Terrier)
CH Bergstaff's Bet On Cabin Creek
Breeders: S. & L. Cabral
Owners: Mr. & Mrs. M. Davi
cabincreek63@gmail.com
www.cabincreekamstaff.com

89 *Rio* (Boxer)
Zeus In Possession Of Power
Owners: Mr. C. Jones & Mrs. S. Rew-Jones
stevierew@hotmail.co.uk

90 *Roman* (Dogue de Bordeaux)
Holgaryn Major Achievement
Owners: Mr. G. & Mrs. H. McKeon
holgarynddb@yahoo.co.uk
www.holgaryn.com
www.welshandwestddbclub.co.uk

93 & 95 *Lullah* (Great Dane)
Owner: Mr. D. Coughlan
dean@deancoughlan.com

96, 97 & 98 *Abbey & puppies* (Chinese Shar Pei)
Abbey Pontshannon Aint I Smart
Owner: Mr. C. & Mrs. L. Walker
ll.walker@live.co.uk
www.pontshannonshar-pei.com

101 *Yogi* (Newfoundland)
Inkomo Harare
Breeders: Inkomo Stud
Owner: Mr. D. Roderick
guy.antoniazzi@btinternet.com

102 *Merlin* (St Bernard)
Mtn Home Merlin The Great
Owners: B. McCarthy & M. Snow
mbmccarthy1@comcast.net

104–105 *Rupert* (Briard)
Crackerbie Crackerjack
Owner: Mrs. C. Cox
caroline_cox1@hotmail.com

106 *Twiga* (Bearded Collie)
Highglade Rags to Riches (AH4)

108 *Boo* (Border Collie)
Owner: Mr. D. Wilson
noblehalf@yahoo.com

109 *Oscar* (Rough Collie)
Cotswoldway Inca Gold
Owners: Mr. J. & Mrs. H. Owens
helendenisesorrento@hotmail.co.uk

113 *Cooper* (Old English Sheepdog)
Llandeilo Prince
Owners: Mr. & Mrs. David
advd11@aol.com

115 *Cassie* (Great Pyrenees)
CH SuePyr's Wild Surprise
SuePyr Great Pyrenees
Owner: Mrs. S. Cole
sue3cole@gmail.com
www.suepyrgreatpyrenees.com

116, 118 & 119 *Bindi, Lash, Shiloh, Belle, & Dozer*
(Australian Cattle Dog)
CH Castle Butte Bindi CD RE HSAdsc HIAsc HXAc NA
OAJ OAP AJP NFP (*Bindi*)
Bar H I'm A Cover Girl HSAs (*Lash*)
CH Castle Cutte Shilho HSAs (*Shiloh*)
Bar H Tinkerbelle Trail PT (*Belle*)
CH Bar H Blue Bulldozer PT (*Dozer*)
Breeders: Mr. & Mrs. P. Myers
Owners: Mr. & Mrs. J. Hampton
barhcattledogs1@verizon.net
www.barhcattledogs.com

121 *Rupert* (Briard)
Crackerbie Crackerjack
Owner: Mrs. C. Cox
caroline_cox1@hotmail.com

123 *Rosie* (Canaan Dog)
Anacan Shoshannah For Amicita
Breeder: Mrs. E. M. Minto
Owners: Mr. P. & Mrs. B. Gould
amicitia9.rosie@ntlworld.com

124, 126 & 127 *Quincy & Murray* (Komondor)
BIS BISS World, Int, Americas, American, Canadian,
Mexican CH Gillian's Quintessential Quincy (*Quincy*)

GCH Quintessential Curious George M. (*Murray*)
Owners: Mrs. J. Cupolo & Mr. J. D. Landis
janrdc@aol.com

129 & 130 *Boz* (Standard Schnauzer)
Owner: Mrs. S. Stone
sharonstone@elpasotel.com

133 *Max* (Pembroke Welsh Corgi)
Llandian's Max
Breeder: D. Connolly
Owner: Mrs. N. Esdorn
nickiesdorn@mac.com

133 *Lady* (Pembroke Welsh Corgi)
Lady Foxway
Owner: Miss R. Crosby
rcc2123@sbcglobal.net

134 *Zeus* (Rottweiler)
Fantasa Free N Easy
Jamado Rottweilers
Breeder: L. Dunhill
Owner: M. Docherty
docherty658@btinternet.com

136 *Kramer* (Doberman Pinscher)
Cosmo Kramer
Owner: K. Fox

139 *Sadie* (German Shepherd)
Sadie Von Defenbaugh
Owners: Mr. & Mrs. G. Gates
hollisgates@aol.com

140 *Mason* (German Shepherd)
Owner: Mrs. S. Vaughan
sian_vaughan13@hotmail.com

142–3 *Onza & Skedaddle* (Bluetick Coonhound)
CH PR NA DEM Koyo Blue Onza Leegend (*Onza*)
CH PR NA DEM Koyo Skedaddle Sundown (*Skedaddle*)
Owner: L. Bolin
indianoutlaw25@hotmail.com

145 & 147 *(Bloodhound)*
Southern Shires Bloodhounds
By kind permission of the Masters of the Southern Shires
www.southernshiresbloodhounds.co.uk

149 & 150 *Cooper* (Bassett Hound)
Malrich Bryn
Breeder: D. Elrich
Owner: Miss H. Anderson
helen.anderson16@gmail.com

153 *Chaucer* (Otterhound)
Teckelgarth Chorister
Owners: Miss M. Lerego, Mr G. Usher, & Mr. M. Branch
maria.lerego@sky.com
www.teckelgarth.org

155 *Bumble* (Beagle)
Blackthorne King of Spellcatcher
Owner: Mrs. K. Denton-Drage
keely-drage@idexx.com

156, 158 & 159 *(American Foxhound)*
Smithtown Hunt
By kind permission of the Masters of the Smithtown Hunt
www.smithtownhunt.org

160 *Jeter* (Catahoula Leopard Dog)
Owner: J. McCulloch
jen@olivesveryvintage.com

163 *Skedaddle, Tule, & Fiddler* (Bluetick Coonhound)
CH PR NA-DEM-KOYO Skedaddle Sundown (*Skedaddle*)
CH PR NA-DEM-KOYO Blue Tule Jewel (*Tule*)
PR NA-DEM-KOYO Blue Grass Fiddler (*Fiddler*)
Owner: L. Bolin
indianoutlaw25@hotmail.com

165 *Jade* (Plott Hound)
PR Fisher's Bearstopping precious Jade
Owner: Mrs. D. Culley-Fisher
culley-fisherd@saccounty.net

166 *Sylvie & Rockin'* (Dachshund)
Dikerdachs Rapunzel (*Sylvie*)
Dikerdachs Rockin' At Midnight From Doxieville (*Rockin'*)
Breeder: V. Diker
Owners: N. Shawriyeh & V. Diker
vtdiker@gmail.com
http://dikerdachs.com

169 & 170 *Shisha* (Rhodesian Ridgeback)
Shisha Tofathin
Breeder: Francine Van Rensburg, Pleasant View Ridgeback
Kennel, SA
Owner: Mr. M. Ammirati
marco.ammirati@gmail.com

172–173 *Molly* (English Cocker Spaniel)
Folderslane Gold Bangle
Owner: Ms. L. Bruce
lynn.bruce@cwgsy.net

174 *Jasmine* (English Springer Spaniel)
Shackleton Bonnie
Breeders: Holloway
Owners: The Plummers
plummers@cprp.demon.co.uk

177 *Bob* (English Springer Spaniel)
Tawney Hill Ted
Owner: Miss S. Ellis
fameliss@aol.com

178 *Molly* (English Cocker Spaniel)
Folderslane Gold Bangle
Owner: Ms. L. Bruce
lynn.bruce@cwgsy.net

180 *Sariyel* (Irish Water Spaniel)
CH Chantico's Light of Land and Sea
Owner: M. Garbarino
mgarbarino1@optonline.net

183 *F.J., Lucille, Winnie, May, & Moody* (English Setter)
Kert-Jo's Black Label On The Rocks (*F.J.*)
CH Kert-Jo's Wild 'N Unfaithful Lucille (*Lucille*)
CH Kert-Jo's Da Winnie Pooh (*Winnie*)
GCH CH Kert-Jo's Maybellene Y-Can't-U-B-True (*May*)
Kert-Jo's In The Mood (*Moody*)
Kert-Jo Setters & All Setter Rescue
Owners: Mr. R. Attleson & Ms. M. Mengel
http://allsetterrescue.blogspot.com

185 *Lacey* (Gordon Setter)
Laurelhach Legacy
Laurelhach Gordon Setters
Owner: Mrs. F. Boxall
frances@laurelhach.co.uk

187 *Zulu & Mally* (German Shorthaired Pointer)
Owner: Mr. E. Jenkins

188 *Maisie* (Vizsla)
Willowhunt Daisy
Owners: Mr. & Mrs. D. Hill
jsmith7@its.jnj.com

191 *Kizzie* (Weimaraner)
Parhelis Minuet (*Kizzie*)
Owners: Mr. B. & Mrs. A. Hargreaves
bill@larkhillfarm.co.uk

192 *Dino* (Spinone Italiano)
GCH CH Brier Creeks Dynoche Know Gunsmoke
Breeders: K. & J. Mann
Owner: H. Key
fieldnfeathers@ymail.com

195 *Zeus* (Chesapeake Bay Retriever)
Zoe's Classic Zeus
Owners: Mr. & Mrs. Prodromakis
alypro42@yahoo.com

197 *Jasper* (Labrador Retriever)
Adula Jade
Owners: Mr. O. & Mrs. F. Morley
ollycooper@btinternet.com

198 *Popcorn* (Labrador Retriever)
Ken Millix Honeybear
Owner: Miss A. Seel
bella@bellaseel.com

200 *Rosie* (Golden Retriever)
Tenfield Coral Sea
www.tenfield.co.uk

202–203 *Bo* (Scottish Terrier)
Rwffys Rockerfeller
Owner: Mrs. C. Adams

204 *Amber* (Manchester Terrier)
Twisel Gregory's Girl
Owners: Mr. B. & Mrs. A. Hargreaves
bill@larkhillfarm.co.uk

206 *Robbie* (Dandie Dinmont)
CH King's Mtn Robert The Bruce
Breeders: Mrs. S. Pretari Hickson & B. A. Stenmark & V. Wilson
Owners: Mrs. S. Pretari Hickson & D. Chambers Bau & V. Wilson
sandra.pretarihickson@gmail.com
www.kingsmtndandies.com

209 *Krystal* (Bedlington Terrier)
GCH WmShire's Krystal Blue Jewel
Breeder: N. Peterson
Owner: N. Peterson & R. Lundin
nadinepet@gmail.com

211 & 212 *Jemima & Bumble* (Border Terrier)
Pourciaux Raz (*Bumble*)
Pourciaux Roselle (*Jemima*)
Owners: Miss S. Wethey & Miss B. Wethey
bellawethey@gmail.com

215 & 216 *Suzi* (Airedale Terrier)
Moonlight Mist

Owner: Mrs. K. Protheroe
kath.protheroe@swansea.gov.uk

218 & 221 *Bo* (Scottish Terrier)
Rwffys Rockerfeller
Owner: Mrs. C. Adams
chuff.wake@tiscali.co.uk

222 & 225 *Zhara, Spencer, & Lady Alice* (West Highland White Terrier)
Rwffys Rockerfeller
Owner: C. Botha
celeste.botha@telkomsa.net

227 *Bear* (Irish Terrier)
Bearnard
Owner: Miss G. Freydl
gabf2000@yahoo.com

229 *Gladys* (Soft-Coated Wheaten Terrier)
CH Heirloom To Infinity & Beyond OA OAP
Heirloom Wheatens
Owners: P. Chevalier & R. Bergman
pjcheval@yahoo.com
www.heirloomwheatens.com

230 & 233 *Karma, Smooch, & Moxie* (Wire Fox Terrier)
GCH Dalriada's Instant Karma (*Karma*)
Rockinfox Sincerely Hugs & Kisses (*Smooch*)
Rushinons Outfoxed Me Once Too (*Moxie*)
Owners: K. Read & S. Loudenburg
read@rmi.net
rockinfox@gobrainstorm.net

234 & 237 *Bentley* (Parson Russell Terrier/Jack Russell)
Bentley Blower
Owner: Mr. Z. Helm
zebhelm@gmail.com
www.zebedeehelm.com

238–239 *Javier* (Pug)
Owner: M. Taylor
mariasdogs@optonline.net

241 & 242 *Rainbow* (Shih Tzu)
Chodeas Eastern Star
Owners: Miss S. & Mrs. M. Dean
cherriedean@sky.com

245 *Bruno* (Lhasa Apso)
Valeview My Cheeky Fella
Owner: The Lees
steve.lee.2@hotmail.co.uk

247 & 248 *Marcus & Finlay* (Pekingese)
Jidorian The Apprentice For Delwin (*Marcus*)
CH Dreamtines Odds On For Delwin (*Finlay*)
Owner: Mrs. G. A. Godwin
toydom@aol.com

250 & 253 *Javier* (Pug)
Owner: M. Taylor
mariasdogs@optonline.net

255 *Sparky* (Chinese Crested)
Hitmonchan Angel Secret
Owner: J. Jones
hitmonchan@btinternet.com
www.freewebs.com/hitmonchancresteds

256 & 259 *Pablo* (Chihuahua)
Owner: Miss R. Jones
rachel.annjones@hotmail.co.uk

260 *Pablo* (Papillon)
Owner: Miss R. Jones

263 & 265 *Tito* (Pomeranian)
CH Velocity's King of Mambo
Mr. J. Bendersky
www.planetjorge.com

266, 268 & 269 *Justin & Patsy* (Poodle)
Donnchada Just Right (*Justin*)
Multiple BIS, BISS CH Donnchada Sweet (*Patsy*)
Donnchada Poodles
Owner: E. Brown
donnchada@yahoo.com
http://www.donnchadapoodles.com

273 *Bowie & Patience* (Boston Terrier)
CH Constellation's Ziggy Stardust (*Bowie*)
Constellation's Patience Is A Virtue (*Patience*)
Owners: Mr. & Mrs. Kaesemacher
timvalk@comcast.net
www.constellationbostons.com

275 & 276 *Charles* (Cavalier King Charles Spaniel)
Owners: Mr. & Mrs. E. Mill
millmob2@comcast.net

279 *Lola* (Yorkshire Terrier)
Owner: L. Hughes
lolajanehughes@gmail.com

281 & 282 *Fleckie* (Dalmatian)
Owner: Mrs. D. Honl

ACKNOWLEDGMENTS

We would like to thank the Kennel Club (www.the-kennel-club.org.uk) and the American Kennel Club (www.akc.org) and the United Kennel Club (www.ukcdogs.com); these websites provided access to official breed standards in addition to extensive and invaluable information on all aspects of dogs.

We would also like to thank all the individual breed clubs, experts, and historians in the UK and US who have been so helpful and generous with their time.

We would like to extend our great thanks to Mark Fletcher, Jane Laing, Dean Martin, Elspeth Beidas, and the rest of the team at Quarto for their patience, support, and expertise, and the following individuals for their time and advice (apologies if anyone has been left out):

Adele Nicholson
Adrian Bicknell
Angela Danvers-Smith
Ann Taylor
Anne Deranmar
Anne Roslin-Williams
Barbara Baese
Barry Bull
Barry Offiler
Beryl Kay
Betty Anne Stenmark
Betty Smith
Bob Plott
Bob Thomas
Bonnie Dalzell
Brenda Willliams
Caroline Riggs
Carl Gomes
Carl Yochum
Carol Cooper
Charla Hill
Chawn Santana
Christopher Adams
Chris Carberry
Chris Hazell
Colin Bowker
Dareen A Bridge
David Crossley
David Webster
Deborah Harper
Dexter Hockley
Diana Allen
Diana Phillips
Don Abney
Dorothy Grayson Wood
Doug And Louise Collier
Ed Thomason
Eileen Geeson
Ellen Minto
Elspeth Kelly
Ermine Moreau-Sipiere
Ernie Hill
Geir Flyckt
Gill Taylor
Gillian Burgoin

Graham Foote
Graham Rogers
Gwen Eddie
Helen Burke
Ian Halbert
Ian Seath
Jackie Jones
Jackie Shore
James Pound
Jan Wakerley
Jill Cowper
Jim Grebe
Jim Todd
Joanne Silver
John French
John Steele
Jorge Bendersky
Judith Ashworth
Judy Creswick
Julia Harris
Kevin Moore
Leslie Bauman
Linda Carnaby
Lisa Cowley
Liz Egan
Lorraine Harvey
Lt. Col Dennis Foster
Lynn Randall
Lynne Luff
Margaret House
Marion Hipkin
Martina Gates
Mary Lowe
Mary Swash
Max Jones
Michael Harrisson
Miranda Brace
Monica Davi
Nick Clancy
Norma Armstrong
Norma Barnes
Officers And Committee Of Basenji Club Of Great Britain
Pat Leach
Pat Muggleton

Pat Munn	Rebecca Berra	Roy Essakow	Sue Nicholls-Ward
Paul Livesey	Rhoda Patience	Sally Sutton	Sue Thompson
Pauline Barnes	Richard Edwards	Sandra Allen	Toni Hyland
Peggy Dawson	Richard Newman	Shaheen Shahani	Valerie Foss
Peter Rousseau	Rita Bartlett	Steve Tillotson	Violet Bruce
Peter Yardley	Rob Hill	Stephen Rew	

Finally, for information on any of the breeds, including the full and official breed standards, we strongly suggest contacting the breed societies, and would like to extend our thanks to the many societies that were particularly helpful, and to those who provided guidance on the descriptions.

Afghan Hound www.afghanhoundclubofamerica.org
Airedale Terrier www.Airedale.org
Akita www.akitaclub.org
Alaskan Malamute www.alaskanmalamute.org
American Eskimo Dog www.aedca.org
American Foxhound www.mfha.org/www.americanfoxhoundclub.org
American Staffordshire Terrier www.amstaff.org
Australian Cattle Dog www.acdca.org
Basenji www.basenji.org
Basset Hound www.basset-bhca.com
Beagle www.clubs.akc.org/NBC
Bearded Collie www.bcca.us
Bedlington Terrier www.bedlingtonamerica.com
Bloodhound www.bloodhounds.org
Bluetick Coonhound www.bluetickbreedersofamerica.com
Border Collie www.bordercolliesociety.com
Border Terrier www.btcoa.org
Borzoi www.borzoiclubofamerica.org
Boston Terrier www.bostonterrierclubofamerica.org
Boxer www.americanboxerclub.org
Briard www.briardclubofamerica.org
Bulldog www.thebca.org
Canaan www.cdca.org
Cavalier King Charles Spaniel www.ackcsc.org
Chesapeake Bay Retriever www.amchessieclub.org
Chihuahua www.chihuahuaclubofamerica.com
Chinese Crested www.chinesecrestedclub.info
Chinese Shar Pei www.cspca.com
Chow Chow www.chowclub.org
Collie www.collieclubofamerica.org
Dachshund www.dachshund-dca.org
Dalmatian www.thedca.org
Dandie Dinmont Terrier www.ddtca.org
Doberman Pinscher www.dpca.org
Dogue de Bordeaux www.ddbs.org
English Cocker Spaniel www.ecsca.org
English Setter www.esaa.com
English Springer Spaniel www.essfta.org
Finnish Spitz www.finnishspitzclub.org
French Bulldog www.frenchbulldogclub.org
German Shepherd www.gsdca.org
German Shorthaired Pointer www.gspca.org
Golden Retriever www.grca.org
Gordon Setter www.gsca.org

Great Dane www.gdca.org
Great Pyrenees www.gpcaonline.org
Greyhound www.greyhoundclubofamericainc.org
Ibizan Hound www.ihcus.org
Irish Terrier www.itca.info
Irish Wolfhound www.Iwclubofamerica.org
Keeshond www.keeshond.org
Komondor www.komondorclubofamerica.org
Labrador Retriever www.thelabradorclub.com
Lhasa Apso www.lhasaapso.org
Manchester Terrier www.americanmanchester.org
Mastiff www.mastiff.org
Newfoundland www.ncanewfs.org
Norwegian Elkhound www.neaa.net
Norwegian Lundehund www.nlaainc.com
Old English Sheepdog www.oldenglishsheepdogclubofamerica.org
Otterhound www.clubs.akc.org/ohca
Papillon www.papillonclub.org
Parson Russell Terrier www.prtaa.org
Pekingese www.thepekingeseclubofamerica.com
Pembroke Welsh Corgi www.pembrokecorgi.org
Pomeranian www.AmericanPomeranianClub.org
Poodle www.poodleclubofamerica.org
Pug www.pugs.org
Rhodesian Ridgeback www.rrcus.org
Rottweiler www.amrottclub.org
Saint Bernard www.saintbernardclub.org
Saluki www.salukiclub.org
Samoyed www.samoyedclubofamerica.org
Scottish Deerhound www.deerhound.org
Scottish Terrier www.stca.biz
Shih Tzu www.americanshihtzuclub.org
Siberian Husky www.shca.org
Sloughi www.sloughi-international.com
Soft Coated Wheaten Terrier www.scwtca.org
Spinone Italiano www.spinoneclubofamerica.com
Standard Schnauzer www.standardschnauzer.org
Vizsla www.vcaweb.org
Weimaraner weimaranerclubofamerica.org
West Highland White Terrier www.westieclubamerica.com
Whippet www.americanwhippetclub.net
Wire Fox Terrier www.aftc.org
Yorkshire Terrier www.ytca.org

The Spirit of the Dog is a historical and cultural review of a selection of our most popular and least known dog breeds—it is a celebration of the dog in all its shapes and sizes and is not intended as a "show dog" compendium or as a breed reference book. The text and the photographs are designed to capture the spirit, essence, history, and nature of the different breeds and as such include dogs from "all walks of life."